THE LURE OF DREAMS

From literary theory to social anthropology, the influence of Freud runs through every part of the human and social sciences. In *The Lure of Dreams*, Harvie Ferguson shows how Freud's writings and particularly *The Interpretation of Dreams* contribute, both in their content and in the baroque and dream-like forms in which they are cast, to our understanding of the character of modernity.

He argues that the recent tendency to view Freud's work mainly as a product of nineteenth-century developments in biology and medicine have obscured what is most important and suggestive for us in his writings. Instead Harvie Ferguson discusses the development of Freud's ideas in the context of the Viennese *fin de siècle* culture in which they were nurtured, and examines the extent to which they reflect a breakdown of classical forms of rationalism in both the sciences and the arts and, more generally, the rehabilitation of dreams in late modernity.

This novel and stimulating approach to Freud and to the dilemmas of modernity and postmodernity will fascinate everyone with an interest in the development of modern consciousness.

Harvie Ferguson teaches sociology at the University of Glasgow.

THE LURE OF DREAMS

Sigmund Freud and the construction of modernity

Harvie Ferguson

London and New York

First published 1996
by Routledge
11 New Fetter Lane, London EC4P 4EE

Simultaneously published in the USA and Canada
by Routledge
29 West 35th Street, New York, NY 10001

Routledge is an International Thomson Publishing Company

© 1996 Harvie Ferguson

Typeset in Baskerville by LaserScript, Mitcham, Surrey
Printed and bound in Great Britain by
Mackays of Chatham PLC, Chatham, Kent

British Library Cataloguing in Publication Data
A catalogue record for this book is available from the British Library

Library of Congress Cataloguing in Publication Data
Ferguson, Harvie.
The Lure of Dreams : Sigmund Freud and the construction of modernity
Harvie Ferguson.
p.   cm.
Includes bibliographical references and index.
(pbk. : alk. paper)
1. Freud, Sigmund, 1856–1939. Traumdeutung.   2. Dream interpretation.
3. Freud, Sigmund, 1856–1939 – Influence.   4. Civilization Modern – 20th
century.   I. Title.
BF175.5.D74F47   1996
154.6'34–dc20   95–38490
CIP

ISBN 0–415–04835–4 (hbk)
ISBN 0–415–04836–2 (pbk)

CONTENTS

PRETEXT

It is just one hundred years since Freud revived the ancient art of dream interpretation and in doing so developed a psychology perfectly adapted to the modern age.

In itself this centenary hardly justifies yet another book devoted to the explication of his classic text. There are already more books on Freud than any reasonable person might wish to read, and new works appear at a rate which is alarming for even the most unreasonable specialist. There seems little enough excuse, even in today's unsavoury academic climate, to add to the existing stockpile of secondary literature on Freud a work which cannot claim to bring to light any new information about his life or suggest any fundamentally new insights into the understanding of his ideas.

The justification for what follows is that it is not actually a book on Freud at all. Freud's text, partly because it is well known and widely available, forms, so to speak, the 'day-residue' from which the present book has been constructed. It seeks to demonstrate the extent to which an entire mode of life, and a characteristic form of experience, is realised in that text as its 'latent content'. It is, therefore, primarily a book about modern society and proposes that Freud's psychology be read as a valuable contribution to the historical sociology of modernity.

This seems at once to raise another objection. Freud was not a sociologist, nor was he particularly interested in society. Indeed, his entire approach to the understanding of behaviour, which links contingent individual experience to universal aspects of 'human nature', seems thoroughly non- (or even anti-) sociological. Yet it is hardly controversial to claim that his work is of some relevance to modern sociology. There are two basic reason for this, usually grudging, acceptance of his significance. Firstly, as personal experience has become a central interest for sociologists, they have been drawn towards Freud as the pre-eminent psychologist of the modern age; and it is in terms of his characterisation of the distinctive forms of inner life that many sociologists have sought to assimilate modern subjectivities to their own traditions of understanding and explanation of society. And, secondly, even where sociologists have neglected the issues which his work raised, they cannot help but meet his reincarnation in contemporary literary theory, cultural studies, the analysis of film, modern social history, social anthropology, philosophy and so on. There is hardly any branch of the contemporary social and human sciences which has not felt in some way the need to respond to Freud's thought, so that his writings have become commonplace. Thus, a certain reluctance to come to terms with his psychology and, at the same time, an irresistible temptation to flirt with some of Freud's more contentious theories, has characterised sociological interest in the founder of psychoanalysis. Ubiquity, however, is no proof against confusion; and it is from the conviction that the 'wrong' version of Freud has been assimilated to sociology that the present work has been written.

Of course, Freud's work can be read in a variety of different ways, and contemporary scholars have not been slow to exploit the richness of his writings by bringing to bear upon it widely divergent perspectives. Much recent Freud scholarship, focused on the history of the biological sciences, on biographical researches, on literary topics and on psychological theory, has, perhaps understandably, had little direct impact on sociology. Yet, the Freud or, rather, the confusing variety of Freuds, which has emerged in recent years through this research is in many ways fundamentally at odds with the conventional sociological understanding of his work. What is interesting in the variety of recent approaches by non-sociologists is the extent to which they suggest an image of Freud which, in fact, 'fits' far better with current interests in sociology than does the figure sociologists have inherited from earlier discussion within their own discipline.

Thus, to mention only the most obvious aspects of these ongoing revisions, it now makes little sense to view Freud's understanding of modernity as an unrelieved struggle between the 'pleasure principle' and the 'reality principle', or, indeed, to read his psychology as claiming that there is any simple relation between 'pleasure' and 'repression'. More generally, it may now seem quite misleading to think of Freud as proposing a 'depth psychology', and, in fact, his openness to all those aspects of modernity that interest sociologists become more obvious if his work is approached as a 'surface psychology' of everyday life. Freud can be read, in fact, as the pre-eminent historical psychologist of modernity and it is in terms of a broad historical context that his work gains a new relevance for contemporary sociology.

It is hardly novel to claim that Freud is essential reading for anyone interested in coming to terms with the nature of modern experience. But just what is the relevance of his work? On this central question we cannot allow ourselves to be guided by Freud himself. His own extensions and extrapolations of psychoanalytic findings to the most general levels of historical, cultural and social understanding do not provide an ideal model for the contemporary sociologist. The important question is not whether sociologists should make judgements on *Civilization and its Discontents*, but how they should respond to *The Interpretation of Dreams*.

Any attempt to establish the particular relevance of Freud's work for the understanding of modernity, then, requires a general exposition of Freud's central texts. A sociological account of his work cannot simply be imposed from the outside. Indeed, an initial surrender to his text is a prerequisite for coming to a more adequate understanding of the context in which it was written. What is equally clear to any reader of Freud's more theoretical works as well as his case histories is the extent to which in them the facile distinction between 'text' and 'context' breaks down. Thus, while the importance of establishing both a convincing reading of the text and a relevant context for its understanding is evident, so far as possible, the distinction between the two has here been dissolved. To wholly abandon such conventions, however, quite apart from the demands it would make of the reader, would assume what should be demonstrated; that is that there is a particular (sociologically significant), contextual way of reading Freud. An initial attempt to establish the relevance of a number of general features in the intellectual and social characteristics of modernity will be made, therefore, before taking up specific issues in Freud's writings. And it is only after a closer reading of his key texts in the light of that provisional orientation that his work can be re-contextualised in its sociologically most significant form. Thus, in what follows the three central chapters can be read as essentially expository and the framing chapters which precede and follow these can be viewed as primarily contextual in nature.

In what follows there is no attempt to replace an older and outdated understanding with a complete and systematic alternative. It is intended only as a provisional and tentative series of suggestions. Thus, while a wide range of Freud's work is touched upon from a variety of perspectives, and some effort is made to follow the direction of his thought in a coherent manner, its ambitions are strictly limited. It is intended, thus, primarily as an introduction to Freud's work for those whose central interests are in sociology and modern cultural history. Any novelty in approach derives simply from the conviction that the history of science, literary theory, philosophy and biography as well as social and political history are all central to contemporary sociology, which can no longer develop, as it were, from its own resources, but requires the continuous stimulation and specialist knowledge of a wide variety of related disciplines.

This self-conscious eclecticism is defensible not only on common sense grounds (it would be foolish to ignore the results of research in other fields just because they were arrived at by unfamiliar means), but as the 'method' best adapted both to the subject matter and to the contemporary situation. Reading Freud's texts is to enter an intellectual labyrinth rather than a system of deductive reasoning. One is led with complete assurance from one astonishing insight to another; an entire and entirely new world is revealed. The long process of uncovering this world, like reading *Don Quixote*, creates an impression of inexhaustible novelty. Freud's world never quite becomes predictable; he endlessly produces surprises, introduces theoretical novelties and ever bolder hypotheses.

Freud's psychology is driven by the demand for descriptive adequacy rather than theoretical rigour. Rather than attempt to tidy up the baroque extravagance of his work by imposing upon it a theoretical framework which is foreign to its spirit as well as to its intentions, a virtue can be made of these tendencies towards continuous inner transformation and metamorphosis. And rather than reflect, through a systematic ordering of its terms and relations, a 'rational' order divined by some undisclosed process to correspond to the underlying structure of reality, it seems better adapted to convey the disordered experience (surely more common) of everyday life; a disorderliness which is, in fact, quite fundamental to the emergence and development of modernity. In Freud's writings, as in the lives of the people it describes, we follow a twisting path, or, rather several paths, from which we cannot stand apart to visualise, in a single panorama, the entire landscape through which they are traced.

Paradoxically, it is just by following these paths that we become aware of the ever-broadening context of his work. Freud's writings, that is to say, themselves possess the qualities of a dream, and any attempt to preserve this essential characteristic of his writing is bound to give rise to the impression that it is little more than an arbitrary succession of comments. Yet, as Freud's interpretations revealed, dreams are not, after all, meaningless jumbles of images; when amplified and contextualised through a variety of associations they are transformed into coherent narratives. The meaning of dreams becomes clear through a continuous oscillation between their text and their context; and, in the same way, the significance of Freud's work for contemporary readers can only emerge through a similar process.

What does emerge through this process might be understood primarily as a contribution to the theory of *representations*, and it is in this respect that Freud's writings continue to exercise their most profound influence on modern thought. That is not to say that psychoanalysis is essentially a theory of language, or is best understood from a semiotic standpoint. In spite of the force with which such a case has been argued in recent years, it can, in fact, be argued that it is just the way in which Freud introduces non-linguistic considerations into his analysis of representations that is most fruitful for a proper historical understanding of modern experience. From a contemporary perspective Freud's fundamental contribution to a new understanding of modernity is focused on the role of the body and of the body-image in the system of representations: psychoanalysis is primarily a way of 'reading' the body as a text. But such a bald statement, typical of the contemporary respect for, and ignorance of, his writings, makes imperative a closer acquaintance with both the text and context of his writings.

NOTE

In the interests of readability a mixed system of referencing has been used in a consistent way throughout the text. Longer quotations have been indented and are identified in the text in accordance with the Harvard System. All other references are identified by traditional endnotes. All references to, and quotations from, *The Standard Edition of the Complete Psychological Works of Sigmund Freud* (24 vols) are identified as SE followed by the appropriate volume and page number.

1

CONTEXT
The dream of modernity

It is commonplace to regard the long-term intellectual and social development of modern society as inimical to dreams. For modernity, established
on the basis of a number of decisive oppositions, apparently champions the
cause of the objective, rational and real against the subjective, irrational
and illusory: and nothing seems more evident than to characterise dreams
as subjective, irrational and illusory. It is not a matter of defining dreams
by reference to a scale of 'more' or 'less', for they belong unambiguously
and completely to the degraded 'other' of every evaluative polarity whose
exalted upper element is claimed to be the unique invention of modernity.
There is, consequently, something detached and alien in the dream; and
unlike the state of irrationality from which children have not yet emerged,
the succession of ephemeral and detached dream-images do not yield to
the growth of 'reason'. The unreasonableness of the dream for the
modern, rational and wide awake individual hinges on the enigma of
personal responsibility. A distinguished commentator remarks that:

> The mystery of the dream originates in the fact that this phantas-
> magoria over which the sleeper has no control is at the same time
> entirely a product of his imagination. When it is unfolded before him
> without his consent, he can hardly believe himself responsible.
> (Grunebaum and Caillois 1966, p. 51)

For modern society, thus, if it is viewed as nothing but the liberation of
reason from the constraints of ignorance and error, the dream is rejected
as a residue of an unenlightened age.

Yet, today, such assumptions need only be stated to make evident the
ambiguity which is the real foundation from which, at one time, sprang an
over zealous condemnation of dreams. Indeed, it is no longer possible to
state the case without recourse to moderating terms – 'apparent', 'seems'
– and the equivocation of inverted commas. Looking back, however, to a
culture dominated by intellectualism and rationalism dreams were, at best,
curiosities. The entire process of enlightenment, in terms of the progressive

1

conquest of nature by scientific means and the associated decay of religious and magical worldviews, legitimated a profound self-confidence and sense of superiority over previous periods of history and other still barbaric or primitive societies which could be characterised, among other childish attributes, by an uncritical valorisation of dreams. It is now all too easy to look back on such optimism with an equally unfounded sense of our own superiority; albeit one which displays itself as a sly relativism. In any event as confidence in modernity was shaken by the persistence of economic crises, war, disease, superstition, death and, in spite of everything, the continuation of a heedless longing for happiness, it became more difficult to claim that modern society had awakened from a long sleep; or to construct from the routinised drudgery of factory production, bureaucratic administration and earnest scientific endeavour an inspiring image of progress. And, perhaps even more significantly, as the programme of scientific rationalism foundered upon the irreconcilable contradictions thrown up by equally essential but incompatible images of nature, it became less necessary to dismiss dreams as uninteresting and meaningless psychic *débris*.

The rehabilitation of dreams might be viewed, then, as a rough measure of our disenchantment with modernity, and of our unwillingness to accept a wholly rationalised conception of life; or, rather, with the civilisation of nineteenth-century Europe which is, somewhat narrowly, the implicit point of reference for many now contested notions of the modern. Of course, for some, the emergence of a modern oneiric science, which is one of the most evident symptoms of this rehabilitation, clung to an older conceit and sought, through explanation of the origins, functions and forms of dreams, to extend the empire of rational self-control.[1]

There is more to this than a fashionable inversion of modern western prejudices. Certainly, it is no longer obvious that reality must be placed above appearance, or that we should cling to being rather than abandon ourselves to becoming, or that either is more likely to be encountered in the crystallised actuality of objects rather than in the fluid potentiality of subjects. Nor is it surprising that, in the light of such radical revaluation, dreams have been accorded a new prominence within all forms of self-understanding. More significant is the extent to which dreams become subversive of *all* such organising polarities. Rather than reclaim neglected and degraded aspects of existence for a generously redefined human domain, dreams place a question mark over all these evaluative certainties and, indeed, over the very acts of distinguishing and judging. The playful character of dreams, so obvious to every self-observation conditioned by a reading of Freud, reproduces within itself, albeit it in a different order, all those distinctions through which reality is defined for the non-dreaming observer. The dream, so to speak, contains its own world; its own inner-sense of subject and object, reality and appearance, being and becoming.

To dream is to enter this other world; rather than to experience a specific segment of what, when awake, we imagine to be a singular reality. It is just this radical difference, the separateness and self-sufficiency of the dream-world, that is productive of so much ambiguity. It is as if in sleep we paradoxically awake to the peculiarities of a reality which has an equal claim on our credulity. The problem of the dream, thus:

> is no longer the question of a single consciousness powerless to distinguish between illusion and reality, but of two beings from two different realms.
>
> (Grunebaum and Caillois 1966, p. 50)

As all distinctions reemerge within it, the dream itself has no defining opposite. The dream is an inclusive term and exhaustive of its own reality. It is both a world apart and a world to itself; so that 'to dream is not another way of experiencing another world, it is for the dreaming subject the radical way of experiencing its own world'.[2] 'Sleeping', rather than 'dreaming', is the opposite of 'waking' and, as a broader context reveals, it is only relatively recently that dreaming has been exclusively associated, though not identified, with sleep. And even now the ambiguity of dreams is evident in our often thinking of them as located in some kind of intermediary and indeterminate zone between waking and sleeping.

The history of dreams, and the history of the interpretation and explanation of dreams is, then, more than a scale of changing values. The reality which constitutes the dream and dreaming itself changes. This can hardly be otherwise when, throughout the development of western society, to say nothing of the variations observed in non-western societies, the mode of defining and grasping reality has undergone such profound changes. The centrality of Freud's writings to contemporary understanding of dreams can hardly be overestimated. In spite of sporadic efforts to reinstate a nineteenth-century scientific disdain of dreams, Freud's influence is now so pervasive as to be almost invisible. Yet Freud is rarely read in terms of the larger context which, it seems, provided the impetus to, if not the inspiration for, his own interest in dreams. It is worth beginning, therefore, with the inception of a distinctly modern discourse on the character of dreaming.

DOUBT AND DREAMS

Many of the most intractable (and fascinating) difficulties thrown up by the modern discourse on dreams were clearly stated at its outset by Descartes. For Descartes the enigma of dreaming (he rightly avoids the casual objectification in referring to a 'phenomenon' – the dream) poses fundamental problems for our understanding of the world and of ourselves.

The illusory character of dreams, which is so much more impressive and general than the accident of waking perceptual error, is taken for granted by Descartes and appealed to as a stimulus to the metaphysical doubt which is the real starting point of his reflection. For the problem of knowledge dreams are important first of all as exemplary instances of deception, and, retrospectively, arouse the scepticism Descartes wishes to extend to other kinds of perceptions. He declares, thus, to have:

resolved to pretend that all the things that had ever entered my mind were no more true than the illusions of my dreams.

(Descartes 1985, p.127)

The distinction between dreams, which are seen as self-generated images occurring during sleep, and waking perceptions, does not seem initially to pose a problem. Descartes assumes everyone is willing to admit that, however unreliable the testimony of our senses, they provide us with some information about the outside world in a way which our dreams never can. But he would like to argue that, contrary to a philosophically naive view, our senses are much more deceptive than is generally assumed:

every sensory experience I have ever thought I was having while awake I can also think of myself as sometimes having while asleep; and since I do not believe that what I seem to perceive in sleep comes from things located outside me, I did not see why I should be more inclined to believe this of what I think I perceive while awake.

(Descartes 1984, p. 53)

More interestingly, he also argues that by standards that might be applied to our sense impressions, our dreams often appear equally as truthful, rather than equally as false. This raises for him the more difficult question of whether or not we can reliably tell whether we are asleep or awake. The deceptiveness of dreams, in other words, goes deeper than at first suspected:

As I think about this more carefully, I see plainly that there are never any sure signs by means of which being awake can be distinguished from being asleep. The result is that I begin to feel dazed, and this very feeling only reinforces the notion that I may be asleep.

(Descartes 1984, p. 13)

Disconcertingly he suggests just such a criteria – 'to feel dazed' – at the very moment of denying its possibility. But this apparent contradiction can be resolved on the assumption that 'to feel dazed', while it may be some sort of vague indication of being asleep, can never amount to the 'sure sign' which he is seeking. The kind of certainty for which Descartes is searching, and in which he hopes to anchor philosophy, is found exclusively, he contends, in 'clear and distinct ideas'. This, in fact, presents a new difficulty, because it is in our dreams that we frequently conceive just such clear

4

and distinct ideas, which, by virtue of their clarity and distinctness, ought to be true. Thus, in spite of 'feeling dazed', Descartes insists that ideas coming to us in dreams are often 'no less lively and distinct' than those we have when awake. It must be remembered, however, that the criteria of 'clear and distinct ideas' refers to the Truth, and not the verisimilitude of ideas. It might be said that, in dreaming, we often experience clear and distinct *images* but not lucid *ideas* which, abstracted from sensory images, have a purely intellectual content.

It now seems that Descartes can unambiguously characterise dreams as internal images devoid of genuinely rational interconnection. At the close of the Sixth Meditation he reports that, between dreaming and waking:

> I now notice that there is a vast difference between the two, in that dreams are never linked by memory with all the other actions of life as waking experiences are.
>
> (Descartes 1984, p. 61)

This seems compelling, but does not in the end lay to rest the doubts engendered by his scattered remarks. His various comments have been made from the perspective of someone who believes himself to be awake. But it is just a characteristic of waking experience that we feel, when awake, that 'we cannot doubt whether we are awake or dreaming'. The difficulty lies in a fatal asymmetry between the two states. The notion of experience through which these distinct states are joined is by no means the same viewed from the perspective of each. It is only when we are asleep that we may doubt whether we are dreaming or not; wakefulness carries with it, as it were, is its own guarantee. Thus, while in a wakeful state we may clearly distinguish between, on the one hand, the rational interconnectedness of our own thoughts and their appropriateness to the world around us, and on the other, the disconnected and uncoordinated images of a recollected dream. But, when asleep, nothing strikes us as odd, and the most absurd images may appear perfectly natural and rational. Descartes quotes the example of a man who dreams of a clock striking 'one, one, one, one' and sees nothing odd in his reacting with the thought that the mechanism had 'gone mad' because it had struck 'one' four times, rather than striking 'four'.

Nor is Descartes alone in this profound equivocation. His contemporary, Thomas Hobbes, is hardly more sanguine. For him, mental images were simply the result of the 'agitation' of the senses, and when asleep, these could be stimulated by the movement of 'the inward parts' giving rise to dreams which were indistinguishable (as images) from the pictures of the external world that we formed when awake. And he concurs in his judgement of the asymmetry of our relationship to the perceived world in the waking as compared to the dreaming state:

it is a hard matter, and by many thought impossible, to distinguish exactly between sense and dreaming. For my part, when I consider that in dreams I do not often nor constantly think of the same persons, places, objects, and actions, that I do waking; nor remember so long a train of coherent thoughts, dreaming, as at other times; and because waking I often observe the absurdity of dreams, but never dream of the absurdities of my waking thoughts; I am well satisfied, that being awake, I know I dream not, though when I dream I think myself awake.

(Hobbes 1962, p. 65)

The search for unambiguous criteria of dreaming leads, then, to a more profound metaphysical scepticism; and what began as the most common exemplar of a distinction which might profitably be applied to all thinking, ends in a paralysis of doubt:

What if dreaming is a single operation which enables you sometimes to dream that you are dreaming, and at other times to dream that you are thinking while awake?

(Descartes 1984, p. 335)

Descartes himself introduces the suspicion that his philosophy is suffused with dreamlike unreality. His conviction that he had 'discovered the foundations of a marvellous science', if not itself born of a dream, was expressed in a dream he reports from November 1619. According to Baillet (who had seen the original and subsequently lost manuscript of the 'Olympica' notebook in which the experience was recorded), Descartes fell asleep in his 'stove-heated room' and had three consecutive dreams which, on waking, he interpreted as evidence of his destiny to transform philosophy through the introduction of a new mathematical and scientific system. Descartes himself reports 'I had a dream involving the Seventh Ode of Ausonius which begins *Quod vitae sectabor iter*' (What road in life shall I follow?).[3] Late in his life Freud was asked by Maxime Leroy for his comments on Descartes' dream. In a brief reply, confirming Descartes' own interpretation, he considered them as examples of 'dreams from above'; that is 'they are formulations of ideas which could have been created just as well in a waking state as during the state of sleep'.[4]

Modern philosophy often presents itself as an 'awakening' from the sleep of reason. Emerging from the dream of superstition and error to a new critical method approaches the simplest matter sceptically and, thus, through a continuous process of reflection, arrives at the Truth. Thus Kant, on reading Hume, declared that he had been 'roused from dogmatic slumbers'. But the coupling of dreaming and philosophy is not easily undone. Does not the quest for certainty and the longing to terminate the self-renewing process of doubt in fact lead further and further away from 'reality'? Are not philosophers rightly called 'dreamers'? And, in spite of its institutionalised self-criticism, is modern philosophy anything other than the dream of a new certainty?

For modernity dreaming is the unexpected meeting point of doubt and certainty, truth and falsehood, reality and illusion. The wish to render experience into a system of pure concepts is one of the most generalised dreams of modern life. The philosopher, gripped by doubt, is led effort-lessly from one idea to another; and, perpetually testing and criticising the human power of representation, there passes through his or her mind an endless succession of thoughts. Doubt detaches philosophy from the con-fusing world of everyday events, and, withdrawing into the tranquillity of an impenetrable privacy, creates there a realm of unlimited freedom. Philosophical reflection, once set in motion, has an involuntary character, and throws up unforeseen 'results' which often appear bizarre to the non-philosophical mind. The detachment and strange lucidity, the fascin-ating insignificance, of modern philosophy is more than trivially oneiric, and betrays more certainly than does all but the finest scientific treatise on the subject, the ambiguity of dreams for modern culture.

THE MECHANISATION OF THE WORLD-PICTURE

Whether the experience of modernity is construed initially in terms of the restless inner-movement of doubt over our knowledge of the world, or in terms of uncertainty over the distinction between appearance and reality, dreams occupied a significant and enigmatic position within it. As either a counter-image, or as a confirmation, of the world of experience, the dream revealed the mind's inability to escape the trap of its own artifice. In becoming an object of reflection the dream stimulated the most intract-able form of that species of doubt, which, as lived experience dreaming in turn abolished. As an analogue of the mind the dream came to represent *both* reflection *and* imagination. Indeed, the plasticity of the dream not only brought to life a picture of the world; its succession of images also revealed the normally hidden process of representation itself.

Such views of dreaming were formed as a minor accompaniment to the general process through which the awareness and understanding of the distinctive character of modern society took shape. This process, in time, was to generate a new institutional order and universalise a principle of rationality held to be immanent within each individual. In the modern world each person would act when fully awake, and, thus, in complete possession of his or her faculties. Social life, consequently, would emerge into the clear light of day. But immediately prior to this enlightenment, and in the awareness of the irreversible destruction of a feudal, hier-archical world view which sanctified a singular and fixed cosmological order, the underlying arbitrariness of social life, and the entrapment of human knowledge within an endless process of representation, brought

7

the dream into prominence as an emblem of human uncertainty and the loss of control over its self-generated reality.

The centrality of dreaming to the culture of the early modern period, and in particular the significance of literary variants of radical doubt for Freud's psychology, will be examined later. For the present it is important simply to note that this prominence faded as the control of nature, and the ordering of society, became better understood in terms of the continuous action of a simple underlying mechanism. It was, in fact, Newtonian science, rather than Cartesian rationalism, which came to provide the authoritative conceptualisation of the world for modern society. In this tradition the cohesion and order of nature was a consequence of the continuous operation of underlying laws which were everywhere the same. Nature was conceived, that is to say, as an emergent totality rather than as a preconceived unity: a totality which could be fully explicated in terms of our knowledge of the irreducible characteristics of its fundamental constituents, together with statements about the rules governing the interaction among them. Beginning from a singular body in empty space Newton developed a precise mathematical description of the interaction of the planetary system, and looked forward to the development of a complete 'system of the world' as a definitive statement of human knowledge of the cosmological order.[5]

Newtonian science reconstructed the universe as a system of rules, rather than as a harmony of substantial forms. Scientific knowledge of nature consisted in a set of elegant equations which, in principle, remained wholly detached from the world whose operation they represented. The truth of this system lay in the representation of the relations among its elements, which, for the purposes of explanation consisted exclusively in indications of quantity and location of what was held to be a uniform and simple substance. The sensory qualities of things remained shrouded in mystery, and the success of the entire enterprise required that reason was identified with science as a system of signs rather than as a body of symbols.

The detachment of the process of representation from the domain of qualities did not, after all, lead to an arbitrary succession of images, but to a new and more powerful expression of the underlying unity of creation. This intellectual certainty, and the apparently growing mastery of nature which, though not wholly or systematically dependent upon the development of new scientific knowledge, was associated with it as a 'progressive' social movement, encouraged the suppression of any alternative conceptions of nature. No other knowledge of nature was possible, or desirable, and the entire process of representation, as a consequence of the formal accuracy of its scientific form, was rendered invisible. There was no further need, now that its inherent doubtfulness had been shrouded in a history of practical triumphs, to reflect upon the process of representation itself, nor, for that matter was there any further point in reflecting on the justice of a society which had become self-regulating simply by allowing individuals the freedom to act rationally (scientifically) in pursuit of their private interests. The system of rules through which the world was explained scientifically could, then, be understood simply as a description of the world itself.

In the context of the developing confidence in scientific reason, dreams, which seemed to be inferior, irrational and fragmented images of a world completely known to science, became devalued. Equally, for a modern society which was understood as the emergent order of individually motivated and rational actions, dreams could only be the insignificant dross of consciousness.

Later sociological views of modern society, even where they originated in a penetrating critique of Enlightenment optimism, were just as hostile to the dream. Following Rousseau the dream was invoked in accounts of the 'primitive' as the characteristic and mistaken form of consciousness typical of archaic and simple societies in which people lived in immediate contact with nature. For whatever reason they had not developed that process of rational thought and accumulated that store of technical knowledge through which we regulated our more detached relationship to nature and to society. With a wealth of ethnographic illustrations Victorian anthropologists tirelessly elaborated on themes drawn from eighteenth-century rationalism. E. B. Tylor, the most incisive of collators, impressed particularly by ethnographic material on what was thought to be the simplest of primitive societies, the Australian aborigine, argued that their attempts to understand themselves and their world were frozen in an archaic mode largely because their conscious mind was dominated by their dreamlife. Indeed, it was claimed that they failed properly to distinguish between waking experience and dream-images.[6]

THE ROMANCE OF DREAMS

But alternative views did persist. The 'longing for total revolution' which was characteristic of every aspect of modernity was a transforming vision of the inner freedom of the human soul as much as it was the submission of nature to rational laws.[7] At the very moment that science seemed to be on the point of defining and describing an order of autonomous objects, withdrawn into a cold, distant and empty space, Romanticism sank itself into modern subjectivity and sought to liberate the spirit from the obscurity of its self-enclosed depths. The Romantic dream was not, as it was for Renaissance writers like Giordano Bruno or Marsilio Ficino, a literal flight from the world into what the astronomer Kepler called the 'dull immensity of space'; it was, rather, an escape by collapsing inwards, upon the self, revealing through an interminable fall the inexhaustible immensity of the subjective world. This fall, and the domain of absolute freedom it opened to experience, was an inner journey mapped by the experience of dreams.

9

For the Romantics, therefore, the dream was cherished at the very time when it was being devalued by the positive sciences. This apparent 'anti-modernism', however, is deceptive. The Romantic flight is not driven by nostalgia for the pre-modern world, but by an insatiable longing to explore the infinite abyss which lies at the centre of everything new. This infinitising movement gives depth and solidity to the superficiality of modern life. The 'poetry of night and of twilight' has the effect of making everything 'alien and yet familiar and attractive'.[8] Through dreaming, the prosaic waking world, as if newly created, recaptures its primordial mystery, so that 'what formerly was ordinary, is now strange and wonderful'.[9] The lure of dreams lies not only in the promise of liberation from an oppressive waking reality, but also in the possibility of consecrating appearance to a renewed substantiality. As opposed to the dominant intellectual tradition of modernity, Romanticism insisted on the broadest possible definition of the dream, which offered, more certainly than the sciences in which many of its poets were well trained, a complete vision of reality. For them, the dream was a privileged mode of participation in a higher form of life.

The inner world of human subjectivity knows the world of objects only through itself. It can become aware only of its own movements. The world of objects withdraws into itself, existing only as the dubious postulate of senses which, entirely reliable in their own terms, can convey nothing of the quality of created being. The human predicament is not so much to be confronted with a world of enigmatic, but interpretable, symbols, as to be wholly contained within a world of arbitrary signs, from which real presence is rigorously excluded. In this context the dream is not distinguished from waking reality directly as subject is to object; for waking reality too is wholly subjective. As the most notable student of Romantic dreams rightly points out, for them, 'the dream was not a phenomenon of sleep', but was rather a privileged form of representation.[10]

The newly developing sciences, therefore, offered little real insight into, and no comfort in the face of, an imperious and impenetrable nature. Novalis, thus, turns inwards and celebrates the Night and Dreams: 'I turn aside to the sacred, ineffable, mysterious night'.[11] And in doing so he does not turn to another kind of day, a time without light; but is drawn into and is shrouded in eternity. The distinction is not a division within a pre-existing continuity, but is, rather, an absolute difference. The power of 'eternal night' is greater than that of light, and in entering into it we find ourselves in a state 'when slumber will be eternal and there will be only one inexhaustible dream'.[12]

In his incomplete novel, *Heinrich von Ofterdingen*, Novalis speaks through the central character, Heinrich, of the power of dreams. Heinrich's father, Friedrich, represents the new enlightened, historical and sceptical view:

Dreams are spindrift, whatever your learned men may think of them;

and you will do well to turn your mind away from such useless and harmful reflection. The times are past when divine apparitions appeared in dreams, and we cannot and will not fathom the state of mind of those chosen men the Bible speak of. The nature of dreams as well as the world of men must have been different in those days.

(Pfefferkorn 1988, pp. 191–92)

Heinrich, like Don Quixote a dreamy character composed of the many texts he has read, is not at all impressed by this rational conceit, and argues differently:

Is not every dream, even the most confused one, a remarkable phenomenon, which apart from any notion of its being sent from God is a significant rent in the mysterious curtain that hangs a thousandfold about our inner life?

(Pfefferkorn 1988, p. 176)

His dream of a blue flower, which inaugurates the novel, has a deep personal significance for him. In an image which recalls Kepler's visionary astrophysics he claims:

Certainly the dream I dreamt tonight was not accidental, without repercussions for my life, for I feel how it reaches into my soul like a vast wheel that is to drive it along in its mighty sweep.

(Kuzniar 1990, p. 105)

As opposed to all pre-modern dreams, the Romantic image is one of oneiric lucidity in opposition to the veil of illusion, obscurity and indefiniteness of waking reality. Heinrich further defends his love of dreams:

Dreams seem to me to be a defense against the regularity and routine of life, a playground where the hobbled imagination is freed and revived and where it jumbles together all the pictures of life and interrupts the constant soberness of grownups by means of a merry child's play.

(Kuzniar 1990, p. 173)

Novalis's view of dreams as the realm of absolute freedom, is associated with a libertarian conception of both children's play and its spontaneous representation as fairy tales, in relation to each of which modern poetry recreates, with deliberate artifice, an image of human transcendence.[13]

And at one with the literary theorists of German idealism, with whom he was closely associated, Novalis praised the fragment and the incomplete expression over any rational and systematic order: the dream is 'without coherence an *assemblage* of miraculous things and events'. The discontinuities and disjunction of framing episodes and narrative in *Heinrich von Ofterdingen* give formal expression to the non-rational structure of dreams

11

and play. Within the dream 'the universe breaks down into infinite worlds, which are always contained by more immense worlds'.[14]

Here the dream is an internal and private illumination; and for that reason, to continue its work of romanticising, it must be aided within the public sphere by poetry. The Romantic dream opened an infinite world to the individual, to every individual. Commenting on Calderón, Novalis remarks: 'Our life is not a dream – but it should, and maybe it will, become one'.[15]

The 'metaphysical ecstasy' of Romantic dream visions encouraged a renewed interest in historical studies of language, and more particularly of myth, as a storehouse of symbolic forms still relevant to the modern world.[16] This tradition persisted throughout the nineteenth century, and, particularly in the writings of Scherner, was well known at the time Freud became interested in dreams. Moreover, the conception of the task of human self-understanding as the interpretation of a stream of images, endlessly unfolding itself from the inner depths of subjectivity, was overlaid, but never wholly eclipsed, by scientific and medical investigations of the machinery of life.

MEDICINE AS A SCIENTIFIC ENTERPRISE

The impact of the rational scientific world view on Freud's intellectual development was profound, and made its most significant and lasting impact in terms of the training he received as a medical student at what was, and had been for some time, one of Europe's leading medical schools. In Vienna scientifically-based medical training had been established towards the end of the eighteenth-century with the emergence of a specialised academic faculty which was not composed simply, as it had been previously, of all medical practitioners within the city.

By the time Freud became a student, the dominant tradition of positivistic medical investigation was well established. Laboratory studies, to which Freud was strongly attracted, was the foundation of an enormously expanded programme of medical education. It is tempting to see a number of Freud's most fundamental ideas as applications of the leading theoretical points of view with which he was familiar from these laboratory studies and the scientific traditions, both in Vienna and Berlin, which sustained them. Further, it seems plausible to argue that some of his more general and fundamental intellectual perspectives were formed through his education within this tradition. The embrace of Darwinism as an integrative theoretical framework for the biological (and psychological) sciences, a commitment to non-vitalistic biological principles in which mechanical processes played the fundamental role, and a view of medicine as primarily a scientific enterprise with which a variety of therapeutic techniques of limited value were loosely associated might all be seen as the inheritance of the years he spent in the Physiological Institute headed by Ernst Brücke.[17] But if that was the full, or even the primary, significance of Freud's scientific training, then his own interest in dreams, and the central part that interest played in the development of his work as a whole, would become puzzling.

The influence of the Vienna Medical School, important as it was in shaping Freud's basic intellectual position, was certainly not the sole source of this orientation, nor, significantly, was its impact as consistent and uniform as has often been assumed. Its modern foundation coincided with the upsurge of Romanticism in European culture, and Vienna's leading physicians during this significant period, Johann Peter Frank and Franz Josef Gall, looked first to French and Scottish paradigms of medical practice. They championed the view that bodily health was based on an optimum degree of 'excitation' (conceived as a combination of the natural irritability of bodily tissues with suitable intensities of appropriate stimulation), rather than of the harmonious mixture of bodily fluids. John Brown, an Edinburgh graduate whose ideas were influential in Vienna, argued that diseases differed fundamentally only in the extent to which stimulation departed from the healthy norm; giving rise to symptoms of 'sthenia' (over-stimulation) or 'asthenia' (under-stimulation).[18] Those seeking a comprehensive grounding to more general and theoretical approaches in biology turned to Kant and Schelling, rather than to traditions of scientific modernism, for inspiration. Intuitive reasoning, a general morphological approach to the understanding of living beings, and the recognition of spiritual and non-material causes in both normal and pathological organic processes were accepted, as was a general perspective within which a parallel was drawn between the development of the individual and the evolution of the species. Such conceptions:

> played a central role in the writings of the *Naturphilosophen*; but they were also important to a much larger body of workers who were striving to achieve a comprehensive scientific understanding of vital processes and structures. Moreover, whereas *Naturphilosophie* enjoyed a relatively brief vogue followed by a rapid decline, the more general movement of a romantic biology pursuing this end with these means persisted until the mid-nineteenth century and beyond.
>
> (Clarke and Jacyna 1987, p. 3)

It was within this tradition that clinical medicine, with a strong humanistic background, non-invasive and non-interventionist techniques, became established in Vienna.[19] It was also in this context that 'alternative' medical therapies flourished. Anton Mesmer, the notorious founder of semi-occult practices associated with 'animal magnetism', was never quite forgotten in Vienna, and, by way of Paris and Nancy, Freud and others were later to re-establish there the techniques of hypnotism that had been developed from his unorthodox example.[20] Homeopathy, hydrotherapy and later electrical treatments were also widely used throughout the nineteenth century as part of a Romantic tradition which restricted therapeutic measures to providing a stimulus to the body's inner capacities to heal itself. This holistic approach to medicine, which saw disease in terms of an internal dynamic rather than as the mechanical outcome of a pathogenic stimulus, was supported by Feuchtersleben, who was not only the most significant figure in the foundation of psychiatry and psychology in Vienna, but was also an influential voice in reforming the university, and more particularly the medical faculty, in the wake of the 1848 Revolution. It is ironic, therefore, that the major consequence of these reforms was to establish a more strictly positivistic, laboratory-based approach to medicine. Though, to a large extent, modelled on developments in Berlin (in many cases, indeed, Berlin scientists were appointed to chairs in Vienna), the new approach probably owed most to the indigenous example of Carl von Rokitansky.[21] As the pathologist in charge of conducting autopsies in Vienna he had literally thousands of cases at his disposal, and it was through his, and his successor Rudolf Virchow's, monumental and careful labour in classifying diseases in terms of anatomical lesions that doctors began to conceive of 'symptoms' as the natural outcome of an underlying 'disease process', rather than as the 'accident' of an internal dialectic.

Given this background, the influx of Berlin laboratory scientists, including Brücke, Billroth and Nothnagel, finally established the superiority of a physiological–mechanistic over a morphological–descriptive approach to clinical medicine in Vienna. A student of Müller's, along with Emile du Bois-Raymond and Hermann Helmholtz, Brücke established physiological research as the foundation of scientific medicine. Du Bois-Raymond wrote that together they had 'conspired to spread the truth that no other forces are effective in the organism but the ordinary physical-chemical ones'.[22] Helmholtz, indeed, who was active in physics as well as biology, infiltrated the idea of physical 'force' and 'energy' into biology and looked towards the ultimate unification of the sciences of living matter, as well as of inanimate bodies, in terms of these fundamental concepts.

It would be misleading, however, to view the 'School of Helmholtz' in a narrowly positivistic framework. Laboratory-based science never wholly ousted the humanistic clinical tradition, especially in terms of therapeutics. And, even more importantly, it must be remembered that, as the teachers of Freud and many others, they shared with their students not only a deep conviction of the scientific validity of their approach to biology, but confidence in a much broader German education which revered Goethe and classical studies as the inspiration behind *both* the literary *and* the scientific traditions of modernity. The Berlin scientific *avant garde* had in common:

14

the precious possession of a philosophy and a set of moral rules which they had assimilated from the new humanism with which they had come in contact at the Humboldt mansion, and the study of Kant.

(Lesky 1976, p. 280)

Brücke, like Billroth, was a painter, as well as a physiologist, Meynert, an authoritative figure in psychiatry, was the son of a writer and an opera singer and Breuer, for several years Freud's senior colleague and collaborator, was deeply interested in music. Artistic interests, as well as scientific pursuits, characterised the Viennese intellectual milieu throughout the latter part of the nineteenth century, as, indeed, they had during the Enlightenment and the Romantic Movement.[23]

It is, therefore, in no way contradictory to claim that Freud was attached *both* to the development of mechanistic biology *and* to the morphological–descriptive approach to clinical work which took its inspiration directly from Goethe. It was, in fact, his reading of Goethe's essay 'On Nature' that first dissuaded him from the study of law.[24] And it is only in retrospect that these seem to be sharply divergent traditions, and that Freud must belong exclusively to one or the other.[25]

In fact, even as a student, Freud did not accept the more aggressive reductionist programme, and he did not restrict himself to narrow scientific topics. He attended a course in philosophy given by Brentano, and seems to have been considerably influenced by his distinctive phenomenological approach to the understanding of consciousness.[26]

THE BREAKDOWN OF BOURGEOIS RATIONALITY

Towards the end of the nineteenth century, while confidence in science, and the mastery of nature which its embodiment in the technology of the second industrial revolution seemed to promise, for many encouraged the most optimistic assessments of human progress, unresolved difficulties within the Newtonian paradigm itself apparent to relatively few threatened the entire edifice of modern rationality.

The development of the natural sciences, from the intellectual revolution of the seventeenth century up to the mid-nineteenth century can be conceived as a dynamic theory of the closed body. The singular 'body in space' was not only the object upon which the enquiring scientist's gaze was fixed, it was, like the vanishing point of a perspective painting, a mirror-image of the enquiring observer. But throughout the second part of the nineteenth century, as the bourgeois ego became aware of itself as an unfounded and ultimately arbitrary bundle of sensations, and the singular and privileged point of view from which the classical sciences had reconstructed reality fractured into a multiplicity of perspectives, the natural bodies which had been the object of such precise observation themselves began to fragment and dissolve.

Two major developments in scientific theory, thermodynamics and electro-magnetism, reflected a new difficulty in quite precisely locating objects in space. For the Newtonian scientist a 'body in space' was just that; an irreducible lump of matter whose mass and position could be unambiguously stated, as could its change of position over any stated period of time. What characterised scientific explanation, indeed, was the belief (if not the fully vindicated practice) of accounting for any specific phenomenon in terms of such simple physical properties as mass and change of position. However the development of thermodynamics – the branch of physics which dealt with the phenomena of heat, including that generated and lost in machines – developed along two rather different lines which it proved to be impossible to reunite. At a microscopic level heat was understood to be connected with the vibration of elementary lumps of matter; the faster they vibrated the hotter a substance became. And at the macroscopic level laws governing heat transfer, radiation, conduction and so on were specified to high degrees of precision. The real difficulty arose when the simple underlying mechanical picture was used as the model from which the macroscopic laws should be deduced. Good approximations were achieved using a statistical approach, and this was not generally thought to create a real methodological difficulty. It was assumed that our inability to specify precisely what would happen to, for example each and every molecule of water in a basin when mixed with a certain quantity of water at a hotter temperature, was a result merely of our temporary ignorance of all the 'facts' of the case. With the advantages of modern high-speed computers, for example, the problem would have been expected to disappear. It was soon realised, however, that the difficulty was more intractable. When liquids of different temperatures are mixed in this way, heat energy is 'transferred' from hotter, more active molecules to cooler, less active, ones. Now, though we can predict just what the overall effect will be, there is no way of specifying in advance precisely which molecules will gain or lose energy. There was no mechanical principle which would lead in an unbroken chain of physical causes (upon which rested the claim to a rational explanation), from the characteristics of individual 'bodies in space', to the dynamic characteristics of the 'system of the world'.

This break was all the more evident in the parallel development of electro-dynamics by James Clerk Maxwell. In his revolutionary physics there were no 'bodies in space' at all, no collisions, and no mechanisms. The fundamental observational data relating to electrical and magnetic phenomena were elegantly synthesised by him into a series of powerful equations which described their effects in terms of ever present, and effortlessly extended fields of force, rather than in terms of the point-mass characteristics of bodies. This 'non-material' dynamics was the foundation of the subsequent dramatic transformation of the physical sciences.

The 'physical world', that is to say, was no longer conceived as made up of interacting bodies precisely located in space. And what imprecisely located bodies did exist displayed unpredictable changes of state. The unbroken continuity essential to a purely quantitative science, on closer examination, and in conformity with both the new statistical laws of thermodynamics and the Maxwell field-equations, proved to be something of a mirage. Elementary particles of matter could be assigned an energy level, depending for example on their temperature and state of motion, but, while at the level of everyday observation we assume such energy levels to be a continuous variable, which could be indefinitely subdivided, its differentiation depending only on our capacity to measure and distinguish minimal increments along some quantitative dimension of value, in reality such increments were made up of simple multiples of a discrete and invariant *quanta* of energy. An elementary body, therefore, could be in a limited number of states, and would spontaneously change from one to another. These changes, at an elementary level, were once again apparently independent of any unifying mechanical cause.

This non-localised, and dematerialised conception of matter reflected, as clearly as had classical mechanics mirrored its previously 'closed' bourgeois form, the new 'open' and dissociated forms of the observing ego.

The implication was that, as no observable body could be finally 'pinned down' in space, neither could an observing subject. The relational mechanics of Mach expressed one half of this equation quite clearly. All bodies were relatively unfixed in relation to all others; but somehow amidst them all a classical ego kept watch upon the kaleidoscope, arbitrarily changing its point of view, but retaining, from each position, the momentary integrity of a first-hand observer. Rather than 'imagine a body in space', we were asked to 'imagine a series of bodies in relative motion to each other'. But fully to take account of the psychological, as well as the dynamical, revolution required that we abandon even a temporary claim to omniscience. Einstein replaced the fixed observer with a new relationalism. Now we were asked to 'imagine two observers in relative motion to each other', and scientific explanation took the form of accounting for their differing observations, rather than in establishing an authoritative and objective statement of the 'facts'. A singular viewpoint was no longer realistic. The aim of science was not to construct a theoretical model of a simple reality thought of as standing behind such observational variations – a true 'system of the world' in which all observational contradictions would be transcended – but consisted in the normalisation of such differences themselves.

In different ways the perspectivism of Ernst Mach, and the philosophical dissolution of the classical bourgeois world view in Nietzsche's philosophy, challenged the validity of any representation of reality reconstructed from a singular viewpoint. Their approaches challenged not only the methodological naiveté of the positive sciences, it also subverted the romantic dream of reawakening nature's depths within us. 'Depth', the artefact of a singular point of view, was as illusory as 'place' or 'substance'.

In the new physics of dispersed forces, matter was absorbed into the general framework of space–time. The radical distinction between matter, on the one hand, and space, on the other, was overcome. The boundary between the two was an area of deformed space–time, a zone of increasing concentration, rather than a qualitatively different kind of region. And though a precise mathematical expression of these relations had to await the development of a General Theory of Relativity, its possibility was clearly stated by William Clifford well before the end of the nineteenth century.[27]

Oddly (for those still attached to nineteenth-century assumptions) this dematerialisation of the physical cosmos had the effect of rendering possible a more realistic representation of its most significant characteristics. For classical mechanics time had no meaning. Newton's equations are precisely that, reversible relations of equality. Classical physics was founded on laws of conservation; quantity was preserved through all the transformations possible to matter in motion. This gave to classical physics its sense of eternity; it treated the cosmos as a vast perpetual motion machine. But the new physics, one branch of which (thermodynamics) came into existence in an attempt to apply classical physics to actual machinery, discovered an arrow of time in every physical change and saw in the continual interchange of physical quantities the shadow of cosmological decay. Energy is continually lost; every interaction exacts a price; entropy increases.

Similarly for social experience which is dislocated and disoriented, fragmented beyond hope of recombination under the fictive unity of the ego, time has more significance than space. The elements of experience have nothing in common but duration. And the more intense the experience, the more certainly does it confront the subject, which is its momentary coeval, with the certainty of once again passing into oblivion. But time, concentrated, so to speak, in the intensity of the moment, itself dissolves into insignificance.

And just as nature became dematerialised and its underlying continuity was sundered, so psychologists began to discover the strange and compelling phenomena of hysterical amnesia, double-consciousness and multiple personality. The fundamental problems of the new age thus became problems of memory and the representation of time, rather than those of epistemology and the representation of space.

Freud's psychology is part of this transformation in *fin-de-siècle* culture. Developing out of the positive sciences which had dominated nineteenth-century intellectual life, he provided an approach to self-understanding which, in common with literary and artistic as well as scientific movements of the period, focused directly on the paradoxical and non-rational elements of experience. And in rejecting both classical bourgeois rationality and its Romantic counter-image he simultaneously articulated the immediate context of social life in late imperial Vienna.

DREAM CITY

Vienna, more than any other European city by the end of the nineteenth century, was the home of all those scientific and cultural transformations which were to be viewed in retrospect as typical of the most advanced characteristics of modernity. That mood of complacent self-confidence which had become synonymous with bourgeois culture was shaken by a profound sense of inner disintegration. Astonishing novelties appeared in every field, giving rise to a curiously stable equilibrium of creation and decay. And it was the most creative individuals who were most acutely conscious of this decay. To Oskar Kokoschka 'the whole world seemed to be in the grip of an existential malaise'.[28] Arthur Schnitzler was aware of 'a constant intermingling of seriousness and play, of reality and farce, of truth and mendacity'.[29] And Stefan Zweig came to recognise in its bourgeois sense of comfort and security 'nought but a castle of dreams'.[30]

The city was both an image and an exemplar of the chaotic flux of sensation into which the secure and rational world of bourgeois egoism had dissolved. Looking back to a period just prior to the outbreak of the First World War, Robert Musil opens his great novel, *The Man Without Qualities*, with a description of Vienna in terms of characteristic impressions of noise and bustle:

> Like all big cities it consisted of irregularity, change, sliding forward, not keeping in step, collisions of things and affairs, and fathomless points of silence in between, of paved ways and wilderness, of one great rhythmic throb and the perpetual discord and dislocation of all opposing rhythms, and as a whole resembled a seething, bubbling fluid in a vessel consisting of the solid material of buildings, laws, regulations, and historical traditions.
>
> (Musil 1968, 1, p. 40)

Mirroring both Simmel's description of the overwhelming stimulation of modern city life, and Nietzsche's imagery of the perpetual flux of nature, Musil emphasises the exhausting effect of a continuously shifting point of attention, and the sheer, crushing weight of this 'world of hurrying forms':

> If one could measure the leaps that the attention took, the exertion of the eye-muscles, the pendulum-movements of the psyche, and all the efforts that a human being must make in order to keep himself

vertical in the flux of the street, then presumably – so he had thought, and had toyed with trying to calculate the incalculable – the result would be a quantity compared with which the force that Atlas needed to hold the world up was trivial, and one could imagine the enormous output of energy, nowadays, of even a man who was doing nothing at all.

(Musil 1968, 1, p. 43)

Given this 'tangle of forces', Ulrich, the novel's central character, realises that 'it doesn't matter what one does'. Reality has no more significance for him than that of a temporary and accidental arrangement of objects and events. Ulrich is continually struck by the thought that everything 'could probably just as easily be some other way,' and that he need 'attach no more importance to what is than to what is not'.

The arbitrariness of experience, the continuous appearance within it of new and disturbing possibilities, renders strangely unreal and insubstantial the thing-like solidity of the urban environment. To Ulrich, the entire world of modern ideas is similarly infected with incoherence and insubstantiality. For him, 'sharp boundaries everywhere became blurred'. The clear distinction between subject and object, force and matter, idea and object; antinomies which had defined a rational bourgeois order, softened and merged. Renovating his new house Ulrich attempts to create an interior suitable to the modern condition and mood, but:

Finally he gave up inventing anything but impracticable rooms, revolving rooms, kaleidoscopic interiors, adjustable scenery for the soul, and his ideas grew steadily more and more insubstantial.

(Musil 1968, 1, p. 52)

The 'vast sensuality' in which all the contradictions of modern life are caught up and reflected does nothing to unify the fragmentation of experience. There is something oppressive and at the same time unreal in the unrelenting objectivity of modern existence.

The 'incoherency of ideas' which Ulrich believes characteristic of the present era is itself an aspect of modern experience. Dream and waking reality are not so much confused, which would imply their separation, as coalesced into the phantasmagoria of modern life. Ulrich, repeating a phrase from Novalis, notices that 'there was something about people's faces that was like spindrift':

All these circular lines, intersecting lines, straight lines, curves and convolutions, of which an interior consists and which had accumulated round him, were a product neither of nature nor of inner necessity, but, down to the last detail, bulged with baroque superabundance.

(Musil 1968, 1, p. 174)

In a world in which anything seems possible, many of the historic dreams of western society might be realised:

> If the realization of primordial dreams is flying, travelling with the fishes, boring one's way under the bodies of mountain-giants, sending messages with godlike swiftness, seeing what is invisible and what is in the distance and hearing its voice, hearing the dead speak, having oneself put into a wonder-working healing sleep, being able to behold with living eyes what one will look like twenty year's after one's death, in glimmering nights to know a thousand things that are above and below this world, things that no one ever knew before, if light, warmth, power, enjoyment and comfort are mankind's primordial dreams, then modern research is not only science but magic.
>
> (Musil 1968, 1, pp. 73–4)

And if this strange intermingling of reality and fantasy, of science and magic, is most dramatically evident in a ubiquitous sense of dreamlike unreality, it equally implies a new realism of the dream. Thus, although, 'we have gained in terms of reality and lost in terms of the dream', and we have been possessed by a demon of hard work and efficiency, it is equally true that 'it may all of a sudden happen' that we fail to 'summon up any sense of reality' and one day appear to ourselves as 'a man without qualities'.

Ulrich is indifferent to a world in which 'everything sparkles with novelty', but he is incapable of condensing within himself any sense of solidity which might betray the presence of a personality. In spite of himself, therefore, he finds he is caught up in the welter of events and relations from which he had attempted to stand apart:

> Has one not noticed that experiences have made themselves independent of man? They have gone on to the stage, into books, into the reports of scientific institutions and expeditions, into communities based on religious or other conviction, which develop certain kinds of experience at the cost of all others as in a social experiment; and in so far as experiences are not merely to be found in work, they are simply in the air. Who today can still say that his anger is really his own anger, with so many people butting in and knowing so much more about it than he does? There has arisen a world of qualities without a man to them, of experiences without anyone to experience them, and it almost looks as though under ideal conditions man would no longer experience anything at all privately and the comforting weight of personal responsibility would dissolve into a system of formulae for potential meanings.
>
> (Musil 1968, 1, pp. 198–99)

Ulrich's dreamy indifference to the world does not stem from introversion so much as from participation in a social world that lacks coherence. Musil, a student of Ernst Mach, like his mentor explores the affinity between the most advanced of modern scientific ideas, and the fragmentation of inner experience. There is a link between physics and psychology which, as Hermann Bahr noticed, also defines a new aesthetics. There is, in every field, a sense of inner dissolution:

> Nothing can save the 'I' says Ernst Mach, Impressionism's acutest thinker. Its 'I' has vanished, and with it the world has vanished also, nothing remains but the sense-illusion of impressions.
>
> (Bahr 1925, p. 47)

Mach, a physicist as well as a philosopher, insisted upon a strictly Humean self-conception. The ego is:

> as little absolutely permanent as our bodies. That which we so much dread in death, the annihilation of our permanency, actually occurs in life in abundant measure . . . . The assumption, or postulation, of the ego is a mere practical necessity.
>
> (Mach 1989, p. 29)

Hugo von Hofmannsthal, the greatest poet of the age, agreed:

> we have no consciousness beyond the instant, because each of our souls only lives for an instant . . . . My ego of *yesterday* is of as little concern to me as the ego of Napoleon or Goethe.
>
> (Bennett 1988, p. 21)

Nothing can prevent this inner dissolution, because nothing exists:

> For me, everything disintegrated into parts, those parts again into parts; no longer would anything let itself be encompassed by a single idea. Single words floated around me; they congealed into eyes which stared at me and into which I was forced to stare back – whirlpools which gave me vertigo and, reeling incessantly, led into the void.
>
> (Field 1967, pp. 11–12)

And this was by no means always a negative experience. For Hofmannsthal, as for Simmel, modernity provided new opportunities; those, who had the means 'to bask in the light of immediate consciousness' and were willing to 'luxuriate in the realm of appearance', perhaps best understood the times.[31]

Fin-de-siècle Vienna was, in some respects, a metropolis which displayed advanced symptoms of cultural decadence (Nietzsche), nervous excitement (Simmel) and dreamy indifference (Musil); each indicative of the most developed forms of modernity. Yet in terms of more conventional historical categories Vienna was far from being a progressive capital city.

As the political and cultural centre of the Habsburg Empire, Vienna presided over a 'grotesque collection of odds and ends', and, half-a-century after its bourgeois revolution of 1848, was a society in which formal and ritual precedence was taken by an aristocracy which looked back to its imperial past.[32] In addition to Austria proper, the Empire included Hungary, Bohemia and parts of Italy and Poland. Strong ethnic and linguistic loyalties meant that, for most of its subjects, including the Viennese, the Empire appeared to be an artificial creation. The modern nation state had little meaning, administratively, politically or culturally for the mass of people who felt themselves to be, first and foremost, German, Czech, Italian, Magyar, Slovene, Slovak, Polish, Ruthene, Serb, Croat, Rumanian, Slav or Jew. 'Austriandom', perhaps not surprisingly, 'was not at all a state consciousness which offered a place for patriotism'.[33] And for the smaller group who felt no national sentiment whatever the Empire had primarily, even exclusively, a merely ritual significance.

But within Vienna ritualism was much in evidence. On the Ringstrasse multicoloured and elaborate uniforms of army officers were a daily spectacle.[34] A compulsory three year military service system fed a large reserve force, that aimed (without success) at being 'a nursery of dynastic feeling'.[35] The title of *Leutenant der Reserve* carried considerable prestige and social standing only because its holder was entitled to wear uniform even when not on active duty.[36] Government officials, of which there were thousands, occupied offices carrying precisely defined status, but ill-defined responsibilities. Official positions were a mark of social standing and, though bureaucratic reforms were initiated by Alexander Bach, who was the first Habsburg state functionary for whom bureaucratic absolutism was an end in itself, government departments and agencies continued to operate on the basis of personal influence, bribery and an elaborate and unreliable network of police spies.[37] The state, in the words of Viktor Adler, the Socialist leader, was 'an absolutism tempered by slovenliness'.[38] Vienna, in terms of its ruling elements, remained rooted in the baroque age. Its political leadership:

> charming and pleasant, was gripped by moral indolence . . . astonishingly ignorant and narrow-minded; shallow, pompous, futile . . . . Bourgeois morality represented a code of personal conduct beneath the notice of the aristocracy . . . (which was) irresponsibly frivolous, irresistibly gay, fundamentally ignorant, devotees of sport and fashion, hopelessly gregarious, and class conscious.
>
> (May 1951, pp. 162–63)

Its political ideas, hardly affected by liberalism, developed from the enlightened absolutism of the late eighteenth century (Josephinism), to repressive conservatism in the style of Metternich.

Nor had Vienna, during its rapid growth in the latter part of the nineteenth century fully developed a modern system of industrial production. Exceptionally for larger European urban areas of the period, small-scale artisan production dominated the suburban development of

Vienna until the financial crisis of 1873, during which a large number of small businesses were bankrupted. It was only when the following depression was finally overcome, which was not until the mid-1880s, that the surviving artisan producers 'were slowly caught up in impersonal economic processes beyond their understanding or control'.[39]

The rapid growth of the population resulted in an acute housing shortage which, it has been claimed, significantly affected the social habits of the Viennese. As distinct from most other urban centres, in Vienna,

> the coffeehouse, the inexpensive restaurant, the public gardens, the spacious Prater, and the woodlands encircling the city were substitutes for the home as a place of relaxation and diversion.
>
> (May 1951, p. 307)

Whatever the significance of these evident signs of political and social backwardness, Vienna, for a relatively brief period, became the centre of the most advanced European culture. It thrived primarily as a secular Jewish culture; and it was the implications of the influx of Jews into Vienna which forms an essential background to Freud's intellectual development. The 'secularized Jewish intelligentsia changed the face of Vienna', which had in the past been notable only for the excellence of its musicians and composers.[40]

In this sense Vienna's modern development was inaugurated by Joseph II's Patent of Toleration in 1781, which reversed those of Maria Theresa's anti-Jewish laws which had excluded all but a handful of Jews from Vienna. The Patent did not grant religious or secular freedom, but defined legal rights for Jews which were equal with those granted to Protestants; they were excluded from the civil service, from a variety of retail trades and professions, from the acquisition of land. Additionally they could not build a house without a special permit, organise their own community, and significantly Maria Theresa's family law was upheld, allowing only the eldest son of Jewish parents to marry.[41] But the new law did grant residence rights to 'tolerated' Jews, and, more significantly opened state schools to Jewish children, making German the official language of the Empire. Joseph's successors were less enthusiastic 'Enlighteners' but a Jewish presence and a core of German-Jewish culture had been established in Vienna. The concessions won in 1848 were short-lived, but the abolition of serfdom and the consequent detachment of the rural population from any legal obligation to the land had important long-term implications for the growth and composition of the Jewish population in Vienna. And in 1867 the new constitution finally granted citizenship rights to Jews.

The growth in the total population of Vienna between 1857 and 1910 was dramatic, though not exceptional for a major European city. The rate of increase, and the total number, of its Jews, however, was unparalleled, as shown in the table below.

As a magnet for Jews Vienna was rivalled only by Budapest. During the

Table Growth of Jewish population of Vienna 1857–1919[42]

Year	Total population	Jews	% Total
1857	476,220	6,217	1.3
1869	607,510	40,227	6.6
1880	726,105	72,543	10.0
1890	827,567	99,441	12.0
1890*	1,364,548	118,495	8.7
1900	1,674,957	146,296	8.8
1910	2,031,498	175,318	8.6

* Includes enlarged boundaries of Vienna in 1890

period of most rapid growth, the 1860s the Jewish population of Vienna grew each year by more than 40 per cent. The spectacular growth, prior to the 1880s, was disproportionately concentrated on an expanding middle class seeking new opportunities for themselves to pursue careers in trade and business, adopt an urban bourgeois style of life, and have their children educated in German scientific and literary culture in the hope that they would, in their turn, join the ranks of the liberal professions. By 1880 about 30 per cent of all students in Vienna were Jewish, and the proportion was even higher in the faculties of medicine and law.[43] Indeed, it was the influx of Jewish students which shifted the centre of gravity of the university away from training an 'official intelligentsia' for civil service posts, to educating a 'liberal intelligentsia' in the arts and sciences. The Jewish commitment to modern education was highly successful. In the early 1880s 60 per cent of all doctors registered in Vienna were Jewish, as, by the end of the decade were 58 per cent of all advocates.[44] The entry of Jews into professional careers seems not to have aroused a 'racial' response. Schnitzler reports that, during the 'late-blossoming period of liberalism' towards the end of the 1870s, 'anti-Semitism existed, as it had always done, as an emotion in the numerous hearts so inclined and as an idea with great possibilities of development, but it did not play an important role politically or socially'.[45]

The first waves of migration had been predominantly made up of Hungarian Jews from medium and larger Jewish communities close to Vienna. But during the latter part of the century mass migration of Jews to Vienna from economically backward, small and geographically isolated rural communities in Galicia became a dominant trend. It was in relation to the influx of Ostjuden, distinct in terms of dress, customs and language, that anti-Semitism in its modern form first developed in Vienna. And it is in this context that two stereotyped images of the Viennese Jew developed.

On the one hand there were those held to represent 'an almost unknown human type full of mystery and wonder'; people 'with their dirty caftans' and 'exotic faces' whose 'ghostly apparitions from time long lost, still haunt the modern present'.[46] On the other hand, there were those seen as having 'abandoned Yiddish for German, traditional Jewish names for proper German ones, Jewish customs for the styles of nineteenth century Europe'.[47] There were also religious differences between these groups. The Jewish Reform Movement encouraged the pursuit of German *Bildung* as an educational ideal for *Judaism*, whereas Eastern Jews for the most part followed the traditional pattern of Hebrew study.[48] Anti-Semitism developed in the context of a lengthy period of successful assimilation, or at least of toleration, which many Jews as well as Gentiles believed to be threatened by the arrival of 'racially distinct' *Ostjuden*. By 1900, middle-class Jewish anti-Semitism was common, and influential given their dominant position in Viennese journalism. For a significant group 'The Eastern Jew was the bad memory of German Jewry come alive and an ever-present threat to assimilation aspirations'.[49]

The triumph of Karl Lueger's Christian Social Party, and his eventual confirmation as Mayor of Vienna in 1897, was based on an appeal to petty-bourgeois prejudice and fear of Jewish banking and big business. As an experienced 'democratic agitator' Lueger ruthlessly exploited popular misconceptions and an outdated electoral system.[50] While there was liberal opposition to Lueger, as there was to the persistence of imperial conservatism with its outmoded longing for absolutism, there never developed in Vienna a political tradition based on economic interests and strong party-based loyalties.[51] In politics, as in so much else, Vienna seemed to have by-passed the nineteenth-century, and leapt straight from baroque absolutism to modern populism. And, for some contemporary observers, as well as for their academic descendants, politics in the imperial city had become dangerously superficial. The moral vacuum of imperial decline, fertile of the *avant garde* in art and science, was, equally, productive of 'democratic agitators' and the transformation of politics into journalism. It was less that, failing to develop a framework for liberal-constitutional politics, intellectuals withdrew into an aesthetically defined private world, than that reality, fragmented beyond any hope of rational reconstruction, became unified as a dream.[52] Hermann Broch, in the most incisive discussion of this culture, notes that 'insofar as by "reality" one predicates something in some sense comprehensive, one is already near to dream'.[53] The 'worldless ego' of the late nineteenth century is nothing other than an 'aesthetic dreamworld'. It is a 'dream induced by reality'; or rather by the dissolution of that particular kind of reality which was the

> style or non-style of the nineteenth-century, in which rationalism, individualism, historicism, romanticism, eclecticism, skepticism are all imbedded and sustained in a kind of Manchesterism calculated for all eternity.
>
> (Broch 1984, p. 82)

In Viennese politics, as in its art, science and public life there was a visible 'convergence of life and dream.'[54] It was as a kind of decorative covering around this 'value vacuum' that Viennese culture promoted a 'lightness of the ever present desire for pleasure and entertainment', and a 'love of spectacle'.[55] The new age was announced in the 'flat cynicism' and 'superficial, careless sensuality' of a view of life devoted to 'the most ephemeral pursuit of pleasure'.[56] One contemporary claimed that 'this city is a paradise without fig leaves, serpent or tree of knowledge'.[57] Its daring cultural innovations were conceived in the coffee-house and theatre rather than in the academy. Its intellectuals and artists communicated through a series of informal relations rather than in terms of formal institutions; its cultural life was a baroque labyrinth organised in terms of the sites of modern urban pleasure.[58]

Freud's texts, like the dreams they interpret, and the culture in which he lived, are labyrinthine structures that continually open on to new perspectives and assimilate fresh material from unexpected and apparently distant sources. It is not sensible, therefore, to attempt to define *the* context, or even the most significant context, for a contemporary reading of his work. Yet, in one way or another, the varied perspectives which Freud opens on to the dream world all take their point of departure in, and return to, the most general characteristics of modernity. Of course, this could hardly be otherwise and little light is shed on either by such an assertion, or by the general considerations which have so far been offered in its support. To establish a more nuanced understanding of the many points of contact between Freud's psychology and the specific character of modern experience it is essential to proceed to a closer reading of the Freudian text. Paradoxically, the relevance of distinctive and related contextual fields to an understanding of this text become more evident through an 'internal' reading of the text itself than they do through a sociologically inspired 'external' interpretation of his work. Such connections cannot be established by intellectual *fiat*, but, rather, must be allowed to emerge gradually through an approach which does justice to the richness of its primary source material.

It would be equally futile to plunge directly into Freud's writings in the naive expectation that they are self-explanatory. Before confronting a series of key texts, therefore, the following chapter proposes in a tentative fashion a series of 'associations' between particular themes in Freud's psychology and a somewhat more specific characterisation of some central aspects of modern experience.

NOTES

1 For a comprehensive review of a variety of research traditions see Foulkes (1978).

2 Foucault, in Foucault and Binswanger (1993), p. 59.
3 The relevant section of Baillet's text is conveniently available in Cottingham (1989). For interesting discussions of his dreams and their role in the formation of his philosophical thought see Maritain (1946), Poulet (1956).
4 SE 21, pp. 199–204.
5 Cohen (1980), Koyré (1973, 1956), Meyerson (1930); this does not, of course, mean that Newton was himself wholly 'rational' in his approach to or understanding of the natural world.
6 Tylor (1871), Burrow (1966), Turner (1974) and for an interesting reworking of the theme Duerr (1985).
7 Yack (1986).
8 Behler (1993), p. 182.
9 Quoted in Kuzniar, p. 118.
10 Bousquet (1964), p. 35.
11 Haywood (1959), p. 55.
12 Ibid, p. 75.
13 Behler (1993), pp. 211–13.
14 Quoted in Kuzniar, p. 114.
15 Ibid., p. 174.
16 Béguin (1946), Bousquet (1964), Firth (1973), pp. 92–118.
17 The Darwinian background in particular is stressed by Sulloway (1980) and Ritvo (1990).
18 Lesky (1976), pp. 8–11.
19 On the scientific tradition stimulated by German idealism and Romanticism see, e.g. Nisbet (1972), Decker (1977), Emmerton (1984), Burwick (1986). More generally Johnston (1972), pp. 223–29 provides a good discussion of the background to 'therapeutic nihilism' in Vienna.
20 Ellenberger (1970), pp. 57–69, 110–23.
21 Lesky (1976), pp. 106–17.
22 Quoted in Lesky (1976), p. 229.
23 The practical scientific interests of the Romantics should not be overlooked, see Ziolkowski (1990).
24 Goethe (1952), pp. 242–44. It seems likely this fragment was written by the Swiss theologian, Tobler, though Goethe accepted it as an accurate rendition of his views; see Gedo and Pollock (eds) (1976), p. 54.
25 Compare, e.g. Sulloway (1980), Ricoeur (1970).
26 McGrath (1986), pp. 94–5.
27 Clifford, William Kingdom (1879). For a sociological perspective on these issues see Ferguson (1990), pp. 158–238.
28 Kokoschka (1974), p. 27.
29 Schnitzler (1971), p. 20.
30 Zweig (1943), p. 16.
31 Hofmannsthal, quoted in Miles (1972).
32 May (1951), p. 2.
33 Jászi (1961), p. 164.
34 Clare (1984) p. 28.
35 Steed (1969), p. 60.
36 Thompson (1990), p. 132.
37 Macartney (1971).
38 Quoted in Jászi (1961), p. 165; the most sensitive treatment of changing military and bureaucratic values is Joseph Roth's novel, The Radetzky March, Roth (1974).
39 Boyer (1981), p. 48.

40 Wistrich (1990), p. vii; le Rider (1993).
41 Wistrich (1990), pp. 19–20.
42 Wistrich (1990), p. 42.
43 Beller (1989), pp. 34–5; more generally le Rider (1993).
44 Macartney (1971), p. 518.
45 Schnitzler (1971), p. 63; Berkley (1988).
46 Jacob Fromer, quoted in Ascheim (1982), p. 12.
47 Rozenblit (1983), p. 6.
48 Wistrich (1990), pp. 132–33; Goldscheider and Zuckerman (1984), pp. 69–70; Gilman (1986); Cuddihy (1987) p. 4; Wertheimer (1987).
49 Ascheim (1982), p. 12; Berkley (1988); Gilman (1993).
50 Schorske (1980), pp. 133–46; Boyer (1981) pp. 184–246
51 Wistrich (1990), pp. 131–63.
52 The first alternative is argued by Schorske (1980), pp. 3–23.
53 Broch (1984), p. 82.
54 Broch (1984), p. 108.
55 Ibid., p. 61.
56 Ibid., p. 77.
57 Heinrich Laube, quoted in Zanuso (1986), p. 35.
58 Timms (1986), pp. 9–10.

2

ARCHETEXT

The texture of the present

Freud's psychology is primarily a description of modern life, and consequently provides invaluable material for contemporary sociology. Indeed, insofar as the experience of modernity is a central issue in sociology, it is in terms of his fundamental psychological works that Freud makes his major contribution to our understanding of society. These works can be approached and effectively linked with the variety of overlapping contexts within which their social meaning comes into sharper focus, through a consideration of what might be termed Freud's 'aesthetic' writings.[1] These works can be read as indicating his interest in, and understanding of, the immediacy of social life. Certainly, more than *Totem and Taboo*, or *Civilisation and its Discontents* his aesthetic works might be considered as contributions to sociological theory; that is, to an understanding of the nature of social experience and social relationships in modern society.

The importance of aesthetics to the understanding of social life has only recently become a central issue for sociological theory; and may be viewed as part of the shift towards a more general cultural understanding of modern society. This, in turn, has been, in part at least, a response to the decline of class-based politics (or, at least, of its associated rhetoric), the emasculation of radical oppositional social movements, the globalisation of networks of communication, and the continuing expansion of consumerism as the 'spirit' of advanced capitalism. While Freud's psychology, in charting with exceptional clarity the breakdown of the nineteenth-century world of experience, is itself a social theory, his insight into the character of everyday social encounters has often been neglected. And, while his psychology in its break with classical bourgeois models of individualism and rationalism, is only now finding itself in a familiar world, his descriptive sociology is equally prescient if less well known.

THE SUPERFICIALITY OF MODERN LIFE

As subject and object, along with all other bourgeois antinomies, were dissolved on the living surface of modernity, the 'soul' merged with the 'body', and the whole meaning of psychology underwent a radical transformation.

Freud was not the first to develop a 'superficial' psychology of modern life, though his work has proved to be the most complete and influential. The emergence of a distinctively modern aesthetics, which is the form in which this psychology was first developed, can be traced to central themes in eighteenth-century philosophy, and became a major preoccupation for Kant and the subsequent development of idealism. And the subtle critique of modern aestheticism offered by Kierkegaard during the 1840s represents the psychologically most insightful contribution within this tradition.[2] In a series of dazzlingly inventive works, imbued with the spirit of Romanticism and exploiting all the resources of idealist philosophy, Kierkegaard demonstrated the extent to which modern life as conceived by its most cultivated and 'advanced' individuals was nothing more than the pursuit of transient pleasures. This modern 'pleasure principle' (which from Freud's perspective might be viewed as a highly sublimated and refined form of gratification), turned out to be self-contradictory. In order to experience the pleasure through which the ego could realise and validate its claims on existence, the individual had to presuppose a continuous self-identity which persisted both before and after the moment of enjoyment. But, in fact, the very concentration of aesthetic value on the momentary present, on immediacy, had the effect of dissolving the ego into a chaotic flux of experience. Kierkegaard's pseudonyms proposed a series of alternatives to this transitory and vanishing selfhood; the development of an ethical or religious identity through which the fundamental melancholy of modern life might be conquered.

Kierkegaard's solutions, in fact, proved either insufficient or more deeply self-contradictory than the aesthetic standpoint from which they departed. In any event Freud's analysis of modern aestheticism, and the possibilities inherent within it, was rather different and held out the prospect of a reconciliation with, rather than a triumph over, the restless character of modern life.

Just as significantly, and more directly linked with Freud in terms of the experience of the culture of 'decadence', Nietzsche can be viewed as establishing the point of departure for a new psychology. Whereas in the philosophical tradition of modernity the human psyche was conceived as an imaging device which, as if viewing in a mirror or through a window, was presented with a visual image of the world, Nietzsche began to chart the landscape of an alternative sensibility, founded upon a tactile register of shocks and excitations. In some ways recalling more ancient modes of grasping reality, Nietzsche suggested that knowledge of the modern world is not so much encoded within the soul in terms of a specular *logos*, as it is inscribed directly on the surface of the body-image. We live through the body not the spirit; or, rather, we exist as a spiritualised body awakened to a new sensitivity as all those abstract infinities to which the soul had been projected re-emerge on the surface of modern life. The *body*, which had for so long in western society been despised, thus comes into a new prominence, not through an inversion of a traditional mode of valuation, but as the *locus* of all those human powers and attributes previously separated and infinitised as spirit, soul, knowledge, consciousness, thought, language and so on.

The animating energies of modern life were conceived as flowing across and through the human body on whose surface they left, as if on a photographic plate or softened wax tablet, an enigmatic trace.[3] Consciousness could no longer be regarded as something separate from the rest of experience; it could not stand apart and observe, but could only become flickeringly aware of itself as part of an operation in which it was itself implicated. This was the environment into which the man without qualities was born:

whatever still remains to him of his 'own person' seems to him accidental, so completely has he become a passage and reflection of forms and events not his own.

(Nietzsche 1973, p. 115)

Though Nietzsche found it difficult to wholly abandon specular imagery, he clearly anticipated its demise.[4] The 'selfless man' is:

a precious, easily damaged and tarnished measuring instrument and reflecting apparatus which ought to be respected and taken care of . . . a delicate, empty, elegant, flexible mould which has first to wait for some content so as to 'form' itself.

(Nietzsche 1973, p. 116)

His is a philosophy, as Freud's is a psychology, awaiting the plastic age. For both, experience leaves its trace not only, or mainly, in terms of an ideal memory, but also, and more significantly, in a morphological history of the body.

The understanding of modernity as a dream, or a dreamlike state, in which experience is moulded to a continuous and unbounded *surface*, (of which the body is one relational aspect), sits uneasily with the widely held view of Freud's psychoanalytic project as a process of excavating the hidden depths of experience. Are not Freud's texts the product of an insatiable curiosity to uncover, to dig down and to bring to the surface everything which has been buried? Is not Freud responsible, after all, for the creation of *depth*-psychology? And are not dreams, as 'the royal road to the unconscious', an invaluable means by which to plumb these depths?

Spatial metaphors are, perhaps, unavoidable but tend to convey more than intended by their user, or is justified by the context. The notion of a depth-psychology grew up among some of Freud's followers, and, more generally has become a popular designation of his method among interested outsiders.[5] Freud himself contributed to some extent to the popularity of the depth metaphor by his repeated comparison of psycho-analysis with archaeology. He claimed, indeed, to have read more archaeology than psychology, and admitted that his passion for collecting antiquities was, with his need for cigars, both an addiction and an extrava-gance.[6] In an early lecture on the aetiology of hysteria he develops at some length the comparison between the problems and methods of under-standing hysteria with that of revealing the historical significance of ancient remains:

> imagine that an explorer arrives in a little-known region where his interest is aroused by an expanse of ruins, with remains of walls, fragments of columns, and tablets with half-effaced and unreadable inscriptions. He may content himself with inspecting what lies ex-posed to view . . . but he may act differently. He may have brought picks, shovels and spades with him, and he may set the inhabitants to work with these implements. Together with them he may start upon the ruins, clear away the rubbish, and, beginning from the visible remains, uncover what is buried. If his work is crowned with success, the discoveries are self-explanatory: the ruined walls are part of the ramparts of a palace or a treasure-house; the fragments of columns can be filled out into a temple; the numerous inscriptions, which, by good luck, may be bilingual, reveal an alphabet and a language, and, when they have been deciphered and translated, yield undreamed-of information about the events of the remote past, to commemorate which the monuments were built. *Saxa loquuntur!* (stones speak!).
>
> (SE 3, p. 192)

And even when this work is not 'crowned with success' and the results are far from 'self-explanatory', archaeology continues to provide for Freud the most relevant model of scientific enquiry and explanation. In the 'Prefatory Remarks' to the Dora case-study he notes that:

> In face of the incompleteness of my analytic results, I had no choice but to follow the example of those discoverers whose good fortune it is to bring to the light of day after their long burial priceless though mutilated relics of antiquity. I have restored what is missing, taking the best models known to me from other analyses; but, like a con-scientious archaeologist, I have not omitted to mention in each case where the authentic parts end and my construction begins.
>
> (SE 7, p. 12)

True, the archaeologist removes surface layers to uncover what was buried, but this kind of excavation should be thought of as a gentle brushing aside of the obscuring shroud of human history, rather than as a forceful boring down through the earth's crust. And the archaeologist can often read the past in visible monuments and relics which have been incorporated into new structures. In a much later and more general work than that quoted above Freud raises a 'hardly studied subject'; the 'general problem of the preservation in the sphere of the mind'. He approaches the question through an extended analogy with the interpretation of the ancient history of Rome through its visible remains. Though a good deal of ancient material is 'buried in the soil of the city or beneath its modern buildings', for someone equipped with 'the most complete historical and topographical knowledge' the past can be traced in remains to be found 'dovetailed into the jumble of a great metropolis'.[7]

Archaeology is a 'superficial' activity in comparison with mining, or palaeontology. It is preoccupied with reconstructing a picture of past life from the corrupted remains of that past itself. It is worth noting that Freud's fascination with archaeology, therefore, is consistent with the spirit of post-bourgeois modernity, and is quite distinct from the conservative spirituality of the Romantics which is revealed in their frequent recourse to the *motif* of life underground. Many of the Romantic writers were professionally involved with mining and engineering, and in their literary works reflected an idealised conception of life in terms of the discovery of living beings deep in the natural caverns at the heart of mountains.[8] Like the Baroque flight of fancy, this Romantic mining locates the human soul in a strange and inaccessible environment which is normally unconnected with the surface of modern life. But Freud's excavations are all carried out on the surface and consist primarily in interpreting what is already visible, and, where he reveals things previously hidden, they are always 'dovetailed' into surface features. The past which he unearths is linked to the present by an unbroken contiguity, and shows itself on the surface in morphological deformations and anomalies which betray the sites of ancient activities.

And when Freud's method bore unexpected results, revealing a hitherto hardly suspected mental landscape, his own description of the process of discovery brought another metaphor into prominence. In a revealing letter to Wilhelm Fliess, written shortly after the publication of *The Interpretation of Dreams*, Freud likened himself to a *conquistador*, to a bold explorer mapping unknown lands:

> For I am actually not at all a man of science, not an observer, not an experimenter, not a thinker. I am by temperament nothing but a *conquistador* – an adventurer, if you want it translated – with all the curiosity, daring, and tenacity characteristic of a man of this sort.
>
> (Freud 1985, p. 398)

Quite apart from the linguistic allusion to the Spanish Golden Age and, by implication, an association with Don Quixote's journey through the imagination, which will be taken up later, the metaphor of exploratory travel is revealing. It suggests that the most remote psychological structure is connected with modern experience by an unsurveyed, or only partially surveyed, but unbroken surface. This is important because Freud places himself on the same level with his subject matter; there is no position, above or below, where the human soul, preserved in an unperished state, provides us with a perspective from which we can gain a panoramic view of the corrupted surface of modern life.

THE SHOCK OF THE NEW

As subject and object merged on the living surface of modernity, and the 'soul' ended its long estrangement from the 'body', a new order of corporeal significance was born. Psychology, along with the experience of the world it sought to understand, was transformed by the shock of the new. And psychology, as a central aspect of the aesthetics of modernity, should begin, therefore, with an analysis of this novel gestural language; should begin, in fact by transcribing, analysing and translating the *inscriptions* wrought upon the body by this shock. This, in fact, is Freud's starting point. His love of archaeology, and its special significance to him as a model of investigation, was equalled by his passion for languages, and the consequently privileged position he accorded the process of translation as a model for understanding immediately incomprehensible mental states and bodily symptoms. His initial problems are conceived as puzzles in a foreign language. Linking two of his great intellectual passions, then, he seeks, to decipher the symptoms his patients display as if their bodies were ancient monuments, or wax tablets petrified after the moment in which some message had been inscribed upon their surface. But these are modern rather than ancient bodies, so he begins by investigating them in their most characteristically modern communicative mode; he begins, that is to say, with hysteria.

It is an appropriately ancient complaint. The notion of hysteria (Greek *hystera*/uterus) had long been associated with 'women's diseases'. Plato, in a text which had been integrated into the western medical tradition through Galen and the Hippocratic writers, asserted that:

> the matrix or womb in women, which is a living creature within them which longs to bear children. And if it is left unfertilized long beyond the normal time, it causes extreme unrest, strays about the body, blocks the channels of the breath and causes in consequence acute distress and disorders of all kinds.
>
> (Plato 1955, p. 123)

If it is not 'appeased by passion and love' the womb moved from its natural position within the body and, attaching itself to soft internal tissues, gave rise to a wide variety of symptomatic disturbances.

35

The uterine theory faded with the rise of modern medicine, based on accurate anatomical knowledge and, more significantly, on new views about the functioning of the brain and nervous system. Thomas Willis (1622–75) adduced detailed observation in support of his contention that hysteria 'the so-called uterine disease is primarily a convulsive disease caused by an alteration of the nerves and brain'.[9] Autopsy showed no general connection between uterine damage and hysteria, and on this basis Carolus Piso claimed hysteria was just as likely to affect men as women. Yet even though William Cullen (1712–90), introducing the term *neurosis*, held that all diseases were deformations of the (sexually undifferentiated) nervous system, the assumption of sexual specificity was unshaken. Thomas Sydenham (1624–89), the most celebrated medical practitioner of the early modern period, argued that hysteria was, next only to fevers, the most common disease and began the process of redefining its protean symptomology as an aspect of gender rather than of sex:

Of all chronic diseases hysteria – unless I err – is the commonest. . . . As to females, if we except those who lead a hard and hardy life, there is rarely one who is wholly free from them. . . . Then, again, such male subjects as lead a sedentary or studious life, and grow pale over their books and papers, are similarly afflicted.

(Veith 1965, p. 141)

Throughout the nineteenth century two leading conceptions of the origin of hysteria were developed, both of which sought to account for the variety of its symptoms and its apparently disproportionate concentration among women, and particularly among young women. One traced the onset of symptoms to a 'trauma', most frequently a physical shock of some kind, while the other claimed symptoms could be explained in terms of the 'suggestibility' of the patient. Linking both views there was an underlying assumption of the constitutional weakness of young women.

The traumatic theory of hysteria owed its popularity to the authority of Jean-Martin Charcot, the greatest of nineteenth-century clinical psychopathologists. He had spent his internship at the Salpêtrière Hospital, in Paris, from 1848–52, returning ten years later as attending physician and professor. This huge hospital, which his assistant Gilles de la Tourette called a 'pandemonium of human infirmities', was for Charcot 'a sort of museum of living pathology' which contained some five thousand patients upon which he could exercise his diagnostic and taxonomic skills.[10] In 1885 Freud was awarded a scholarship to visit Paris and study with Charcot for a period of six months. He was captivated both by Charcot and by Paris.[11]

Charcot specialised in neurological complaints, and his published lectures contained many examples drawn from the Salpêtrière, of conditions arising from specific lesions of the nervous tissue, whether caused by accident or by disease. In many cases, however, no specific physical damage could be detected. These 'functional' disorders were as varied as the symptoms of organic disease, and additionally, were quite frequently labile and unpredictable. Thus, although in general, hysteria was 'an affection remarkable for its permanence and obstinacy', many of its local symptoms were typically 'mobile and fleeting', and 'the capricious course of the disease', he claimed, 'is frequently interrupted by the most unexpected events'.[12]

In what were themselves somewhat theatrical performances, Charcot would remove hysterical symptoms from hypnotised patients (usually prepared before the lecture by an assistant). Under hypnosis he would suggest the symptom had disappeared, an apparently paralysed limb would suddenly move, or feeling return to an anaesthetised area of skin. This 'recovery' would continue, for some time at least, after the patient had been awakened. Conversely, Charcot demonstrated that if a 'normal' person were hypnotised hysterical 'symptoms' could be induced, and would persist on waking. The connection between hysteria and hypnosis, Charcot suggested, lay in a constitutional weakness of the nervous system of the individual. Only potential hysterics could be hypnotised, and in this abnormal state, their disorder would manifest itself.[13]

The hysteric was characteristically, though not universally, female; that is they tended to be weaker, more excitable and more subject to 'nervous attacks' than 'normal' men or older women. In comparison the majority of adult men were more 'in control' of their affections, less impressionable and were affected less intensely and less immediately by their surroundings. Charcot's therapy, thus, centred on calming the patient, and on removing her from the source of excitation. Normally he advised isolation from the family which, in most cases, 'serves only to perpetuate the excitable nervous condition'.[14] The controlled use of static electricity and hydrotherapy was also recommended. Charcot argued that hysteria was often consequential on a traumatic accident of some sort. The new phenomena of railway-spine and railway-brain were in fact hysterical symptoms precipitated by the 'psycho-motor commotion' of the accident.[15]

On this view hysteria, though an ancient disease, was increasing dramatically due to the intense pace of modern life.[16] Many potential hysterics, who in pre-modern society might well have gone through life without developing any symptoms whatever, fell ill as a result of the 'nervous shock' of modern living. One of Charcot's assistants, Gilles de la Tourette, describes how such a sensitive, but hardly abnormal, individual experiences the vertigo of city life:

> a sensation of cerebral emptiness accompanied by weakness of the lower limbs. . . . A veil spreads before the eyes, everything is gray and leaden; the visual field is full of black spots, flying patches, close or distant objects are confused on the same plane.
>
> (Roth 1994, p. 17)

Charcot's conception became the point of departure for an important tradition in French psychology, neurology and psychiatry. In the present context his significance lies primarily in drawing attention to the 'disintegrative' effects of modern life. The primary features of hysteria was a loss of control, or sensitivity (alternatively hypersensitivity) and responsiveness, of some part of the body. It was as if part of the body 'had a mind of its own' and refused to respond spontaneously and effortlessly to the will of the patient.

If Charcot's elaborate botanising in the Salpêtrière had its alarming aspect, hinting at a deeply disintegrative tendency in modern life, he at least viewed its effects as confined to a minority of unfortunate constitutional sufferers. Some bodies were naturally formed to respond in this way to the overburdening stimulation of life. Hippolyte Bernheim, on the other hand, placed no such optimistic limit on the spread of hysteria. Or, rather, there were no constitutional limitations on suggestibility which, Bernheim argued, was the real foundation of most of Charcot's observations.

Bernheim insisted that 'suggestibility' was the fundamental phenomenon of hypnosis, and that 'nothing could be further from the truth than the assertion that only hysterics are hypnotisable'.[17] The already classic diagnostic portraits from the Salpêtrière were, in fact, 'cultivated hysteria'. Charcot's patients may have been unusually suggestible, and unwittingly prompted by Charcot's own discourse and his assistants diligent preparation of the subject, produced the symptoms as an artificial construct of the situation. 'We do not realise how easy it is to make unconscious suggestions', he argues, and 'by projecting onto the patient our own conceptions, we fabricate an observation with the preconceived ideas that we have in mind'.[18] It was hardly surprising, therefore, to find that, in the Salpêtrière at least, 'it is rare for hypnotic suggestion not to rid the patient of the principal manifestations of hysteria'.[19]

If, for Charcot, hypnosis was assimilated to a general notion of 'nervous shock', for Bernheim it was simply a form of suggestion. Charcot regarded the physical 'deformation' of hysteria as the 'reality' actualised through hypnosis. Bernheim, however, regarded 'suggestibility' as the underlying reality masked by hysteria. Unlike Charcot, Bernheim was not an academic engaged in studying a captive mass of patients, but had been directly influenced by Liébeault's medical practice in unfashionable Nancy. Bernhaim described the distinctive approach of the Nancy school as 'the systematic and reasoned application of suggestion in the treatment of the ill'.[20]

For them suggestion was not a passive act, 'not a simple imprint deposited within the brain', but always a form of 'autosuggestion'.[21] 'Suggestion is in everything' was the fundamental principle of 'ideodynamism'. Sensation, Bernheim argued, is always formed into ideas, and ideas can frequently give rise to direct sensation, and their therapeutic effort was directed at exploiting the 'considerable action of the morale on the physique, of the mind on the body, of the psychic functions of the brain on all organic functions'.[22] Hypnosis, which is a type of sleep, 'in suppressing control, creates suggestibility'.[23] In a state of physical torpor the imagination is more active, and we are more receptive to suggestions arising from outside ourselves. This, Bernheim insisted, is an old insight which has been revived by the enthusiastic and often misguided followers of Mesmer. In fact, he claims, the valid method of hypnosis was clearly outlined by the Abbot Faria, one of Mesmer's original followers, in his *Traité du Somnambulisme*, which Liébeault followed. The method of hypnosis is very simple. As outlined by Liébeault, it is primarily a matter of speech. 'The simplest and best method for impressing the subject is by words', he argued, and quotes Liébeault in support:

> While the subject keeps his eyes on those of the operator, his senses are isolated from external and internal impressions. You direct him to simply imagine sleep and healing. You announce the initial phenomena of sleep to him – heaviness of the body, the desire to sleep, heaviness of the eyelids, and insensibility.
>
> (Bernheim 1980, pp. 64–5)

He argues, in fact, that there is no special hypnotic state, but only various levels and forms of suggestibility. And as external impressions can only become suggestions through the inward transformation into images by the subject himself or herself – that is to say 'somnambulists can only accomplish what they can imagine' – then it follows that 'the sole characteristic of natural somnambulism is active hallucinating or dreams in action'.[24]

Charcot's patients, thus, like the subjects of popular entertainments, imagined the 'symptoms' described to them, and transformed these images into corresponding sensations (or anaesthesias). Suggestion might be thought of as the inversion of the process of perception as it had been conceptualised in the empirical tradition of psychology from Locke and Hartley onwards. Bernheim's notion of 'ideodynamics' suggested that the boundary between the 'body-image' and the world was insecure and subject to continuous transformation; there was not only some means by which parts of the 'external world' became 'internal' to the body-image, but also means whereby such internal images were sensed as external objects.

Charcot and Bernheim presented two alternative and distinctively modern accounts of significant alterations in the classical bourgeois body-image. For Charcot hysteria became a typically modern disease; it was a bodily protest against the 'unnatural' excitement of modern life. For Bernheim hypnotism was a phenomena of suggestion and suggestion was, in different ways, also increasingly a feature of public life. More and more people were being urged to walk about in a 'waking dream'. The somnambulist was, then, in many respects an ideal citizen of the modern world. The 'dream-world' of modern consumption depended upon suggestibility, and encouraged it in every possible way. The visitor to the new Parisian department stores was entranced by the variety and luxuriousness of displays, lulled into a physical torpor in which the slightest external stimulus was sufficient to create a potent mental image of a desirable object, and the sensation of an urgent longing for its possession.[25]

Bernheim's criticisms of Charcot were effective, though they were not immediately accepted. But Bernheim's views created difficulties of their own. Hysteria, apparently, was more common than ever before; not just among the inmates of the Salpêtrière, but among the populace at large. And if it was plausible to suppose both 'nervous shock' and 'suggestibility' were peculiarly features of modern society, it was not clear why (discounting Charcot's constitutional theory) either should give rise to hysterical symptoms.

Towards the end of the century, in fact, there seemed to be a near epidemic of hysteria. And as more investigative studies and reports were published, the more unusual and dramatic the symptoms seemed to become.

In 1860 Azam, a doctor in Bordeaux, reported the puzzling symptomology of a patient of his, Felida X, who subsequently became one of the most celebrated and widely discussed cases in French psychology. Azam's patient oscillated unpredictably between two quite distinct states; states in which, to all appearances, she seemed to be two quite different personalities. It was as if she were two individuals, complete in themselves, each with their own store of memories, although 'in one she possessed her memory entire; in the other she had only a partial memory of all the impressions in that state'.[26] An outsider was forced to treat her as either of two individuals, depending on which persona she presented on any one occasion. In fact Felida X was not the first or clearest case of 'double-consciousness'; McNish had reported the similar case of 'an American lady' as early as 1830. In that case while one of the 'individuals' had complete knowledge of the other, the 'secondary' personality believed itself to be in sole possession of the 'American lady' and, from its point of view (amnesia of all intervening periods being complete) was convinced of its own continuous presence.[27] But the significance of such bizarre symptoms could hardly be guessed at while the assumptions of bourgeois egoism held sway. And when, during the latter third of the nineteenth century, these assumptions did begin to disintegrate, evidence of 'dissociation', 'double-consciousness' and 'multiple personality' was promptly found everywhere.

Common hysterical symptoms were reinterpreted as minor forms of dissociation, and multiple personality became seen as full-blown hysteria. Hysterical symptoms were viewed, in other words, as the result of some sort of 'breaking apart' of consciousness. In most cases, in fact, they might be seen as disturbances of 'normal' memory. The integration of consciousness as an 'ego' was seen to depend on the continuous function of memory, which, linking together the various states of consciousness in an unbroken sequence, created an irresistible impression of a singular inner observer. Theordore Ribot thus writes that 'the *ego* subjectively considered consists of a series of conscious states'.[28] He elaborates as follows:

> The *ego*, its present perpetually renewed, is for the most part nourished by memory; that is to say, the present state is associated with others which, thrown back and localized in the past, constitute at each moment what we regard as our personality.
>
> (Ribot 1882, p. 107)

This was the view upon which the 'associationist' psychology had been built. But it was just this model which was inadequate to the new psychological phenomena brought to light in studies of somnambulism, hysteria and double-consciousness. It seemed, rather, that the memory worked in a selective fashion, binding together as a continuous narrative only those events and experiences which could be meaningfully integrated with some specific image of the self. Those elements in the past which fell outside such an image, or even seemed to contradict it, would form the centre of a mentally dissociated state with its own bodily consciousness, recollection and self-image. For many individuals such dissociated elements remained insignificant and unobservable in relation to their 'major' ego, but in many they formed the nucleus of hysterical symptoms, which were the beginning, so to speak, of an alternative body-image, and an alternative personality.

Ribot, in fact, following Maudsley, argued that the foundation of personality was not the work of a conscious memory at all, but of the unconscious *coenaesthesis* of bodily states which are 'ever-present, ever-acting, without repose or respite, knows neither sleep nor exhaustion, lasting as long as life itself, of which it is only an expression'.[29] But this resort to unconscious bodily habit as the underlying integrity of the personality, a view later espoused, among others, by Proust, hardly avoids the difficulty. It merely transfers to an unconscious, and therefore unexamined, level the bourgeois prejudice in favour of unity and completeness. The *ego*, rather than being explained in relation to it, simply reappears as the body-image.

During the same period Alfred Binet, more famous now as the originator of intelligence testing than as an investigator of 'double-consciousness', urged a frank recognition of the radical dissociation in such cases. The many cases of 'natural somnambulism' or sleepwalking that had been noted during the previous century, as well as all the more recent studies of hysterical 'splitting' of the personality, should not be interpreted as differing states of the same personality. In reality

41

these noctambulists are two persons. The person who rises in the night is entirely distinct from the one who is awake during the day, since the latter has no knowledge or memory of anything that has happened during the night.

(Binet 1977, p. 3)

He insisted, similarly, that 'Felida X is really two moral persons'.

Binet suggested that 'a kind of spontaneous breaking up' of the personality is not uncommon. Frequently the dissociated 'part' of the personality is pathological in some way, so that the whole process can be seen as an exercise in psychic hygiene. The transition from one personality to another, in some cases at least, 'is made in an instant, almost unconsciously'.[30] And in place of the singular identity of 'a body in space', he proposes a new and striking image, related to Freud's own preferred archaeological metaphor:

the personality of our subjects of observation and experiment seems to me like a complicated and frail building, of which the least accident might overthrow a part; and the stones that have fallen away from the mass – and this is a very curious thing – become the point of departure for a new structure, which rises rapidly by the side of the old.

(Binet 1977, p. 347)

The most sustained and exhaustive studies of all the various 'disintegrative' tendencies at work in the modern psyche – and thus of the modern body-image – was the work of one of Charcot's students, and eventual successor at the Salpêtrière, Pierre Janet. Though loyal to the pioneering insights of his master, a considerable shift in emphasis is evident in his work. From early attempts to specify the conditions under which more or less independent 'automatisms' emerged, controlled by pre-existing bodily disposition, he became increasingly interested in reconstructing the 'mental structure' of hysteria, and, thus, of 'making sense' of the individual symptoms. In this way Janet found many instances of a personality dissociating under the impact of 'fixed ideas', themselves related to a traumatic event. There was an intermediary level, in other words, between the trauma, as discovered by Charcot, and the resulting symptom, which otherwise appeared to be an arbitrary affliction.

He reports, for example, the case of a young woman who, after a failed love affair, unsuccessfully attempted suicide by refusing to eat. This entire episode had been forgotten, but thoughts of death and suicide continue to play an undetected part in her daily life. She developed a curious symptom affecting voluntary action; a disturbance of the will, or aboulia. When asked politely to reach out and grasp a cup, she would claim to be able to comply, but despite making an evident physical effort her hand would not move.

However, if abruptly commanded, she would say that she could not comply, yet would at once seize the cup. Alternatively when Janet, passing behind her suggested in a whisper that she lean forward and take the cup, she would at once do so. The 'fixed idea' of suicide by fasting, though consciously forgotten, here interferes with the higher functions associated with voluntary action. The patient remains unconscious of the 'obstacle' to her taking nourishment, but the doctor can activate more 'primitive' levels at which the will operates, bypassing, as it were, the conscious will of the patient in favour of another level of unconscious organisation.[31]

Adducing many related examples Janet stressed the systematic character of hysterical symptoms in relation to, usually unacknowledged, 'fixed ideas'. In cases of a localised anaesthesia, for example, the significance of the area involved had to be understood. Or a patient might suffer some impairment of the visual field, but this would turn out to be specific to a meaningful group of objects, or to a specific person, in relation to whom the patient had in the past suffered some undisclosed trauma. The systematic character of the symptoms was related to the patients' own 'representations' and 'images' of themselves, rather than (as Charcot had assumed) an underlying 'disease process'. Thus while the hysteric is 'capable of completely paralysing a part of their body', it is an 'imaged' part, rather than a physiological unity. A patient's hand, for example, might be paralysed without any noticeable insensitivity or immobility in the corresponding forearm where, in fact, the major nerves and muscles controlling the affected area are located.[32]

The dominance of 'fixed ideas' or 'intellectual automatisms' give to the hysteric the character of 'dreamers'. They exhibit a tendency to 'ceaseless reverie':

> Hystericals are not content to dream constantly at night; they dream all day long. Whether they walk, or work, or sew, their minds are never wholly occupied with what they are doing. They carry in their heads an interminable story which unrolls before them or is inwardly conceived.
>
> (Janet 1977, p. 201)

Hysterics had succeeded in detaching themselves, or part of themselves, from the reality in which, for the most part, they still manage to live. They draw back from the complexity of real life, and substitute for it 'variable, incoherent images', which become typified and systematised into fixed ideas: 'It is always the same monotonous story.'[33] The hysteric becomes indifferent to the world, endlessly repeating a reverie, every detail of which they can control, its outcome assured from the very beginning. The advantage of the 'fixed idea' is just this predictability; the mental world 'instead of changing incessantly, according to the thousand incidents of life, has a mechanical regularity and remains always the same'.[34]

In the repetition of fixed ideas the hysteric unwittingly relives the past, over and over again. The 'deformation' of the body image which results – the host of local anaesthesias, hypersensitivities, abulias, paralyses and distortions of normal voluntary actions – are so many physical signs of some past event. And the alterations of the body-image connected with the splitting apart of consciousness in hysteria, is, at the same time a hidden history of the soul. But Janet did not fully develop this insight. His training under Charcot, his exposure to such a mass of pathological material, urged upon him the neverending task of classification, typification and characterisation, as a task of greater significance than was diagnostic analysis. The result was a comprehensive exposition of the entire range of hysterical symptoms systematised from a physiological standpoint. But his central insight was to undermine just such a point of view. The 'body' of the hysteric was a 'fixed idea'; a representation or image which bore a direct relation to popular ideas about the body, and had little to do with the carefully organised chapters and subheadings of an anatomical text. Janet demonstrated, but somehow could not accept, the coming of an autonomous post-bourgeois body-image; one which had decisively entered into the field of modern *representations*.

ON MODERN BODY LANGUAGE

It was not from congenital weakness, but, more simply, as a consequence of their greater exposure to the genuinely novel elements of modernity which made middle-class young women particularly prone to hysteria. It was this new leisure class, able at last to claim a position in public life, albeit that of the transient *flâneuse*, that first entered the world of modern consumerism and spectator culture. More than their husbands and fathers, for whom the shock of the new was absorbed, to a large extent, by a network of professional and public relationships which sustained for them the myth of bourgeois egoism, middle-class young women were abandoned to the new world of commodities. This was a liberation into a magically unreal existence of endless, aimless and ultimately self-defeating pleasure. Initially, of course, this release was viewed in terms of a *bourgeois* principle of pleasure – on the notion of enjoyment as self-aggrandisement and self-realisation through possession – but, theory not withstanding, when they did escape the constraints of domestic life women discovered a strangely ambivalent world.

For this most advanced of modern social groups the (by men) highly valued realm of rational self-control and equally rational self-expression was held (also by men) to be of little significance.[35] Such young women, not surprisingly, experienced intense conflict between the demands of domestic life and their new public freedom as consumers of modern culture. Bourgeois egoism played little part in either. At home they were contained within semi-feudal forms of relations, entirely dependent for

44

their being upon the status, wealth and personality of their menfolk; while in public they became absorbed into the new play culture of instantaneous wish-fulfilment. The conflict between these two worlds, as well as the ambiguities of 'pure modernity', were literally bodied forth as symptoms.

Freud, impressed by both Charcot and Bernheim, whose major work he translated into German, combined elements of both the traumatic and suggestion theory when he turned to the practical study of hysteria. More importantly, however, in developing his own 'archaeological' approach to understanding the superficiality of modern life, Freud unearthed the meaning, as well as the cause, of bodily complaints. Symptom formation, which he treated as a hermeneutic problem – that is as a text which could be understood in its own terms – was a double process of inscription and encoding. The pliant female body, unprotected by a hard reflective shell of intellect, was continually falling into a state of helpless torpor in which it was receptive to a multiplicity of uncontrolled and disordered impressions. If these external forces reached traumatic intensity a lasting trace would be left on the body in the form of an energetic somatic 'conversion' which did not simply register, but also signified, its 'exciting cause'.

> The symptoms which we have been able to trace back to precipitating factors of this sort include neuralgias and anaesthesias of very various kinds, many of which have persisted for years, contractures and paralyses, hysterical attacks and epileptoid convulsions, which every observer regarded as true epilepsy, *petit mal* and disorders in the nature of *tic*, chronic vomiting and anorexia, carried to the pitch of rejection of all nourishment, various forms of disturbance of vision, constantly recurrent visual hallucinations, etc.
>
> (SE 2, p. 4)

The inexhaustible array of bodily symptoms were chosen primarily for their powers of signification. It surprised Freud less than he claimed, perhaps, that his case histories should read like short stories, and that, compared to detailed reports of psychotic patients there was an evident and 'intimate connection between the story of the patient's suffering and the symptoms of his illness'.[36] From his first full-length case study, in fact, he assimilated the interpretation of symptoms to the recounting of each patient's 'story'.[37]

There was no fixed rule by which such signification should be assigned, and Freud relied on *post hoc* interpretation, validated by the conscious acceptance of the account by the patient herself, and by the general integration of the clinical picture which such construction allowed. Looking back on his earlier cases he regretted his failure to track down in every instance the 'special kind of symbolism' implicated in symptoms.[38] But even in his first published case study, that of Frau Emmy von N., he feels compelled to defend the view that the smallest details of a case point infallibly to the originating cause of the symptoms:

I may here be giving an impression of laying too much emphasis on the details of the symptoms and of becoming lost in an unnecessary maze of sign-reading. But I have come to learn that the determination of hysterical symptoms does in fact extend to their subtlest manifestation and that it is difficult to attribute too much sense to them.

(SE 2, p. 93)

Frequently many physical symptoms could be understood as unambiguous 'mnemic symbols' of an original, emotionally painful, situation which had been subsequently forgotten. In the case of Frau Emmy von N., indeed, her *tic*-like facial movements, and hand-clasping, were a simple repetition of aspects of a traumatic scene; the death of her husband, which, Freud conjectures, was too painful for her to recall as a plastic image, but the memory of which had survived in the abbreviated form of physical reactions to the original event. However, her symptoms were also, in part, an attempt at 'fending off' these very memories themselves and constituted a kind of 'protective formula' through which she could retain her peace of mind. Other characteristic symptoms, including an intrusive 'clacking' sound Freud observed in another of his cases at this period, were better understood as 'putting an antithetic idea into effect'. Thus, the effort of remaining completely silent while watching over her sick child expressed itself through its opposite, as an involuntary disturbing noise. Further, Freud assumes that it was her horror at the noise which made its production traumatic, and that the effort to control it resulted in her equally characteristic stammer, which was thus 'made into a symbol of the event for her memory'.[39] And once the process of interpretation has begun the patient herself may spontaneously suggest new and relevant material. Frau Cäcilie, whom Freud claims to have known better than any other of the patients featured in the *Studies on Hysteria*, though he discusses her only partially, and in footnotes, to highlight various points brought up in the context of other cases, developed many new symptoms in the wake of the interpretative breakthrough, each uncovering, almost of its own accord, further particulars of the traumatic incident. These symptoms 'were like a series of pictures with explanatory texts'.[40]

In their 'Preliminary Communication' Breuer and Freud had provided what was to become a famous formulation: 'Hysterics suffer mainly from reminiscences.' But in the case studies and discussions which were to follow in the text of *Studies on Hysteria* differences in approach between the two authors became more apparent. In fact, rather than write a joint account of their studies they simply divided the book into sections which each wrote separately. Breuer, as the senior author, was responsible for the 'theoretical' section, as well as for the first, and most celebrated, case study, that of Anna O. (Berthe Pappenheim), usually regarded as the first patient of psychoanalysis.[41]

Breuer's clinical practice was unusual above all in its intensity. Daily visits with hypnotic treatment over a period of weeks represented an unprecedented level of professional commitment to his patient. But his understanding of hysteria remained much more closely bound by French preconceptions than did Freud's, in spite of (or possibly because of) the latter's much closer involvement with the studies of Charcot and his school as well as with Bernheim's work.[42]

Breuer maintained that the 'mnemic symbol' was formed in a 'hypnoid state' and that hysterical attacks were spontaneous recurrences of such states. The symptoms, as Charcot had demonstrated could be removed by direct suggestion during hypnosis. This amounted to a restatement of the 'dissociation theory' of Janet and others, who had taken the distinction between waking and sleeping, between reality and dream, to represent two distinct phases of existence and ultimately two separate, but linked, personalities.[43] In his first case study Freud at points seems to concur with such a view. Frau Emmy von N.'s facial contortions revealed a rich inner world of dissociated processes:

> What we had here was a hysterical delirium which alternated with normal consciousness, just as true *tic* intrudes into a voluntary movement without interfering with it and without being mixed up with it.
>
> (SE 2, p. 49)

Later, however, in a lengthy footnote to the same case study, Freud makes it clear that the hysteric's tendency to create 'false connections' and symptomatic behaviour does not depend on any abnormal splitting of their personality, but is a general feature of normal consciousness. Indeed, in this connection, he draws on his own experience and likens the hysteric's compulsive associations, which give rise to many apparently odd and disconnected actions, to dream recollections. What is typically involved in all such cases is the survival, as a recollection, of an element associated with some more complex situation. In a state of dreaming, or hypnosis, but more generally in any situation in which affect is heightened, the normally 'rational' limits on associations are in some way relaxed, allowing many accidental, but not wholly arbitrary connections to form and persist in memory. It is not just in sleep, but, as it were, in states of super-wakefulness, of heightened attention and emotional involvement, that the ability to register a wider variety of associations can be found. Sleeping states, or better dream states, have their own peculiar receptivity to the manifold currents of life to which modern young women seemed to be particularly prone.

More generally Freud viewed the formation of hysterical symptoms at this point (prior, that is, to his systematic study of dreams) in terms of defence; as 'the refusal on the part of the patient's whole ego to come to terms with this ideational group'.[44] In the early case which most closely resembled the classic French type, that of Fräulein Elisabeth von R., the 'splitting of consciousness' was just one consequence of this defensive measure and not itself the cause of the primary symptoms. Thus:

> in place of the mental pains which she avoided, physical pains made their appearance. In this way a transformation was effected which had the advantage that the patient escaped from an intolerable mental condition; though, it is true, this was at the cost of a psychical abnormality – the splitting of consciousness that came about – and of a physical illness – her pains, on which an astasia-abasia was built up.
>
> (SE 2, p. 237)

Hypnotic therapy was not wholly successful because, quite apart from the unpredictability of the technique, the patient would spontaneously produce new symptoms as soon as existing ones were 'cleared up'. Both Breuer and Freud had found, as their intensive analytic treatment advanced, that they would be confronted with a daily succession of new symptoms linked to current events. Indeed, there seemed, quite contrary to the medical orthodoxy within which Freud had been educated, a marked imbalance between the single presumed cause of hysteria, and the luxurious growth of a multiplicity of its effects.

These early studies of hysteria are remarkable now for their reliance on a realistic approach to the understanding of the emotional and moral conflicts current in the lives of their *dramatis personae*. Frau Emmy's symptoms were related to the conflict between responsibilities to her sick husband and to her simultaneously sick child. Fräulein Elisabeth von R., was torn between similar demands to nurse her father and the freer and wider role which had become available to young women of her class and to which she felt temperamentally suited. Freud remarks on these characteristic circumstances, fertile, he believes, of hysterical symptoms:

> I have described the patient's character, the features which one meets with so frequently in hysterical people and which there is no excuse for regarding as a consequence of degeneracy: her giftedness, her ambition, her moral sensibility, her excessive demand for love which, to begin with, found satisfaction in her family, and the independence of her nature which went beyond the feminine ideal and found expression in a considerable amount of obstinacy, pugnacity and reserve.
>
> (SE 2, p. 161)

It is, quite commonly, the duty to care for sick relatives that sets up painful conflicts within such gifted and ambitious individuals. Here, in spite of the misleading pronouns, Freud expresses himself in a somewhat more sympathetic manner:

Anyone whose mind is taken up by the hundred and one tasks of sick-nursing which follow one another in endless succession over a period of weeks and months will, on the one hand, adopt a habit of suppressing every sign of his own emotion, and on the other, will soon divert his attention away from his own impressions, since he has neither the time nor strength to do justice to them. Thus he will accumulate a mass of impressions which are capable of affect, which are hardly sufficiently perceived and which, in any case, have not been weakened by abreaction. . . . If the sick person recovers, all these impressions, of course, lose their significance. But if he dies, and the period of mourning sets in, during which the only things that seem to have value are those that relate to the person who has died, these impressions that have not yet been dealt with come into the picture as well; and after a short interval of exhaustion the hysteria, whose seeds were sown during the time of nursing, breaks out.

(SE 2, pp. 161–62)

The other set of circumstances which may typically precipitate the development of hysteria involves the arousal of sexual feelings which, for reasons of propriety, cannot be adequately expressed. But again it is important to note here that the entire situation is understood in terms of conscious motives and meanings.

Yet more is revealed by, and concealed in, hysteria than these conscious conflicts suggest. Increasingly impatient of Breuer, Freud, by the mid-1890s, had developed his own theory of its sexual aetiology. Hysteria was the consequence, he argued, of a specifically sexual trauma, which had occurred in childhood, the conscious memory of which had been suppressed, but the emotional response to which, unexpressed at the time, provided the 'psychical energy' expended in the process of 'conversion' into physical symptoms. In hysteria, then, 'what is played out in the body takes the place of a discourse that cannot be uttered'.[45] It is the hysterical body, inscribed with visible signs of its own past, rather than the secretive spatial consciousness of the rational mind, which is the true analogue of the modern world.

Freud's so-called 'seduction theory' of hysteria has been extensively discussed in recent years, but a proper understanding of the issues involved requires a prior examination of both his dreambook and the circumstances and results of his self-analysis. For the present it is worth noting that it represents, in the combination of trauma and the development of meaningful symptoms suggestive of the event, the most extreme meeting point of his two French mentors, Charcot and Bernheim. It is also worth noting that, by displacing the genesis of the symptoms onto childhood, he views hysterics as victims of the breakdown of idealised bourgeois family relations, rather than as victims directly of the over-excitement of the modern age.

JOKING AND THE ECONOMY OF PLEASURE

In spite of their appearing after the publication of *The Interpretation of Dreams*, some further developments of Freud's aesthetics of modernity can be introduced at this point and will, in fact, serve as a useful introduction to that key text.

Transience, flux, fragmentation and incompleteness are all characteristics of experience in advanced societies and might in another perspective be viewed as the *playful* aspect of modern life. Its inner, subjective freedom and apparently rootless liberty means that, as well as being fecund of dreams and hysteria, modernity is the ideal medium for joking. Freud notes the:

> peculiar and even fascinating charm exercised by jokes in our society. A new joke acts almost like an event of universal interest; it is passed from one person to another like the news of the latest victory.
>
> (SE 8, p. 15)

The joke establishes playful connections of similarity and difference among things and people that are usually kept apart. Freud quotes Jean Paul approvingly, 'freedom produces jokes and jokes produce freedom. . . . Joking is merely playing with ideas'.[46] Reviewing the work of a number of contemporary philosophers and psychologists, Freud defines a series of divergent, though not incompatible, definitions and characteristics of joking. Thus, in addition to making playful judgements, and linking dissimilar things, the joke typically draws attention to unexpected contrasts, discovers 'sense in nonsense', produces a succession of bewilderment and enlightenment, brings forward hidden ideas, and is formulated with essential brevity. But all these notions, Freud remarks, constitute '*disjecta membra*, which we should like to see combined into an organic whole'.

Prior to suggesting such an organic view, he illustrates his own analytic approach. Noting that jokes typically depend for their effect upon specific verbal techniques, he recounts an example which plays a similar role in his subsequent discussion as does the specimen dream to *The Interpretation of Dreams*. The joke is taken from Heinrich Heine, and features a comic character, Hirsch-Hyacinth, a lottery-agent and corn-extractor, invented for a series of short stories and journalistic writings. Claiming to have met Baron Rothschild, Hirsch-Hyacinth boasts that 'he treated me quite as an equal – quite familionairely'. The joke (such as it is), seems to hinge, as Freud points out, on the mode of expression used for the thought, which, in an expanded form might read 'Rothschild treated me quite as his equal, quite familiarly – that is, so far as a millionaire can'.[47] The underlying thought conveys none of the comic effect which seems to result from the compression of these two sentences. The condensation, typical of dreams, can be represented as a literal compression of two statements:

Rothschild treated me quite *familiär*,
that is, so far as a *Millionär* can.

The second statement can be represented by fusing *familiär* and *Millionär*, producing a composite expression *familionär*. This expression is meaningless in itself, but in the context of the story conveys the disillusioned truth of the suppressed second statement with surprising economy. This technique of joke construction, 'condensation with substitute-formation', is instructive though, in fact, it is not widespread. Freud quotes as further examples of the type de Quincey's remark that old people are apt to fall into their 'anecdotage', and the description of the Christmas season as the 'alcoholidays', as well as a number of Viennese illustrations which originated with Josef Unger, a Professor of Jurisprudence and President of the Supreme Court, who was well known in the city for his wit.

There is an apparently wide variety of joking techniques. Many employ multiple use of the same material, as a 'play upon words', double meanings, and so on, and quite generally treat words 'as a plastic material with which one can do all kinds of things'. The confusing diversity of joking techniques, however, all resolve themselves into so many different means of condensation. Freud argues that brevity is, indeed, the soul of wit. But, he asks, 'what does a joke save by its technique?' From a more inclusive point of view this 'tendency to economy' in joking technique seems to be 'more than balanced by the expenditure on intellectual effort' required for its construction.[48] From an economic point of view joking does not seem to make any sense.

Again, following the model of the dream, Freud shows that joking techniques also makes use of displacement. In such cases the joke may be completely free of verbal play, and consist entirely in an unexpected diversion of a previously established train of thought. Freud's key example concerns borrowing money from friends, a situation well known to him from his period as a student and early years in private practice:

An impoverished individual borrowed 25 florins from a prosperous acquaintance, with many asseverations of his necessitous circumstances. The very same day his benefactor met him again in a restaurant with a plate of salmon mayonnaise in front of him. The benefactor reproached him: 'What? You borrow money from me and then order yourself salmon mayonnaise? Is *that* what you've used my money for?' 'I don't understand you', replied the object of the attack; 'if I haven't any money I *can't* eat salmon mayonnaise, and if I have some money I *mustn't* eat salmon mayonnaise. Well, then, when *am* I to eat salmon mayonnaise?'

(SE 8, pp. 49–50)

Many jokes, of course, combine the condensation of a word-play with displacement of a train of thought. Thus, among the several jokes involving

Jewish marriage-brokers (*Schadchen*), quoted by Freud, he gives the follow-ing as displaying a combination of techniques:

> The *Schadchen* had assured the suitor that the girl's father was no longer living. After the betrothal it emerged that the father was still alive and was serving a prison sentence. The suitor protested to the *Schadchen*, who replied: 'Well, what did I tell you? You surely don't call that living?'
>
> (SE 8, p. 55)

The appearance of forming a syllogism, a kind of 'secondary revision' of the joke work, is a favourite with Freud. Another *Schadchen* story is typical:

> The bridegroom was most disagreeably surprised when the bride was introduced to him, and drew the broker on one side and whispered his remonstrances: 'Why have you brought me here?', he asked re-proachfully. 'She's ugly and old, she squints and has bad teeth and bleary eyes . . .' – 'You needn't lower your voice', interrupted the broker, 'she's deaf as well'.
>
> (SE 8, p. 64)

Such examples make it obvious that the technique of construction (as is the case also with hysterical symptoms) 'is only the outer shell, the façade, of the joke', whose meaning or purpose is something quite distinct. The 'joking envelope', which can be either verbal or conceptual, is quite distinct from, and independent of, the purpose of the joke, which may be either 'innocent' or 'tendentious'.

While some jokes, such as Lichtenberg's, work simply by providing an innocent intellectual pleasure, more generally successful jokes are ten-dentious. And as the technique of jokes is the same in both cases, the tendentious joke 'must have sources of pleasure at their disposal to which innocent jokes have no access'.[49] Where a joke is not an aim in itself, Freud claims there are only two fundamental purposes it can serve: 'It is either a *hostile* joke (serving the purpose of aggressiveness, satire, or defence) or an *obscene* joke (serving the purpose of exposure)'. In both cases the situation is complicated by a consideration of the social situation of such joking, which calls for at least three people:

> in addition to the one who makes the joke, there must be a second who is taken as the object of the hostile or sexual aggressiveness, and a third in whom the joke's aim of producing pleasure is fulfilled.
>
> (SE 8, p. 100)

Freud considers the case of 'smut' as on the borderline of this joking relationship. In that case sexual aggressiveness is expressed towards a defensive individual, apparently for the benefit of a third party. Smut is technically less demanding than joking, and is therefore popular, he claims, among poorly educated and unrefined members of society:

It is remarkable how universally popular a smutty interchange of this kind is among the common people and how it unfailingly produces a cheerful mood. But it also deserves to be noticed that in this complicated procedure, which involves so many of the characteristics of tendentious jokes, none of the formal requirements which characterize jokes are made of the smut itself. The uttering of an undisguised indecency gives the first person enjoyment and makes the third person laugh.

(SE 8, 100)

In 'refined' society smut is only acceptable under the guise of a joke. The joke, thus, makes possible 'the satisfaction of an instinct (whether lustful or hostile) in the face of an obstacle that stands in its way'.[50] The tendentious joke 'provides a means of undoing the renunciation and retrieving what was lost' by accepting the conventions of politeness. Freud argues that through the process of repression, the sexual encounter has been removed from the directly erotic realm of touch, to that of vision, and then to speech, before finally distinguishing within forms of speech a 'coarse' and a 'refined' variant. Yet, though the ultimate source of the pleasure is the same, even such close relatives as smut and the joke represent quite distinct 'levels' and 'forms' of pleasure:

When we laugh at a refined obscene joke, we are laughing at the same thing that makes a peasant laugh at a coarse piece of smut. In both cases the pleasure springs from the same source. We, however, could never bring ourselves to laugh at the coarse smut; we should feel ashamed or it would seem to us disgusting. We can only laugh when a joke has come to our help.

(SE 8, p. 101)

Similarly, hostile jokes have developed as means of alluding to feelings which, in modern society, cannot be expressed directly. Here joking is a refined form of verbal invective and insult and, therefore, particularly suited to criticising authority figures. The diverting façade of jokes conceals something forbidden. In the sophistical jokes which feature the marriage-broker, it is not really he, but the suitor who is mocked and ridiculed for leaving out of account the real basis of marriage in mutual affection. Typically such jokes also attack, through their victim, the institutions of morality and respectability to which members of society are supposed to be bound. This gives rise to a special subgroup of hostile jokes which Freud terms *cynical* jokes.

Freud notes that tendentious and cynical jokes are frequently directed against the person relating the joke, and this is particularly the case with Jewish jokes, of which he quotes a large number. These examples, however, are not jokes against Jewish characteristics in general, but are more

53

particularly aimed at the *Osjuden* among whom Freud counted his own father in their early years in Vienna. Their supposed slovenliness, poverty and appearance are all the butt of jokes which are only acceptable when originating within the Jewish community itself. Jokes are unnecessary among outsiders for whom Jews are already 'comic figures', while 'the Jewish jokes which originate from Jews admit this too; but they know their real faults as well as the connection between them and their good qualities'.[51]

Thus, in addition to jokes about marriage-brokers Freud also relates several in which a *Schnorrer* (beggar) figures as a potentially embarrassing but also guilt-rousing figure. Thus, for example:

> A *Schnorrer*, who was allowed as a guest into the same house every Sunday, appeared one day in the company of an unknown young man who gave signs of being about to sit down to table. 'Who is this?' asked the householder. 'He's been my son-in-law' was the reply, 'since last week. I've promised him his board for the first year.'
>
> (SE 8, p. 112)

In treating the rich man's money as his own, the *Schnorrer* is laying claim to the traditional protection of the community, if not to an ancient individual right. The ambivalence attaching to the *Schnorrer* figure is directed, in fact, against an oppressive and demanding Law. This is well illustrated by another example, of the Baron who, moved by the *Schnorrer's* supplications, rang for his servants and commanded, 'Throw him out! He's breaking my heart!'

Freud then asks from what point of view these two sources of pleasure, the technique of joking, and their purpose, can be brought together. In the case of tendentious jokes it is easy to see that pleasure results from the evasion of obstacles to the expression of sexual or hostile impulses. The pleasure seems to be greater when this obstacle is an internal prohibition rather than an external constraint. From an economic point of view Freud asserts that to erect and maintain an internal inhibition requires a continuous 'psychical expenditure', and that the joke's yield of pleasure corresponds to the saving of this expenditure. He argues, further, that the pleasure derived from innocent jokes and the technical element in joking, such as word-plays, can also be understood in terms of a psychic economy. The joke often focuses on the sound rather than on the meaning of words, and by this means links disparate thoughts. These 'short-circuits' are based on the regressive plasticity of language, which assimilates 'thing-presentation' to 'word-presentation', and thus effects a saving on normal mental processes which require the continuous differentiation between the two.

There is also an important source of innocent pleasure in topicality. Most jokes have a certain length of life, and the processes which created them work continually on new material. In modern society this external source of pleasure seems especially important. Topicality, 'ephemeral it is true but particularly abundant', supplements the joke's own resources, by linking it to the sphere of current interests. The joke thus 'economises' by making allusions to a potentially vast range of psychical contents. Freud regards topicality as a particular form of recognition, a species of the familiar, qualified by 'the characteristic of being fresh, recent and untouched by forgetting'.[52]

The nonsense and absurdity which characterises many joking techniques is a further potent source of pleasure. The process of inhibition which has mapped our mental life into more or less logical shapes also requires a continuous expenditure of energy, which the joke (or intoxication) overcomes. Pleasure in 'liberated nonsense' becomes ever more inaccessible as the power of critical reason is increased. However, the replacement of thing-association by word-association and the use of absurdity succeed in 're-establishing old liberties and (in) getting rid of the burden of intellectual upbringing'.[53]

Further, where that tradition of aesthetic valuation had been viewed as a matter of individual taste, indeed as the cultivation of personal taste, Freud's analysis of jokes revealed the essential social relation involved in aesthetic judgement. It is not sufficient, Freud points out, to enjoy a joke by oneself. If a joke occurs to someone they feel compelled to broadcast it, and if one hears a good joke there is an equally strong compulsion to relay it to another. The urge to tell the joke 'is inextricably bound up with the joke-work'; communication is essential to its nature.

The repetition of a joke includes a third person within the joking relationship. The person who makes the joke, the object of the joke (who may not be present), and a third person, on whose reaction the success of the joke seems to depend. This third person laughs at the joke, while its originator cannot; 'he has bought the pleasure of the joke with very small expenditure on his own part'.[54] In the hearer an internal inhibition of some kind has been lifted by the joke, thus freeing a quota of energy which is, literally, 'laughed off'. The construction of jokes must attend equally to what makes its formation possible in the first person, and what allows its greatest pleasurable effect in the third person. Indeed, 'everything in jokes that is aimed at gaining pleasure is calculated with an eye to the third person', and the suspicion arises that 'we are compelled to tell our jokes to someone else *because* we are unable to laugh at them ourselves'. And, thus, 'we supplement our pleasure by attaining the laughter that is impossible for us by the roundabout path of the impression we have of the person who has been made to laugh'.[55] The joke-teller, in fact, uses the laughter of the third person to arouse his or her own laughter.

Through joking a self-absorbing instinct of play is transformed into a social mechanism. As with sexuality, our passions are turned outwards and our pleasure becomes dependent on forming relationships with others.

Freud shared with his contemporaries an interest in the 'aestheticisation' of everyday life, but where this is generally viewed as a form of 'distance' from, or even of disenchantment with, reality, he views it as a pre-eminently social mechanism. Joking links people together in everyday situations and introduces a certain viscosity into the fluidity of modern life.

PARAPRAXES AND THE CONVENTIONS OF EVERYDAY LIFE

The flow of everyday life, which has been established as an external and given fact of life for the modern psyche, also plays an important part in generating 'parapraxes', which might be viewed as an inverted form of joking. Everyday incidents of forgetting, misremembering, clumsy or bungled actions and apparently accidental and insignificant interruptions in intentional activity, all of which quickly became known as 'Freudian slips', frequently occur in situations that would be eased by joking.[56] But the conditions for joke formation are relatively testing, and, where they cannot be met successfully, a 'slip' is likely to occur.

The specimen case of faulty recollection in *The Psychopathology of Everyday Life* involves a characteristically modern situation which also featured in Freud's book on joking. While being driven with a stranger through Dalmatia for a destination in Herzegovina the conversation turned to travel in Italy. Freud asked his companion if he had ever had the pleasure of visiting Orvieto and seeing the frescoes there, but found that he could not recall their artist's name, *Signorelli*. And, though he knew they had no connection with that work of art, found the names *Botticelli* and *Boltraffio* had come into his mind instead. A typically intricate analysis revealed that the substitution occurred as a result of Freud's attempts to prevent a potentially disruptive line of thought from entering the conversation.

Immediately prior to this memory failure Freud had been discussing with his travelling companion the customs of the Turks in *Bosnia* and *Herzegovina*. According to Freud they have great confidence in their doctors, but are resigned to fate. If they are informed that nothing can be done for a sick relative their typical reaction is to say '*Herr* [Sir], what is there to be said? If he could be saved, I know you would have saved him.' At that point, however, Freud was reminded of another anecdote revealing a further characteristic attributed to the Turks; namely that they 'place a higher value on sexual enjoyment than on anything else'. One of Freud's colleagues had reported a Turkish patient with a sexual disorder as saying '*Herr*, you must know that if *that* comes to an end then life is of no value.' However, as he 'did not want to allude to the topic in a conversation with a stranger', he diverted his attention from the interconnected subjects of death and sexuality. Or, rather, he tried to, but found his train of thought, by a more indirect route, returning to the forbidden topics. *Signorelli's* frescoes at Orvieto are of the 'The Four Last Things', Death, Judgement, Hell and Heaven, and presumably continued to stir up ideas with which, in the circumstances, he felt uncomfortable.[57] A joke would have eased the situation, but the unconscious processes of word-play, disaggregation and recombination, instead produced a paramnesia. Further analysis revealed that the association of death and sexuality was also connected to the recent suicide of one of his own patients 'on account of an incurable sexual disorder'; news of which had reached Freud while he had been staying at a small town called *Trafoi*. The forgotten name had undergone a series of transformations. It was first divided into two syllables, the second of which appeared without alteration in one of the substitute names (Bottic*elli*), while *Signor*, translated into *Herr* formed numerous associations with the repressed topic of death and sexuality. In a manner characteristic of joking, but aimed at maintaining rather than removing inhibitions in the conduct of everyday life, 'the names have been treated in this process like the pictograms in a sentence which has had to be converted into a picture-puzzle (or rebus)'.[58] And although the analysis of any particular case involves considerable complexity, Freud claims that all the instances he had examined could be understood as 'motivated by repression'.

Like jokes, the forgetting of proper names is contagious, indicating that a heightening of formality and inhibition, as well as of its relaxation, is also the work of unconscious mental processes. The one situation can be turned into the other by the discovery of some hitherto unknown connection between the participants. Freud quotes a case in his book on jokes:

A Galician Jew was travelling in a train. He had made himself really comfortable, had unbuttoned his coat and put his feet up on the seat. Just then a gentleman in modern dress entered the compartment. The Jew promptly pulled himself together and took up a proper pose. The stranger fingered through the pages of a notebook, made some calculations, reflected for a moment and then suddenly asked the Jew: 'Excuse me, when is Yom Kippur (The Day of Atonement)?' 'Oho!', said the Jew, and put his feet up on the seat again before answering.

(SE 8, pp. 80–1)

Jokes and parapraxes, the first relaxing and the second tightening the conventions of everyday social behaviour, illustrate the subtle dialectical interplay of disguise and revelation which is realised in normal behaviour.

Freud's aesthetics is intimately connected with the notion of play, and with a new highly sensitised and sensuous body-imagery. The coalescing of these ideas reveals Freud's intimate but ambivalent relation to the Romantic movement.

The notion of the inner freedom of play connects his work directly to the writings of Schiller and Lessing, who defined for modern German

57

culture an ideal of aesthetic valuation which was not only fundamental to the philosophical discourse of art, but also served, more generally, as the central arena of *Bildung.* Freud as a youngster had identified strongly with that tradition, distancing himself, as did other middle-class Jewish migrants of his generation, from the culture of the *shtetl.*[59] And while it might be argued that to make a theory of play central to an analysis of joking was, in some sense, to demean the cultural prototypes responsible for introducing this concept into modern literary and philosophical discourse, what emerges as more significant is that, by linking jokes to play, he provides a theoretical basis for the autonomous valuation of the aesthetic. The aesthetic, of which joking is an everyday form, can then be viewed as the continuation and elaboration of play, rather than, or at least in addition to, the 'sublimation' of sexual or aggressive instincts.

At the same time the spectacle of hysteria – a kind of semi-permanent parapraxis of the body – is conceived by Freud as a critique of Romantic psychology. In the modern world there is no possibility of the soul establishing contact with a transcendental realm of ultimate meaning and significance. Meaning begins and ends in the body, from which there is no escape into any more liberated domain.

Freud's aesthetics, therefore, unlike the Romantic and idealist tradition to which it is nonetheless linked, is not concerned primarily with distancing the ego from the world of objects. Rather, as it was also for Kierkegaard, aesthetic immediacy is regarded as a mode of participation in a disordered world.

NOTES

1 In this sense almost all Freud's works could be regarded as 'aesthetic'. Of particular relevance here, however, are his *Studies in Hysteria,* which is usually read as a 'clinical' work, *The Psychopathology of Everyday Life,* and *Jokes and their Relation to the Unconscious.* Spector (1972) usefully discusses the latter work in relation to Freud's works more explicitly devoted to conventionally defined artistic and aesthetic subjects.

2 Adorno (1989), Ferguson (1995); on possible links between Kierkegaard's and Freud's psychology see Cole (1971), Nordentoft (1972).

3 In a late essay Freud returns to the difficulty of combining in one mechanism the functions of registering impressions and of storing permanent memory traces, illustrating the difficulties by describing 'the mystic writing pad', a device which combines two wax surfaces through which these functions can be separated; SE 21, pp. 227–32.

4 On the older background to specular imagery see Grabbes (1982), Nolan (1990) and for its modern influence, Rorty (1980).

5 Eugene Bleuler was the first to use the term.

6 Schur (1972), p. 247; Gay (1988), pp 170–73. He closely followed the career of Heinrich Schliemann, who was as much a showman as an archaeologist; see Schliemann (1978), Bacon (1976), Calder III and Traill (1986).

7 SE 21, pp. 69–70.

8 Ziolkowski (1990) pp. 18–63.
9 Quoted in Piñero (1983), p. 2.
10 Charcot (1987), pp. xxiv, xxiii. His extensive programme was a significant phase in the 'secularization' of clinical neuro-pathology, and his anti-clerical views won government support; Goldstein (1987).
11 See, for example, his letters to Martha Bernays, during his stay in Paris. Freud (1961), pp. 182–223; McGrath (1986), p. 152; Gay (1988), pp. 47–51.
12 Charcot (1889), 3, p. 223.
13 Ellenberger (1970), pp. 89–102; Harrington, in Bynum and Shepherd (1988), interestingly points out the sense in which hypnosis as 'action at a distance' broke with mechanistic biology.
14 Charcot (1889), 3, p. 94
15 For an early example see Erichsen (1836), and for a general discussion Schivelbusch (1986) pp. 56–60
16 A view taken up independently in an American context by Beard (1881). For a general discussion in an English context see Oppenheim (1991), Showalter (1987).
17 Bernheim (1980), p. 122.
18 Ibid., p. 127.
19 Ibid., p. 160.
20 Ibid., p. 18.
21 Ibid., p. 22.
22 Ibid., p. 36.
23 Ibid., p. 37.
24 Ibid., p. 73.
25 Williams (1982).
26 Ribot (1882), p. 103.
27 McNish (1830).
28 Ribot (1882), p. 107 and more generally Hacking (1995).
29 Ibid., p. 110.
30 Ibid., p. 44.
31 The relative independence of different levels of mental organisation which this and other cases revealed was already familiar to Freud through his study of aphasias, and his resulting familiarity with the works of Hughlings Jackson: Freud (1953), Forrester (1980), Jackson (1931).
32 Janet (1965), p. 138.
33 Ibid., p. 202.
34 Janet (1977), p. 211.
35 Dijkstra (1986) for an excellent discussion of male views of women in *fin-de-siècle* culture; see also Showalter (1993).
36 SE 2, p. 161.
37 E.g. note 1 to SE 2, p. 62.
38 E.g. SE 2, pp. 55, 62.
39 SE 2, p. 93.
40 SE 2, p. 177. Swales, in Stepansky (1986) identifies this important patient as Anna von Lieben, born Baroness Anna von Todesco. See also Appignanesi and Forrester (1993) pp. 86–91.
41 Since the researches of Swales, reported in Stepansky (1986), Masson (1985) and the publication of the complete Fliess correspondence, which brought to light the Emma Eckstein incident, this is now something of a disputed title.
42 Freud soon ended the collaboration, but later claimed not only that Breuer had been significant in the discovery of the new method of psychoanalysis, but that his distinction between 'bound' and 'unbound' psychical energy was

fundamental to the development of his own 'metapsychology'. For an important reassessment of Breuer's work see Hirschmüller (1989). Sidis and Goodhart (1905) developed Breuer's notion of 'hypnoid states', which they regarded as 'sudden upheavals from the depths of the subconscious', and indicative of the normality of multiple personality.

43 This tradition is also represented in America by Prince (1906), and reached a high-point of clinical-descriptive virtuosity in Meige and Feindel (1907).

44 SE 2, p. 237.

45 David-Ménard (1988), p. 3.

46 SE 8, p. 11.

47 SE 8, pp. 16–17.

48 SE 8, p. 44.

49 SE 8, p. 96.

50 SE 8, p. 101.

51 SE 8, p. 111; Oring (1984), expands on the Jewish background to Freud's jokes.

52 SE 8, p. 124.

53 SE 8, p. 127.

54 SE 8, p. 148.

55 SE 8, p. 156.

56 Timpanaro (1976), argues that the single term 'parapraxes' conceals a diversity of quite different phenomena requiring separate explanation. His re-analysis of the specimen and other examples, however, depends on a psychologically unexplicated process of 'banalisation'.

57 Vitz (1988) suggests additional reason for difficulties over Signorelli.

58 SE 6, p. 5.

59 Cuddihy (1987) overstates the case; for an ethnographic study of the *Osjuden* see Zbrowski and Herzog (1952), contentiously, but using jokes; ref. to 'Life with people'.

3

TEXT

Hermeneutics of the dream-life

Clinical studies convinced Freud that hysterical symptoms could be analysed; they could be replaced, that is to say, by a series of immediately understandable and coherent statements expressive of some underlying and perfectly logical thought which, rather than represent in a normal fashion, the patient had chosen instead to disguise by the use of unconventional body-symbolism. And, from first principles, he had also convinced himself that dreams exhibit certain formal similarities with hysterical symptoms. In fact, dreams had played a significant and growing part in his clinical practice. Many of his patients spontaneously reported dreams, and interpreting them within the context of the general clinical picture had become a regular, if not a commonplace, analytic device for Freud. There was a sense in which hysterics seemed to dream while still awake, and Freud was frequently struck by the hallucinatory clarity of their recollections. They recounted their memories as descriptions of plastic scenes which seemed to appear before them as an independent reality rather than as conscious recollections of past events. Instead of pursuing his plans to write a general work on psychological theory, therefore, Freud embarked on a comprehensive study of dreams, and in the process raised in a new way most of the issues with which any such comprehensive theory would have to deal. His dreambook presents a new psychology, as well as a new understanding of dreams; and the implications of his new understanding of dreams spilled over into his subsequent clinical and theoretical writings.

DREAM INTERPRETATION

The very possibility of dream interpretation, as also of the analysis of symptoms, hinges on the belief that their puzzling and apparently nonsensical elements in fact contain a series of clues from which their originating ideas can be deduced. Hysterical symptoms, if they were in some sense designed to conceal events which it would be painful for the patient to recall nonetheless did so in such a way as still to communicate, albeit it in a disguised and indirect form, those very events. There seems to be an elaborate process of partial concealment, both the mechanism and function of which required elucidation.

Shortly before abandoning the unfinished *Project for a Scientific Psychology*, Freud had begun to analyse his own dreams. Indeed, he had been immensely excited by the analytic insight which he believed his first dream interpretations had produced. Over four years after the occasion in 1895 when, on holiday at Bellevue, near Vienna, he had completed his first dream analysis, and shortly before the publication of his dreambook, while again at Bellevue, he wrote to his friend Wilhelm Fliess (12 June, 1900) about his discovery. Obviously still excited by the intellectual breakthrough which he believed his interpretations represented, he asked (one suspects not quite facetiously):

Do you suppose that someday one will read on a marble tablet on this house:

> Here, on July 24, 1895,
> the secret of the dream
> revealed itself to Dr. Sigm. Freud.

(Freud 1985, p. 417)

The dream in question became known as the Dream of Irma's Injection, and serves as the 'specimen dream' which Freud uses as the starting point for *The Interpretation of Dreams*. The details of the interpretation have been much discussed in the Freud literature, particularly since the publication of an unexpurgated version of the Fliess letters.[1] An essential part of the background to the dream, not mentioned by Freud, is concerned with his and Fliess's treatment of one of Freud's patients, Emma Eckstein. During the period in which Freud formulated his basic psychoanalytic ideas he was infatuated with Fliess, and extremely gullible in relation to his friend's esoteric biological theories and medical therapies. Fliess, an ear, nose and throat specialist in Berlin, was convinced, on the basis of highly speculative biological theories, that the nose could be understood, anatomically and physiologically, as a displaced sexual organ. The condition of the nose, he believed, exercised a general regulating function on psychic and bodily health. He persuaded Freud to allow him to operate on Emma Eckstein, to remove a portion of bone from her nose, as a means of relieving her of severe hysterical symptoms. Fliess, who was in fact an inexperienced surgeon, failed to remove a length of gauze packing from the wound, with near fatal consequences. Emma did not recover well, bleeding continued, and eventually Freud called in another surgeon who discovered the oversight, and removed the gauze. Clearly shaken by the incident, Freud nonetheless subsequently assured Fliess of his continuing confidence in him.

There are several allusions to this situation in the Dream of Irma's Injection, which Freud analyses as a series of self-reproaches and

counter-claims. The dream is organised in terms of the relationship between criticisms of his professional competence, and demonstrations of his
medical skill. It is a complex dream, and, for the present purposes, the
more controversial background issues have become somewhat distracting.
For reasons of clarity, therefore, as well as brevity, the basic lines of Freud's
approach to dream interpretation can be more readily illustrated by considering another, related example; the Dream of the Botanical Monograph.
Freud reports his dream as follows:

> *I had written a monograph on a certain plant. The book lay before me and I
> was at the moment turning over a folded coloured plate. Bound up in each
> copy was a dried specimen of the plant, as though it had been taken from a
> herbarium.*

(SE 4, p. 169)

The interpretation of this dream, as of any other, depends on the spontaneous associations of the dreamer to each of its elements. It is the
dreamer, and not an analyst, who provides the interpretation. Freud begins
his analysis, therefore, with his own immediate reactions to the dream. He
had, he tells us, on the morning of the dream-day, seen a new book in the
window of a bookshop, a *monograph* on *The Genus Cyclamen.* He continues
at once with the observation that cyclamens, which had not figured directly
in the dream, were his wife's *favourite flower*, and he reproaches himself for
'so rarely remembering to *bring* her *flowers'.* The phrase 'bring her flowers'
then acts as the point of departure for a new train of thought concerning
a previous patient who had forgotten to buy his wife flowers on her
birthday. He had recently cited this anecdote to illustrate his view, subsequently incorporated into *The Psychopathology of Everyday Life*, that
'forgetting is very often determined by an unconscious purpose'.[2]

Freud's initial analysis was interrupted at this point, but later that day
Freud recalled:

> I really *had* written something in the nature of a *monograph on a plant*,
> namely a dissertation on the *coca-plant*, which had drawn Karl Koller's
> attention to the anaesthetic properties of cocaine. I had myself indi-
> cated this application of the alkaloid in my published paper, but I had
> not been thorough enough to pursue the matter further.

(SE 4, p. 170)

He recalled, furthermore, that during the day he had fantasised that, in the
event of his contracting glaucoma, he would travel incognito to Berlin and
have his friend Fliess arrange treatment for him. This daydream had
caused him to reflect on the ethical difficulties involved in a doctor
approaching his medical colleagues for treatment on his own behalf. It was
only at this point that Freud realised his day-dream, and the dream with
which it was continuous, referred to a specific event:

Shortly after Koller's discovery, my father had in fact been attacked by glaucoma; my friend Dr. Königstein, the ophthalmic surgeon, had operated on him; while Dr. Koller had been in charge of the cocaine anaesthesia and had commented on the fact that this case had brought together all of the three men who had a share in the introduction of cocaine.

(SE 4, p. 171)

He was reminded of the previous occasion, just a few days earlier, on which the cocaine incident had figured. He had been perusing a *Festschrift* (rather than a monograph) in honour of a senior colleague in which, as part of the laboratory's claims to distinction, Koller had been credited with the discovery of the anaesthetic properties of cocaine.[3]

The dream clearly makes sense in the context of the dreamer's current waking preoccupations and activities. The 'dream-thoughts' seem absorbed in characteristically mundane themes. However, in considering what at first appear to be incidental elements in the dream, Freud recalls events from a more remote past. The *dried specimen of the plant*, as if from a *herbarium*, he reports, 'led me to a memory from my secondary school'. Freud had been among those given the task of cleaning the school's herbarium, but, accurately judging his weakness in botany the head teacher had entrusted the young Freud with only a few sheets. These had included the group of flowers known as Crucifers, which he could now recall clearly, but had failed to identify during the preliminary examination in botany which formed part of his first year studies at Vienna University. Cruciferae at once reminded him of another flower group, Compositae, and it struck him that *artichokes*, which 'I might fairly have called my *favourite flowers*', were Compositae; flowers which his wife 'being more generous than I am' often brought him from the market.

Distant events were connected with incidents from the previous day through an unpredictable series of links. The *folded colour plate*, for example, is connected both with another self-reproach directed at his extravagant book buying habits and at an incident from the age of 5. In what he claimed to be 'almost the only plastic memory that I retained from that period of my life', he recalled that his father had encouraged him and his sister (then aged 3) to destroy a book with *coloured plates*. They had 'blissfully' pulled it apart, 'leaf by leaf, like an *artichoke*'. These various trains of thought, which seem heterogeneous and widely dispersed, are linked not only through a series of connecting associations which Freud is able to specify in detail, but with a conversation with his friend, Dr Königstein, which had taken place on the afternoon of the dream-day. Though not revealing the subject matter of that conversation beyond saying that a number of issues important to them both had been discussed, and that Freud's preoccupation with *favourite hobbies* (another reference to monographic studies) had come up, he has said enough to justify the claim that the *manifest* content of the dream is related not to a single preceding event, but that it has at least two separate sources in the dream-day.

As in the more elaborate specimen dream of Irma's Injection there is a strong element of self-reproach in this dream, in relation both to his treatment of his wife and to his own professional competence. At the same time there is a counter-claim in defence of his intellectual significance and importance as an individual:

> All the trains of thought starting from the dream – the thoughts about my wife's and my own favourite flowers, about cocaine, about the awkwardness of medical treatment among colleagues, about my preference for studying monographs and about my neglect of certain branches of science such as botany – all of these trains of thought, when they were further pursued led ultimately to one or other of the many ramifications of my conversation with Dr. Königstein. Once again the dream . . . turns out to have been in the nature of a self-justification, a plea on behalf of my own rights. . . . What it meant was: 'After all, I'm the man who wrote the valuable and memorable paper (on cocaine).'
>
> (SE 4, p. 173)

Indeed, it anticipates a more compelling excuse. The expense of and self-absorption in his studies will be justified by the production of a much more significant monograph (his forthcoming book on dreams). Among his associations to the dream he notes that he had received a letter from Fliess on the previous day, in which his friend, anticipating the completion of the dreambook, writes that, '*I see it lying finished before me and I see myself turning over its pages.*'

It is worth noting that, when the dreambook was finally completed, Freud's letter to Fliess immediately prior to its publication prefaces the imaginary memorial plaque with a miniature 'botanical monograph':

> life at Bellevue is turning out very pleasant for everyone. The evenings and mornings are enchanting; the scent of lilac and laburnum has been succeeded by that of acacia and jasmine; the wild roses are in bloom and everything, as I too notice, happens suddenly.
>
> (Freud 1985, p. 417)

Indeed, Freud tends to associate new ideas with botanising and botanical forms with everything fundamental in psychic life.

The dream-thoughts are consistent and logical, it is only the complexity of the allusions through which they are expressed which gives rise to the appearance of over-complication and arbitrariness. The 'indifferent material' relating to the botanical monograph served as a useful bridge between two sets of events on the previous day, one insignificant (his

sighting of the botanical monograph) and one which had been emotionally arousing (the conversation with Dr Königstein). All the issues
relating to the second were represented in the dream through associations
with the former. At first sight the analysis, like the deciphering of hysterical
symptoms, seems to depend upon a wholly incredible series of coin-
cidences, but, on reflection, Freud maintains that this is not the case:

> If these chains of thought had been absent others would no doubt
> have been selected. It is easy enough to construct such chains, as is
> shown by the puns and riddles that people make every day for their
> entertainment. The realm of jokes knows no boundaries. Or, to go a
> stage further, if there had been no possibility of forging enough
> intermediate links between the two impressions, the dream would
> simply have been different. Another indifferent impression of the
> same day – for crowds of such impressions enter our minds and are
> then forgotten – would have taken the place of the 'monograph' in
> the dream, would have linked up with the subject of the conversation
> and would have represented it in the content of the dream.
>
> (SE 4, p. 176)

It is quite characteristic, Freud claims, for each element of the dream's
content to be 'overdetermined', that is to be represented in the dream-
thoughts many times over. 'Botanical monograph' is one such 'nodal
point' in which a number of different lines of thought intersect. Furthermore, both 'botanical' and 'monograph' separately constitute such nodal
points. In various ways these mnemic symbols allow the indifferent material
of the previous day to be recalled as a kind of cryptogram of thoughts which
were, in fact, stimulated by a quite different series of events.

In further associations to the dream Freud mentions a connection
between 'artichokes' and his thoughts about Italy. He does not elaborate
on this link, but he goes on at once to liken the dream to 'a factory of
thoughts' where might be found:

> . . . a thousand threads one treadle throws
> Where fly the shuttles hither and thither,
> Unseen the threads are knit together,
> And an infinite combination grows.

These lines from Goethe's *Faust*, in conjunction with references to Italy,
links another two of Freud's favourite hobbies. Since his schooldays
Goethe had been a writer with whom he was on intimate terms and
innumerable direct and indirect references to Goethe's writings, and to
Faust in particular, are sprinkled throughout Freud's work. His passion for
Italy is just as evident from his frequent mention of its Renaissance master-
pieces and his extensive travels there to view them. Hence, indeed, the fact
that his failure to recall the name of the artist of the Orvieto frescoes

(Signorelli) was a parapraxis worthy of analysis. It is tempting to suppose, therefore, that the botanical monograph of his dream refers to Goethe's *The Metamorphosis of Plants*, as well as to Freud's own monograph on cocaine and the still unfinished dreambook.

In 1786 Goethe had travelled to Italy in search of artistic and scientific cultivation. It was in southern Italy that he thought he had discovered the *Urplanze*, the primitive vegetative form from which he believed all plant life had evolved.[4] Freud, though no botaniser, was an avid mushroom hunter, and occasionally referred to dreams as primitive plant-like or fungus-like forms. More significantly, Italy and Goethe provided for Freud a model of *Bildung*, of initiation into and ultimately mastery over, the highly-valued German speaking culture of modernity. Goethe radiated the peculiar combination of literary skill and scientific curiosity which Freud felt to be in his own makeup. His effortless visualisation and his unorthodox morphological approach to understanding nature had a direct impact on Freud's approach to psychology.[5]

Though Freud occasionally refers to 'the ultimate meaning' of a dream (usually at a point where, for reasons of discretion, his interpretation breaks off), or of 'solving' its cryptogram, the meaning of a dream consists simply in the dreamer's articulation of associations to its images. In fact, this process of anatomising, and connecting the elements of the dream with memories of both indifferent and significant events might be continued indefinitely.

DREAM ANALYSIS

What makes this whole process difficult to understand is the particular mode of representation which characterises the process of dreaming. Freud uses the botanical monograph example to illustrate several general features of dreams, or more accurately of the dream-work, through which the dream-content is related to underlying dream-thoughts. Significantly he discusses the problem of connecting the two, as he did of understanding hysterical symptoms, in terms of translation:

> The dream-thoughts and the dream-content are presented to us like two versions of the same subject-matter in two different languages. Or, more properly, the dream-content seems like a transcript of the dream-thoughts into another mode of expression, whose characters and syntactic laws it is our business to discover by comparing the original and the translation. The dream-thoughts are immediately comprehensible, as soon as we have learnt them. The dream-content, on the other hand, is expressed as it were in a pictographic script, the characters of which have to be transposed individually into the language of the dream-thoughts. If we attempted to read these

characters according to their pictorial value instead of according to their symbolic relation, we should clearly be led into error.

(SE 4, p. 277)

Most evident, perhaps, is the diversity and richness of the meaningful associations that emerge from what was dreamt as a simple plastic image. The dream-thoughts undergo a process of *condensation*. Often dreams are extremely abbreviated. Once the process of interpretation is begun we have the impression that it might be extended, almost at will; that new lines of thought would come to light and that more and more material would be drawn into an expanding network of associations. The botanical monograph also exhibits the tendency within dreams for particular thoughts to be expressed in terms of images from a related, but quite distinct field of association. This *displacement*, like the formation of hysterical mnemic symbols, is a way of alluding to thoughts which the ego is simultaneously 'fending-off'.

Both processes of condensation and displacement are basic elements of the 'dream-work' which result in the immediately incomprehensible character of many dreams.[6] They are processes which may be visualised in terms of a flowing stream, branching at points into tributaries, gathered at others behind dams. They may also be conceived of as particular types of 'associations'. Having abandoned the *Project* Freud no longer employed the notion of 'paths of association' in a precise physical sense, but the term remained as an effective metaphor to convey the idea of tracing out a path through an interconnected network. The network is now viewed in terms of 'thoughts' rather than of 'periods of excitation', and, perhaps more aptly in this case, can be imagined as a pattern of connected 'nodal points' inscribed upon a waxy surface.

Dreams are continuous processes of which we become aware during sleep. Or, rather, the initial stages of dream-formation take place continually in the waking state, but are broken up and reordered according to the linear rational connectedness of the ego. In the waking state the ego constitutes a privileged path of association and might be visualised as a straight line into which flow innumerable tributaries. The ego possesses a vectorial quality which draws together associative paths into a single temporally organised stream. As the ego sinks into sleep all these elliptical associative pathways are reconnected with each other. Non-ego, dream consciousness, thus, extends itself in all directions simultaneously. In dreams all representations exist simultaneously and are organised according to non-temporal principles. Dreams, thus, 'may include impressions which date back to earliest childhood, and which seem not to be accessible to waking memory'.[7]

If a clear division between dreaming and waking is to be made then, in principle, it could be established in terms of the presence or absence of the ego as the seemingly coherent point-mass which results from the continuous process of forgetting to which the 'arrow of time' of our waking experience is inescapably subordinated. Thus, although the material of dreams is as unsuited to the representation of logical relations as is the material of the plastic arts to the expression of speech, in a similar manner this limitation has been partially circumvented. Ancient artists, Freud notes, did not hesitate to hang labels from the mouths of persons they depicted 'containing in written characters the speeches which the artist despaired of representing pictorially'. Thus:

> just as the art of painting eventually found a way of expressing, by means other than the floating labels, at least the *intention* of the words of the personages represented – affection, threats, warnings, and so on – so too there is a possible means by which dreams can take account of some of the logical relations between their dream-thoughts, by making appropriate modification in the method of representation characteristic of dreams.
>
> (SE 4, pp. 313–14)

Similarly, and in a general way, logical interconnectedness is represented by simultaneity in dreams; the unity of the dream-thoughts is transformed into a more or less unified scene. Logical implication or dependence, on the other hand, may be represented by a relation between two dreams, in which the dependent clause serves as a minor introductory dream to the main dream. A certain freedom still exists here, so that the introduction may follow rather than precede the main dream. Alternatively a causal relation may be represented by an image of a person or thing in the dream being transformed into a different person or thing. In either event logical connections cling to a remnant of the ego and are expressed as temporal relations.

Relations of similarity or consonance, however, are actively favoured by dreams. Where the ego arises through establishing difference, non-ego consciousness delights in the discovery of a multiplicity of similitudes which go unremarked in the waking world. Identifications and combinations of persons and places abound in dreams and is also a feature of the condensation so typical of oneiric images. As the similitude lies in the dream-thoughts and not in the plastic images which represent them, this gives rise to the 'composite structures . . . which so often lend dreams a fantastic appearance'. In another botanical specimen, the biography of one of his patients was represented oneirically in 'the language of flowers' as an impossible plant, combining the blossom and flowers of different species, each one of which indicated a different period in her life.

The most significant formal relations to emerge in dreams, however, are expressed through variations in the sensory intensity among different dream-images, or of entire dreams. Freud insists that there is no evidence for the view, common among the nineteenth-century dream investigators including Maury and Scherner, that 'real sensations' experienced during sleep, originating in external sounds, vibrations and so on, or internal organic processes, are given special prominence in dreams. 'The factor of reality', he claims, 'counts for nothing in determining the intensity of dream images.' Nor is the vividness or clarity of dream-images indicative of their psychical value; in fact there is a complete 'transvaluation of all psychical values' between the dream-thoughts and the dream-images. What is most significant in the dream-thoughts is frequently represented by a fleeting and apparently unimportant detail of the dream content, while the most vivid dream-image often represents peripheral thoughts. It is, rather, the number of associative connections it makes with various trains of thought alluded to in the dream to which the intensity of the image is directly related. In the case of the botanical monograph, for example, the dream is little more than a single intense image which serves as a 'nodal point' for an immense variety of associations. This, again, follows directly on the withdrawal of the ego, for which the centrality and intensity of its experiential contents are synonymous. Yet it is just the meaningless super-ficiality of the intensity of dream-images which makes the dream an ideal image of modernity; and rather than viewing it negatively as the rejection of everything rational and intentional which defines waking experience, the dream comes instead to signify the incomprehensible interconnected and yet fragmented character of modern life.

The dream has also supplanted the ego as an emblem of modernity in terms of its emotional incongruity. Affect in dreams has always been harder to dismiss than their ideational content. And because these are unaffected by the dream-work they are expressed in relation to the latent dream-thoughts rather than in connection with the often inappropriate dream-images. Thus:

> In a dream I may be in a horrible, dangerous and disgusting situation without feeling any fear or repulsion; while another time, on the contrary, I may be terrified at something harmless and delighted at something childish.

> (SE 5, p. 460)

But, although 'whenever there is an affect in the dream, it is also to be found in the dream thoughts', the reverse is not the case, and as a general rule dreams are less rich in affects than are their originating thoughts. Freud finds that:

> When I have reconstructed the dream-thoughts, I habitually find the most intense psychical impulses in them striving to make themselves felt and struggling as a rule against others that are sharply opposed to them. If I then turn back to the dream, it not infrequently appears

70

colourless, and without emotional tone of any great intensity. The dream-work has reduced to a level of indifference not only the content but often the emotional tone of my thoughts as well. It might be said that the dream-work brings about a *suppression of affects.*

(SE 5, p. 467)

Freud specifically mentions the dream of the botanical monograph in this regard. The dream-thoughts 'consisted of a passionately agitated plea on behalf of my liberty', yet the dream that arose from these thoughts was strangely indifferent. And, remarks Freud, like the 'peace that has descended upon a battlefield strewn with corpses; no trace is left of the struggle which raged over it'. While it is quite generally the case that 'it is never possible to enter into the dream-thoughts without being deeply moved', the majority of dreams present a spectacle of anaesthetised images. Though Freud speculates that this may have something to do with the organic effects of sleep, it is to be understood from a psychological point of view primarily as a consequence of the multiplicity of differently 'coloured' trains of thought which go into the 'compromise formation' which constitute the dream-image. Occasionally affects may remain more or less intact because the dream-work is itself of an indifferent nature, but, more often, the dream-work itself introduces contrary emotions which tend to cancel out the original feeling. The indifference of the dream, in other words, is like the anaesthetised sensibility of Musil's 'man without qualities' who, rather than being withdrawn from it, is overwhelmed by the contradictory character of modern life,

Freud argues that some formal relations cannot be expressed in dreams; and these are just the relations through which the ego establishes its own identity as a psychic content. Thus, the relation of 'either/or', which as Kierkegaard had established was fundamental to the emergence and development of the ego, finds no oneiric equivalent. The dream knows only 'both/and', and simply presents alternatives as if they were equally valid, and equally possible. Similarly negation has no meaning within dreams.

The formal characteristics of dreams can be understood through a reductive process of 'thinking away' the ego. But as dreams are all recalled experiences, and, only in that form enter into waking life, their original contents undergo a process of 'secondary revision' which recasts them into a more coherent and logically ordered whole. Connecting thoughts are interpolated into the dream, particularly during the process of waking-up, as the ego re-establishes its psychic hegemony. Secondary revision provides a logical façade (Freud was fond of architectural as well as archaeological metaphors) to dreams and is frequently based on daydreams which, in fact, are unrelated to the dream-thoughts proper. This anticipatory reassertion of the ego in practice has the result of prolonging sleep by presenting the dream in a less disturbing form. This process can be far reaching and, in Freud's view, gives rise to those puzzling dreams which appear to present a long and coherent narrative leading up to an event which can be traced to the sensory stimulus which, in fact, has wakened the dreamer. Freud accounts for Maury's famous French Revolution dream in this way. The entire sequence of images which Maury recalled as a connected narrative of his living through the Reign of Terror, his appearance before the Revolutionary Tribunal, his condemnation, his being led to the place of execution before the mob, mounting the scaffold, being prepared for execution and the sound of the falling guillotine blade was a previously formed daydream which was 'alluded to' by a small piece of food falling across his neck as he slept, simultaneously waking him and releasing the fantasy, which infiltrated and wholly transformed some existing dream-content.[8]

The dream-work is a process of translation between experience gathered up and ordered as a rectilinear ego (point-mass in motion) and experience dispersed across a broad interconnected surface (field of force). Might this difference be expressed less negatively; not as experience minus the ego, but in terms rather of an inner-principle and significance of its own? It is to this end that Freud introduces the notion of wish-fulfilment; wishing, it might be said, is the specific mode of interconnecting egoless experience.

This throws up a number of conceptual difficulties which Freud allows to emerge only towards the end of *The Interpretation of Dreams*. Initially his appeals to the notion of wishing and of wish-fulfilment seems unproblematic and corresponds to common-sense usage. The specimen dream is, thus, not only interpreted in terms of the associations to which it gives rise, but is coherently analysed as the fulfilment of a wish. There is nothing very remarkable about this wish, which expresses a desire on Freud's part to be highly regarded by his colleagues. Similarly, the botanical monograph dream can be understood in terms of his professional ambition and the wish for freedom to indulge his leisure interests. These, clearly, are psychic contents known to the ego. It might even be claimed that such wishes constitute the very core of the ego, informing, as they did for Freud, both long-term intentions and the energetic organisation of daily life.

Of course a good many dreams, and particularly the dreams of children, are frank wish-fulfilments. But where they are not the distortion of the dream-work, like the formation of hysterical symptoms, can be understood 'as if' a second ego were at work as a censoring mechanism prohibiting the direct expression of socially inappropriate wishes in consciousness. The notion of a 'censorship' as a kind of alert secondary ego, as a paradoxical unconscious ego, undoubtedly creates an awkward complication for Freud's approach. Yet it carries him an impressive distance along the new analytic path which had been opened up by his new interpretive approach.

72

This approach, indeed, has become stereotyped as 'Freudian' and for the popular understanding of Freud the 'repression' of sexual and aggressive wishes prohibited in polite society is effected within the individual psyche by this secondary ego or censoring device. Yet, from his first case studies in which he rejected the French understanding of hysteria as 'double-consciousness', and in the light of the many subsequent revisions and several major changes to his entire psychological system, it is clear that Freud was often uneasy with the implications of this initial approach which, however subtle his own understanding of the issues involved, encouraged a simplistic reading of his dreambook.

The difficulty is two-fold. If the prohibited wish can be readily deciphered why should it have been disguised in the first place? It is one thing to argue, as Freud was to do in relation to joking and parapraxes, that, in the context of organised social life, such wishes should not be directly expressed or acted upon, but their appearance in dreams hardly seems to constitute a danger, either to society or to individual psychic health. Even if we assume many of the wishes imaginatively fulfilled in dreams are far more destructive and disruptive than the professional jealousies and ambitions to which Freud owns up in his botanical dream, the waking ego is hardly distressed by their acknowledgement. Indeed, are such wishes not the more easily controlled in being acknowledged? And would not dreams be an effective means of dispersing resentment, anger and frustration if they were openly wish-fulfilments?

Secondly, and more seriously, how can the dream, which is to be understood as experience outside of the organising mechanism of the ego, simultaneously be regarded as a wish-fulfilment if the notion of the wish is itself assimilated to the ego? If, that is to say, the prohibited wish is understood as an intention, or as a desire, then there is no need for disguise, and if it is a process wholly outside the ego, then it would seem that it cannot be represented at all. This is a recurrent difficulty in Freud's work, and can be pursued well beyond his writings specifically devoted to the elucidation of the dream process.

Certainly, within the body of *The Interpretation of Dreams*, the idea of wishing becomes gradually transformed. It is not simply that more 'dangerous' wishes progressively emerge in the interpreted material, but these wishes, in terms of their associations, refer to memories of earlier and earlier events in the life of the dreamer. This progressive revelation of wishing as essentially related to childhood, and, moreover, to periods of childhood normally forgotten and inaccessible to the waking ego, confirms the view that the wish ought to be regarded as an egoless process.

The ego has an essential relation to time and conceives of itself as a process of unfolding, a kind of plant-like growth. Thus, the fact that dreams contain associative links with experiences in the dreamer's childhood is, perhaps, not surprising. The botanical monograph dream had contained references to events from Freud's early childhood which seem logically related to his adult ego. At first this seems to be no more than a certain enhancement of the normal function of memory. But 'the copious and intertwined associative links' of the dream-work in that particular instance, as in others, could not have been established on the basis of projecting his waking ego into the past, as if it could travel backwards in time and, like an interested tourist observing a once visited city, look about for features that appeared similar to known landmarks. It is rather the case that, as the dream originates in processes foreign to the ego, associations with childhood exist *simultaneously* with contemporary events. Biographical time has no meaning within the dream, for which all experience coexists on the same timeless plane.

Childhood experience, thus, becomes contemporary with adult life and frequently, as in the case of the botanical monograph, it transpires that 'the ultimate meaning of the dream . . . is intimately related to the subject of the childhood scene.'[9] And we find not only the child's experiences 'but the child's impulses still living on in the dream'. Freud thus suggests that his professional ambition, which was focused for a long time on his wish to be made *professor extraordinarius* at the University of Vienna, and which had figured in a number of his dreams, originated in an incident from his childhood. At the age of 11 or 12, when dining with his parents in the Prater, a poetic improviser had predicted the young Freud would become a cabinet minister. At the time this was an inspiring possibility; the liberal government of 1867 had, for the first time, included Jews and, indeed, for some years Freud had intended to study law as a preliminary to fulfilling this prediction. However, in later life regarding his long-delayed academic promotion to be the result of anti-Semitism, allusions in his dreams to this incident served not only to remind him of the source of his ambition but also of the more liberal times in which it might have been realised. Similarly, though a series of dreams in which his wish to visit Rome had been related to contemporary impulses, 'it had received powerful reinforcement from memories that stretched far back into childhood'. For many years, in fact, he had avoided visiting Rome. Freud traces these still active childhood wishes, and their apparent thwarting, to his early identification with Hannibal, a Jewish general who, though triumphantly crossing the Alps, had never entered Rome. To his 'youthful mind', he suggests 'Hannibal and Rome symbolised the conflict between the tenacity of Jewry and the organisation of the Catholic church'.[10] Again, current anti-Semitism, which was an obstacle to his professional ambition, was represented by a childhood memory of Jewish success.

Freud points out that Hannibal had continued to play an active part in his fantasies as a result of another incident from his childhood. His father told him of an occasion when a Christian had knocked his new hat into the roadway, accompanying the blow with a shout of 'Jew! get off the pavement.' The young Freud was unimpressed with his father's response which was peacefully to step on to the road to retrieve his hat:

This struck me as unheroic conduct on the part of the big, strong man who was holding the little boy by the hand. I contrasted this situation with another which fitted my feelings better: the scene in which Hannibal's father, Hamilcar Barca, made his boy swear before the household to take vengeance on the Romans. Ever since that time Hannibal had a place in my phantasies.

(SE 4, p. 197)

But he does not stop there, further analysis reveals even earlier sources of his 'enthusiasm for the Carthaginian general', and he speculates that:

the development of this martial ideal is traceable . . . to the times when, at the age of three, I was in close relation, sometimes friendly but sometimes warlike, with a boy a year older than myself, and to the wishes which that relation must have stirred up in the weaker of the two playfellows.

(SE 4, p. 287)

And if the wish is traced back to this early experience we reach back beyond the point at which conscious experience is organised in terms of an ego; to a point at which anger, love, hatred, and other states of feeling which we too readily qualify as personal characteristics and attributes, are active as more or less blind forces. Thus, while early incidents may be used as 'screen memories' upon which to project later material (as the childhood scene associated with the botanical monograph dream was for Freud's later bibliophile propensities), analysis revealed, equally, that the earliest wishes persisted in the most highly developed and individuated dream-content. Indeed Freud is 'compelled to ask' whether 'trains of thought reaching back to earliest childhood' are not the invariable accompaniment, or even a precondition, of dreaming. And not only dreams proper, but daydreams reveal this typical characteristic giving rise, like hysterical symptoms, to 'compromise formations' in which the most varied material from widely divergent periods is included. Reverting to his favourite archaeological metaphor Freud insists that in all essentials daydreams are like dreams:

Like dreams, they are wish-fulfilments; like dreams, they are based to a large extent on impressions of infantile experiences; like dreams, they benefit by a certain degree of relaxation of censorship. If we examine their structure, we shall perceive the way in which the wishful purpose that is at work in their production has mixed up the material of which they are built, has rearranged it and has formed it into a new whole. They stand in much the same relation to the childhood memories from which they are derived as do some Baroque palaces of Rome to the ancient ruins whose pavements and columns have provided the material for the more recent structures.

(SE 5, p. 492)

As Freud became convinced that infantile wishes instigate, but are normally successfully disguised within, almost all dreams, he insisted more vehemently on the peculiar character of the dream-work. Distortion in dreams is not simply a matter of censoring thoughts unacceptable to the waking ego but, more profoundly, involves processes in which egoless forces shape and transform the contents of experience. Summarising his long discussion and many examples of dream-work Freud concludes:

> Two separate functions may be distinguished in mental activity during the construction of a dream: the production of dream-thoughts, and their transformation into the content of the dream. The dream-thoughts are entirely rational and are constructed with an expenditure of all the psychical energy of which we are capable. . . . On the other hand, the second function of mental activity during dream-construction, the transformation of the unconscious thoughts into the content of the dream, is peculiar to dream-life and characteristic of it. This dream-work proper diverges further from our picture of waking thought than has been supposed even by the most determined depreciator of psychical functioning during the formation of dreams. The dream-work is not simply more careless, more irrational, more forgetful and more incomplete than waking thought; it is completely different from it qualitatively and for that reason not immediately comparable with it. It does not think, calculate or judge in any way at all; it restricts itself to giving things a new form. It is exhaustively described by an enumeration of the conditions which it has to satisfy in producing its result.

(SE 5, p. 506–7)

DREAM SYMBOLISM

Freud's approach to interpretation through spontaneous association, and his analysis of the process of representation through the guiding idea of wish-fulfilment, was formulated in distinction to what he took to be the major historical tradition (for which dreams were acknowledged as carrying any meaning at all) of symbolic understanding.

Freud rejects what he calls the 'symbolic' method of dream interpretation, in which an entire dream is assigned a meaning on the basis of an analogy conceived by the interpreter. The pharaoh's dream of seven fat kine followed by seven lean kine, for example, is understood by Joseph as a 'symbolic substitute' for a prophetic warning of the approach of seven years of famine. Freud also rejects a method of interpretation based on

76

assigning particular and fixed meanings of specific dream images. He calls this the 'decoding' method, which:

> treats dreams as a kind of cryptography in which each sign can be translated into another sign having a known meaning, in accordance with a fixed key.
>
> (SE 4, p. 97)

His own method of translation, founded on contextualisation of each image and a consideration of 'the means of representation', cannot lead to the assembling of such a catalogue of fixed symbolic meanings. Initially Freud attempted to treat all mnemic symbols as fully explicable in terms of biographical materials; as so many hysterical symptoms. However, influenced by some of his early followers, particularly Wilhelm Stekel, Freud acknowledged the independent significance of modes of symbolic representation 'as old as language itself'. It is not, however, primarily for the light they shed on the meaning of particular dream-contents but, rather, for the connection they offer with a much wider field representation that Freud became interested in symbolism:

> this symbolism is not peculiar to dreams, but is characteristic of unconscious ideation, in particular among the people, and it is to be found in folklore, and in popular myths, legends, linguistic idioms, proverbial wisdom and current jokes, to a more complete extent than in dreams.
>
> (SE 5, p. 351)

Symbolism became important to Freud because it allowed him to transform psychoanalysis into a general and fundamental cultural science.

However, although symbols in dreams are 'habitually employed to express the same thing', they are always subject to the 'peculiar plasticity of the psychical material in dreams', and cannot simply be treated as elements of fixed meaning. In dreams symbols:

> frequently have more than one or even several meanings and, as with Chinese script, the correct interpretation can only be arrived at on each occasion from the context.
>
> (SE 5, p. 353)

Nevertheless, he quotes a number of common examples of fixed symbolic meanings in dreams, and, quite unjustifiably, this has become popularly identified as the typically 'Freudian' method of dream-interpretation. Thus:

> all elongated objects, such as sticks, tree-trunks and umbrellas (the opening of these last being comparable to an erection) may stand for the male organ – as well as all long, sharp weapons, such as knives, daggers and pikes. . . . Boxes, cases, chests, cupboards and ovens

represent the uterus, and also hollow objects, ships and vessels of all kinds. . . . Rooms in dreams are usually women. . . . Steps, ladders or staircases, or, as the case may be, walking up or down them, are representations of the sexual act. . . . It is highly probable that all complicated machinery and apparatus occurring in dreams stand for the genitals. . . . Nor is there any doubt that all weapons and tools are used as symbols for the male organ: e.g. ploughs, hammers, rifles, revolvers, daggers, sabres, etc. – In the same way many landscapes in dreams, especially any containing bridges or wooded hills, may clearly be recognised as descriptions of the genitals.

(SE 5, pp. 354–57)

In addition, therefore, to the personal associations and the analytic transcription of the dream-work, quite general symbols of 'flowering', 'deflowering', and so on, might be expected to have played their part in the Dream of the Botanical Monograph. Indeed, Freud himself provides a discussion of flower symbolism in one of his more extended examples of representation by symbols. He reports, in English, the following short dream from an engaged young woman, 'not neurotic but is of a somewhat prudish and reserved character' who was preoccupied by the likely post-ponement of her marriage:

I arrange the centre of a table with flowers for a birthday.

Freud is at once able to offer an interpretation based on 'popular symbolism';

It was an expression of her bridal wishes: the table with its floral centre-piece symbolised herself and her genitals; she represented her wishes for the future as fulfilled, for her thoughts were already occupied with the birth of a baby; so her marriage lay a long way behind her.

(SE 5, p. 374)

But, with the aid of the dreamer's own associations, further symbolic elements emerge and become meaningful in the specific context of her personal circumstances. Freud asked what kind of flowers they were and was informed, also in English, that they were 'expensive flowers; one has to pay for them' composed of 'lilies of the valley, violets and pinks or car-nations'. Freud assumes that 'lily' appeared 'in its popular sense as a symbol of chastity', which was confirmed by her own association with it of 'purity'. Further, as 'valley' is a 'frequent female symbol in dreams; so that the chance combination of the two symbols in the English name of the flower was used in the dream-symbolism to stress the preciousness of her virginity'. In 'the language of flowers', 'violets' (violates) express 'the dreamer's thoughts on the violence of defloration', and the dream refers to the cost involved in being a wife and a mother. 'Carnations' symbolises

78

male sexuality (carnal, incarnation), and her *fiancé's* frequent gifts of these flowers suggests that 'she was making a gift of her virginity and expected a full emotional and sexual life in return for it'.

Flowers, Freud claims, commonly have a sexual meaning in other contexts, and 'symbolises the human organs of sex by blossoms, which are the sexual organs of plants'.[11] In arranging the table for a birthday, in her dream, she was 'identifying with her *fiancé*, and was representing her as "arranging" her for a birth – that is, as copulating with her'. The latent dream-thought was of the form 'If I were he, I wouldn't wait – I would deflower my *fiancée* without asking her leave – I would use violence.'

Freud infers the meaning of dream-images from general symbols only to provide initial clues to interpretation, or to forge provisional links in an otherwise broken chain of associations. Symbolism remains, for Freud, essentially one part of the dream-work, which becomes effective only when it is convenient for the construction of the finished dream-image, that is, when its use provides a means of expressing the latent wish. This cautious approach again distinguishes Freud from the Romantic tradition within which symbolism is treated, particularly in myth and fairy tale, as an autonomous, supra-personal mode of signification.[12]

DREAM SYNTHESIS

Dream interpretation is a process of following various undirected lines of thought from the dream-images to dream-thoughts which exist in a time-less plane of psychical interaction. It is, then, a process in which the dreamer is gradually divested of the ego and encourages the reasonable (i.e. 'egoistical') objection that it is an arbitrary process which depends only upon the ingenuity of the interpreter.[13]

Freud himself raised this difficulty, in relation to the interpretation of hysterical symptoms as well as to dreams, and regretted that circumstances rarely admitted of the possibility of a 'dream synthesis' which, beginning from the analysed dream-thoughts, would reconstruct in its entirety the process through which the dream was formed. Indeed, he claims to have performed such syntheses for his own satisfaction but, as this process depends for its starting point upon a completely analysed dream, he felt unable, for 'reasons which are of many kinds and which will be accepted as valid by any reasonable person', to reproduce these examples from his own dreams.[14] To illustrate the principles of interpretation he was able to use his own dreams without pursuing the analysis to its (provisional) conclusion, and at various points he drew attention to the incompleteness of his illustrative examples which stemmed from the requirement for personal discretion. A synthesis of any of his own dreams would require an unprecedented frankness that, ironically, would render his work even less likely to be taken seriously within the scientific community.

Shortly after the publication of *The Interpretation of Dreams*, however, Freud was able to offer an example of dream-synthesis taken from the case study of one of his patients; and, through the same case study was able to discuss at a more general level the relation between the formation of mnemic symbols in dreams and in hysteria.[15] In October of 1900 Philipp Bauer, a wealthy manufacturer in his late forties, brought his daughter, Ida (Dora), for treatment with Freud. He was already known to Freud who, some four years previously, had successfully treated him for a syphilitic infection. Dora's father, in fact, had a history of illness which played a significant role in the formation of his daughter's symptoms. During Dora's sixth year, which marked the onset of her own history of ill health, her father contracted tuberculosis and thereafter spent lengthy periods in health resorts. When she was 10 her father suffered a detached retina and had to spend several weeks in a darkened room, and two years later he underwent a slight paralysis, accompanied by confusional states.

At this period Freud was by no means opposed to the idea that somatic, and particularly heritable organic weaknesses, played an important part in the aetiology of hysteria. He draws attention to her father's history of illness, and particularly to his sexually transmitted infection, as an indication of likely predisposing constitutional factors in Dora's case. The suspicion of an underlying 'somatic compliance' was reinforced by what Freud took to be unmistakable signs of neurosis in her father's siblings. He also knew a sister of Philipp Bauer's, a woman who 'gave clear evidence of a severe psychoneurosis' though 'without any characteristically hysterical symptoms'.[16] And he had once treated his elder brother, 'a hypochondriacal bachelor'. It was, furthermore, not only Dora's hysteria, but her 'natural gifts and her intellectual precocity' that she had 'derived' from her father's side of the family.

But it was the 'purely human and social circumstances' of Dora's family circle that held the key to understanding the development of her hysteria. In spite of his illnesses her father was a dominating and successful individual with whom his daughter had been very much in sympathy. Her mother, whom Freud never met, he describes as 'an uncultivated woman and above all as a foolish one, who had concentrated all her interests upon domestic affairs'; and claimed she displayed the typical symptoms of a 'housewife's psychosis' which had intensified as a result of her husband's various illnesses and 'the estrangement to which it led'.[17] Dora sided with her father in any family disputes, doted on her father's sister, and slowly grew distant from her brother who remained close to his mother.

Freud was presented with a history of nervous disorders stretching back to Dora's childhood. At the age of 8 'chronic dyspnoea' (asthma attack), which occurred after a short mountain trip, was put down to over-exertion and responded to an extended period of rest. At the age of 12 Dora began to suffer from migraine, which cleared up by the time she was 16 without any particular treatment, at which point attacks of *tussis nervosa*, with occasional loss of voice, supervened. There was nothing very exceptional in Dora's medical history, which was 'merely a case of *"petite hystérie"* with the commonest of all somatic and mental symptoms . . . together with depression, hysterical unsociability, and a *taedium vitae* which was probably not entirely genuine'.[18] In common with so many other young women from wealthy families Dora had been subjected to hydrotherapy, electrical treatment, and enforced stays at health spas.[19] She had not responded to these various treatments and, in spite of them, had developed 'into a mature young woman of very independent judgement' who, not surprisingly, distrusted doctors and resisted any proposed consultations.

In the two years prior to Freud seeing her, Dora's condition was described in such non-specific terms as, 'low spirits and alteration of her character'. She had, in fact, recovered, and occupied herself with attending lectures and engaging in 'more or less serious studies'. However, after the discovery of a suicide note in her room (though she had made no attempt on her life), her father insisted she consult Freud.

The immediate circumstances connected with the suicide note were not, in fact, directly related to Dora's history of presumed neurosis, but, indirectly to her father's continuing ill health. While recently at a health resort with her father she had been the subject of an 'indecent proposal' by a friend of her father's, Herr K. To be more precise he was the husband of a friend of her father's, Frau K., with whom he had formed a close friendship some years earlier. She it was, and not his wife, who had nursed Dora's father through his more recent illnesses. Dora had known them both for many years and Frau K. had replaced her aunt (who had died) as an idealised feminine figure, and on several occasions she had looked after the K.'s two young children.

Faced with the prospect of staying with the K.s for several weeks while her father returned home, Dora insisted that their original plan be abandoned and that she would accompany him. Some days later she told her mother of Herr K.'s 'audacity' and her father confronted him with this accusation. He denied the story and convinced Dora's father that, obsessed by sexual matters which she continually discussed with Frau K., she had 'merely fancied' the entire scene. Freud quotes a letter from Philipp Bauer in which he presents his daughter as a victim of her own 'over-excited' state: 'I myself believe that Dora's tale of the man's immoral suggestion is a phantasy that has forced its way into her mind.'[20]

Whatever Freud's initial reaction it is clear that as the case unfolds that he came to accept Dora's side of the story. It is evident that Dora's father had hoped Freud would 'persuade' his daughter that, in fact, nothing had happened; that she had imagined the incident and that, consequently, there was no reason to break off friendly relations with the K.s. Dora's 'unreasonable behaviour' in her father's eyes is essentially reduced to this demand: 'She keeps pressing me to break off relations with Herr K. and more particularly with Frau. K., whom she used positively to worship formerly.' And, though admitting he has 'no very high opinion' of Herr K., and that Frau K. is 'most unhappy' with her husband, he protests that there is 'nothing wrong' in his relations with her: 'We are just two poor wretches who give one another what comfort we can by an exchange of friendly sympathy.'[21]

Freud was clearly suspicious of the motives leading Dora's father to force his daughter into consulting him. He uses the beautifully controlled untangling of her symptoms not only as a demonstration of interpretive technique, but as a means of revealing Herr Bauer's unedifying behaviour (and, thus, of revenging himself on a poorly calculated attempt to misuse his professional standing).[22]

The incident with Herr K., Freud argues, should not be thought of as a psychical trauma which acted as the inciting cause of Dora's symptoms:

> For, as so often happens in histories of cases of hysteria, the trauma that we know of as having occurred in the patient's past life is insufficient to explain or to determine the *particular character* of the symptoms; we should understand just as much or just as little of the whole business if the result of the trauma had been symptoms quite other than *tussis nervosa*, aphonia, depression, and *taedium vitae*.
>
> (SE 7, p. 27)

To explain Dora's symptoms in terms of Herr K.'s attempted seduction would be similar to accounting for a dream exclusively in terms of the connection between its manifest content and the 'day residues'.

Dora's symptoms, Freud argues, all originated at a much earlier date, and had merely been revived by recent events. And, indeed, the scene by the lake proved to be a repetition of a similar incident that had occurred when Dora was 14. Dora revealed to Freud that, on that occasion, finding themselves alone together, Herr K. had taken the opportunity of kissing her. But this too, is dismissed by Freud as unlikely to have been the precipitating trauma of her recent hysterical symptoms. He asserts that 'the behaviour of this child of fourteen was already entirely and completely hysterical' on the grounds that, rather than 'call up a distinct feeling of sexual excitement . . . Dora had at that moment a distinct feeling of disgust'.[23] Her reaction, in Freud's view, involves both a reversal of affect, from pleasure to disgust (Herr K. 'was still quite young and of prepossessing appearance'), and a displacement, from a genital sensation to the stimulation of the mucous membrane at the entrance to the alimentary canal. In Freud's view the feeling of disgust indicates a still earlier process of repression which had distorted Dora's recollection of this event, when 'she felt not merely his kiss upon her lips but also the pressure of his erect member against her body'. This forgotten aspect of the experience persisted as a symptomatic cough, loss of appetite and occasional hallucinated sense of pressure on the upper part of her body, as well as in a phobic avoidance of men in public places who were engaged in animated conversation with women, and who might, therefore, be in a state of sexual excitement.

Several other of Dora's symptom's yielded to a process of interpretation, or, rather, of reinterpretation of her recollections of the tangled relationships among her parents and the K.s. Her periodic aphonia, for example, was linked to the presence or absence of Herr K., with whom, Freud claims, she had, in fact, been in love. However, 'the determination of Dora's symptoms is far too specific for it to be possible to expect a frequent recurrence of the same accidental aetiology'.[24] To understand her general predisposition to form symptoms requires some more comprehensive insight into the origins of her 'somatic compliance', and the reconstruction of events from a much earlier period in her life. To this end Freud provides an exemplary analysis/synthesis of a recurrent dream related by Dora as follows:

> A house was on fire. My father was standing beside my bed and woke me up. I dressed quickly. Mother wanted to stop and save her jewel-case; but Father said: 'I refuse to let myself and my two children be burnt for the sake of your jewel-case.' We hurried downstairs, and as soon as I was outside I woke up.
>
> (SE 7, p. 64)

Dora could recall having had the dream at the lakeside resort where Herr K. had approached her, but the 'day residues' upon which it seized during the analysis itself related to a dispute between Dora's parents over the locking of the dining-room door at night. Her brother's bedroom could be reached only by way of the dining-room and her father did not want him to be locked in as 'something might happen in the night so that it might be necessary to leave the room'. This, she confirmed, had made her think of the risk of fire, and, in doing so, brought back to mind the fact that, on the first occasion of the dream, her father had openly expressed his fear of fire on their arrival at the lake during a violent thunderstorm which he had felt threatened the small wooden house in which they were to stay.

Freud's synthetic interpolation is carried on simultaneously with his interpretation. As a meaningful association emerges, he reconstructs the sequence of events and wishes leading to the formation of that particular element within the dream. With further prompting Dora recalled that, on this first visit to the lakeside, she had gone to lie down during the afternoon (immediately following the attempted seduction), and after a short sleep had suddenly awakened to find Herr K. *'standing beside me'*; just as, Freud points out, she had seen her father standing beside her bed in the dream. She had subsequently obtained a key to the bedroom so that she could lock herself in while dressing, but the next day it went missing; she supposed because Herr K. had removed it from the door. Thereafter, again as in the dream, she *'dressed quickly'*. Freud's initial interpretation, thus, runs 'I shall have no rest and I can get no quiet sleep until I am out of this house', and the last part of the dream expresses this meaning by representing the opposite, *'as soon as I was outside I woke up'*.

Dora associated the jewel-case that her mother had wanted to save in the dream with another dispute between her parents involving the gift of an expensive but unwanted bracelet, in place of the pearl drops his mother had actually wanted. Further pressed she admitted, also, that Herr K. had made her a present of a jewel-case, and a jewel-case (*Schmuckkästchen*), Freud points out, is a favourite expression for the female genitals. The meaning of the dream now reads; 'this man is persecuting me; he wants to force his way into my room. My "jewel-case" is in danger, and if anything happens it will be Father's fault'. And once again an element of the meaning is disguised by being represented through its opposite; in the dream her father is saving her.

Freud's interpretation has so far concentrated on the current 'exciting cause' of the dream, but he returns at this point to Dora's initial association with the dream; that 'something might happen in the night so that it might be necessary to leave the room', and connects it with a childhood situation. Freud deduces that as a child Dora used to wet her bed, and that her father had been in the habit of waking her from sleep (as he did in the dream), in order to prevent this occurring. It is significant that, rather than develop a general psychological account of the case, Freud then goes on to discuss a series of semiotic connections between the childhood situation and the manifest content of the dream. What allows the dream to form, the key to the synthesis it effects among a wide variety of heterogeneous contents, are linguistic and logical connections between separate contexts within which 'water' or 'wetness' is contrasted with 'fire' or 'burnt'.

In the manifest dream Dora's mother wanted to save her jewel-case from being *burnt*, but in the latent dream-thoughts it was a matter of saving her 'jewel-case' from being *wetted*. And as 'fire' is used directly to express the notion of love (*consumed* by love):

> one set of rails runs by way of symbolic meaning to thoughts of love; while the other set runs by way of the contrary 'water', and, after sending off a branch line which provides another connection with 'love' (for love also makes things wet), leads in a different direction . . . to bed-wetting.
>
> (SE 7, p. 89)

Freud is then able to synthesise the dream as follows:

> The dream-work began on the afternoon of the day after the scene in the wood, after Dora had noticed that she was no longer able to lock the door to her room. She then said to herself: 'I am threatened by a serious danger here', and formed her intention of not stopping in the

house alone but of going off with her father. This intention became capable of forming a dream, because it succeeded in finding a continuation in the unconscious. What corresponded to it there was her summoning up her infantile love for her father as a protection against the present temptation.

(SE 7, p. 88)

The dream transformed her intention of flying to her father into the fulfilment of the wish that he should save her even though, in fact, her present danger was largely due to her father's own behaviour. Freud is particularly impressed by the ingenuity with which the dream has, in this case, been able to use a chance occurrence (that Herr K. stood by her bed just as her father had done when Dora was a child) to form a connection between the current situation and childhood. This enabled Dora to substitute, in the dream, her father with Herr K., which 'aptly symbolised' the 'whole trend of her thoughts'.

The chance that, on their arrival at the lake, fire had been a real threat, also provided material for the dream. It was from the risk of fire that her father rescued her. The opposition of fire and water allowed 'ideas relating to sexual temptation' also to find expression in the dream:

Dora knew that there was a kind of getting wet involved in sexual intercourse, and that during the act of copulation the man presented the woman with something liquid *in the form of drops*. She also knew that the danger lay precisely in that, and that it was her business to protect her genitals from being moistened.

(SE 7, p. 90)

And further associations between the 'jewel-case' and a parental dispute over 'pearl drops' allowed Dora's jealousy of her mother to be clearly expressed. Within the dream, thus, both current wishes (that her father should rescue her from Herr K. *and* that she should yield to Herr K.) and childhood wishes (that she should take the place of her mother in relation to her father) were represented through the same images.

But dream synthesis does not produce, any more than does the processes of interpretation and analysis, a complete account of the meaning of dreams. Freud had demonstrated that dreams were meaningful representations and that they could be understood as part of the psychic life of the dreamer. Just as hysterical symptoms were abbreviated memories, dreams were condensed wish-fulfilments; and both dethroned the paramount place of the ego in the organisation of normal waking experience, coalescing past and present into a new domain of representation. Yet, in spite of the patience and care with which he traced out the complex network of meaningful associations, a sense of arbitrariness in dream construction could not be avoided.

Dora terminated her treatment before Freud had completed the analysis. But the fragmentary character of the case history is not a result simply of its incompleteness.[25] Chance events played a significant role in their formation that often rendered them incomprehensible other than through the direct associations of the dreamer. What progressively came to preoccupy Freud was an attempt to establish a non-arbitrary basis for the initial formation of mnemic symbols. If psychic reality is a kind of intermediate zone, spread out across the surface of modern life, and upon which impinge external stimuli and internal organic processes *neither* of which can be directly known, how is 'experience' realised in terms of what seem to be very generally shared and communicable features? What governs the formation of images, which, either from a purely empirical, or from a purely logical, standpoint, seem to be accidental and yet constitute the medium of social interaction and mutual understanding?

DREAM EXPLANATION

As well as assigning a meaning to dreams, or rather a multiplicity of meanings defined through separate but overlapping contexts, Freud also tried to explain the process of dreaming in terms of a general theory of the functioning of what he termed the 'psychical apparatus'. In this way he hoped to link the characteristics of dreams to structural features of the organism and, thus, to the more general phenomena of sleep and wakefulness.

The most general and fundamental characteristic of dreams which his study had revealed was that all dreams could be understood as representations of wishes as fulfilled. From a more general biological point of view this became understandable as a mechanism to ensure the prolongation of sleep. If instinctual demands could be (temporarily) appeased by dreams in which the wishes to which they gave rise were fulfilled then the sleeper need not be roused. Dreams are guardians of sleep; but how do they succeed, for however short a period, in 'fooling' the instincts?

Unlike waking fantasies, the radical irrationality of the dream-work is joined to a second fundamental character of dreams; their ideational content is transformed from thoughts into sensory images 'to which belief is attached and which appear to be experienced'.[26] Freud argues that the compelling reality of dreams can be understood in terms of the 'psychical locality' in which they take place. This notion is evidently linked to his discussion of the 'psychical apparatus' in the unpublished *Project*. But now he is content to 'remain upon psychological ground' and proposes that we 'entirely disregard' the physical structure of this apparatus. He suggests that we picture this apparatus 'as resembling a compound microscope or a photographic apparatus'.[27] The notion of 'psychical locality' is then compared to the various points within such a compound apparatus, at which the preliminary stages of the completed image is formed.

In the metaphorical form of 'the fiction of a primitive psychical apparatus' Freud re-proposes the structural model of psychical functioning he had first outlined in the *Project*.[28] The 'agencies' or differentiated 'systems' are renamed. Elaborating on a comment of Breuer's, that 'the mirror of a reflecting telescope cannot at the same time be a photographic plate', the receptive end of the apparatus is conceived as a perceptual system which remains unaltered by the impressions it is capable of conveying directly to a series of 'mnemic systems' on which memory traces are inscribed and progressively altered in such a way as to facilitate interaction with other traces. Sensory 'associations' are established at the perceptual end of the apparatus, while 'attention' in relation to motor activity issues from the perceptual end. We are normally aware of processes at both ends of the apparatus, and only of such processes. Consciousness, that is to say, is qualitatively distinct from the forms which retain memory, or processes which prompt the apparatus to motor activity.

The hallucinatory vividness of dreaming is a consequence of *regression*, of a general reversal in the direction of excitation within the psychical apparatus itself. This is exactly what happens when we intentionally remember something, but in that case the regression never extends beyond the mnemic images, while in the case of dreams it reaches the perceptual end of the apparatus and produces sensory images. Or, rather, the withdrawal of the ego during sleep has the effect of lowering the barrier between these systems which allows such a regression to take place, and the resulting stimulation of the perceptual system is experienced as dream-images. It must be remembered that Freud, influenced by Brentano, viewed the perceptual world, including sensory images, as related in a wholly incomprehensible way to the 'reality' of nature (matter in motion) of which we can have only a theoretical knowledge. In a similar fashion, at the motor end of the apparatus, the discharge of energy which gave rise to inner feelings of pleasure or unpleasure, and tended towards motility, were completely alien to consciousness and could be understood only in terms of the haziest psychological concepts:

> The unconscious is the true psychical reality; in its innermost nature it is as much unknown to us as the reality of the external world, and it is as incompletely presented by the data of consciousness as is the external world by the communications of our sense organs.
>
> (SE 5, p. 613)

Dream-images, which have their origin in childhood wishes, reach a pitch of sensory vividness, just as the scenes of trauma underlying hysterical seizures are recollected with hallucinatory completeness because the original mode of operation of the psychical apparatus, the 'primary process', is itself a 'path of excitation' from unconscious organic process towards sensation rather than towards motility. This is another way of saying that the new-born infant is helpless, cannot act for itself, and, its entire psychic apparatus bound up within itself, stimulates its senses directly from sources of tension within its own body. But the images to which this process give rise are not to be confused with the energetic process itself. The 'infantile scenes' which are later reproduced in dreams are mnemic images formed at an early age as a result of this process. At this stage Freud is content with providing illustrative examples of this idea; the formation of mnemic images themselves became a central issue in his theoretical work immediately following the publication of *The Interpretation of Dreams*.

Infantile scenes, partly because of the censorship, but more generally because conscious modes of representation soon afterwards take shape as an ego, can find their way into our experience only as dreams. Recent experiences act as *lures* for infantile wishes and the mnemic symbols through which they were first experienced:

> the day's residues, among which we may now class the indifferent impressions, not only *borrow* something from the *Ucs.* when they succeed in taking a share in the formation of a dream – namely the instinctual force which is at the disposal of the repressed wish – but that they also *offer* the unconscious something indispensable – namely the necessary point of attachment for a transference.
>
> (SE 5, p. 564)

Appropriate associative connections established in waking experience attract unconscious wishes as a means of discharge. This provides Freud with an account of the function of dreams, without which unconscious wishes would increase bodily tension and waken the sleeper.

What is equally significant, from the present point of view, is the remarkable way in which the 'fiction' of the psychical apparatus itself acts as a 'mnemic symbol' for the major cultural and intellectual traditions within which Freud's theory of dreams was formed. The historically significant metaphors of mirror and writing pad, of reflection and inscription, are here combined into a single contradictory mechanism. Both outer (objective) and inner (subjective) reality became fused to a single depthless surface upon which dimensionless associations are fleetingly brought to life. The unconscious, whether conceptualised as the alien otherness of the 'thing in itself' outside the body, or posited as an unfathomable 'being within the self' inside the body, cannot exist for us. It is only as representations upon the same interactive surface that we become aware of anything, and it is only in terms of these that we can attempt to suggest the unconscious as the necessary deduction of a permanent process supporting the illumination of transitory signs.

Freud's great monograph is wrongly titled; *interpretation* is only one of the hermeneutic techniques he deploys to transform what had seemed to be impoverished fragments of consciousness into the fundamental data of a new psychology. It is a measure of the centrality and significance of dreams for modern experience that they do not yield to a single method of analysis, and cannot be understood through a formula; but that methods of interpretation, analysis, symbolic intuition, synthesis and explanation all grasp something characteristic, and essentially different, in their nature.

As decisively as had Clerk Maxwell's formulation of the laws of electro-magnetism overthrown the materialism of the physical sciences, Freud's analysis of dreams dissolved the 'point-mass' of the bourgeois ego into an unfamiliar field of forces which gathered itself in localised interactions. But it is just the character of contemporary experience that the ego has dissolved, or, at least, is in the process of dissolving. Our waking experience of the modern world has something of the timeless, and therefore aimless, quality of a dream-state. Modern experience can no longer be represented as a journey, as directed movement through a three-dimensional space, but, rather, emerges as a continuously changing plastic image for which time and space have lost both extension and directionality.

NOTES

1 Freud (1985), prior to that publication Schur (1966, in Loewenstein, Newman, Schur and Solnit and 1972) had elaborated on some of the details from unpublished sources. See also Masson (1984), Appignanesi and Forrester (1993), pp. 117–45.
2 SE 4, p. 170. Later incorporated in *The Psychopathology of Everyday Life*.
3 Byck Freud (1974).
4 Goethe (1952, 1970).
5 Steedman (1995), provides many fruitful connections between Goethe's botancial speculations and the emergence of new ideas about childhood, sexuality and 'interiority'.
6 Given the extent to which he viewed interpretation as a problem of translation, it is hardly surprising that Freud rediscovered and renamed a number of mechanisms well known to the older disciplines of rhetoric and grammar; Todorov (1977), pp. 247–54.
7 SE 4, p. 189.
8 Maury (1862), pp. 133–4; SE 4, pp. 26–7; SE 5, pp. 496–7.
9 SE 4, p. 191. At this point Freud admits he has not disclosed the 'ultimate meaning'.
10 SE 4, p. 196; McGrath (1986), pp. 62–4, 180–3.
11 The symbolic 'language of flowers' has a long tradition in Europe, and popular 'florigelia', not unlike popular dreambooks, were common in Paris when Freud studied there; Goody (1993), pp. 232–53.
12 Bousquet (1964).
13 A good deal of the debate over the 'scientific' status of Freud's theories is focused on this issue. See e.g. Kline, Grünbaum (1993).
14 SE 4, p. 310.
15 Written in the autumn of 1900, the publication, in fact, was delayed until 1905. For the background to the case see Decker (1991), Appignanesi and Forrester (1993), pp. 146–67, Hughes (1994), pp. 46–50, 118–25.

16 SE 7, p. 19.
17 SE 7, p. 20. There is a suspicion that Freud is, in part, expressing his view of his own wife, Martha, in this passage.
18 SE 7, pp. 23–4.
19 Good descriptions of popular treatments can be found in Showalter (1987), and for a classic account, Mirbeau (1990), Skram (1992).
20 SE 7, p. 26.
21 Ibid.
22 His dreams, indicated, after all, that he was sensitive to charges of professional incompetence or impropriety.
23 SE 7, p. 28.
24 SE 7, p. 40.
25 Thus Freud's case histories read not just like short stories, but are fine examples of the 'unreliable narration' typical of modern fiction. See the remarks of Marcus, in Bernheimer and Kahane (1985).
26 SE 5, p. 535.
27 SE 5, p. 536.
28 SE 5, p. 757.

4

SUBTEXT
The prehistory of the ego

The Interpretation of Dreams focused attention on the penumbra of waking experience; on the presence of an intimate but unfamiliar reality. The past, neither dead and buried, nor even buried alive, had merely slipped from view as experience gathered itself into the ordered consciousness of an ego. And as the ego developed, tracing, as it were, a 'world-line' *through* the dispersed field of the pre-conscious, it carried with it an energetic halo of associations. Mnemic images, temporally extended as the intentional memory of self-development, were fused with, and distorted by, the continuous present of originating wishes. In the distorted imagery of dreams, the ego was presented with a deformed translation of its own pre-history.

Freud's initial attempts to discover a 'zero-point' in the process of image formation were directly related to his self-analysis and took the form of uncovering the circumstances under which earlier and earlier mnemic symbols were formed, in the expectation that, ultimately, some completely general and non-arbitrary level of symbolism would be revealed. When the ego's subtext is deciphered, it reveals both a narrative of its own formation and a description of the dissolving world of experience from which it emerged. Freud pursued this line of thought through a number of significant publications following *The Interpretation of Dreams* but, as an initial approach, it is tempting to turn his own method of interpretation against its originator. The manner in which Freud broke off many lines of association with his own dreams, for 'reasons of propriety', the sensational aspects of his case histories, and the controversial character of his theories among both his critics and his supporters has encouraged a process of extension and revision of his own dream-interpretations. And though he castigated some of his medical colleagues for reading case histories as *romans á clefs*, he would hardly have been surprised at recent scholarly attempts to re-read, and to some extent re-write, his major work as an autobiographical study. Indeed, the concentration of recent scholarship on making good the *lacunae* in his own confessions is justified by Freud's own psychological theories which directly and indirectly link childhood experience, dream-images and the development of civilisation. *The Interpretation of Dreams* remains, with the autobiographical psychology of St Augustine and Rousseau, one of the most significant attempts to investigate the general character of reality through the particularities of personal existence.

LOOKING BACK

One possible starting point for such an endeavour – to fill out the autobiographical aspects of his dreambook and link them with the development of his general psychology – is with Freud's discussion of 'The Means of Representation' in dreams. Freud points out that the relation either/or cannot be represented in a dream, which normally presents both possibilities as an inclusive both/and. He provides a brief example:

During the night before my father's funeral I had a dream of a printed notice, placard or poster – rather like the notices forbidding one to smoke in railway waiting-rooms – on which appeared either
> *Your are requested to close the eyes*
or
> *You are requested to close an eye*
I usually write this in the form:
> the
> *You are requested to close   eye(s)*
> an

(SE 4, pp. 317–18)

Each version, Freud argues, has a distinct meaning. One line of thought runs as follows:

I had chosen the simplest possible ritual for the funeral, for I knew my father's own views on such ceremonies. But some other members of the family were not sympathetic to such puritanical simplicity and thought we should be disgraced in the eyes of those who attended the funeral. Hence one of the versions: *You are requested to close an eye*, i.e. to 'wink at' or overlook.

(SE 4, p. 318)

Freud does not tell us precisely what line of thought is represented by the alternative reading, and merely states that:

The dream-work failed to establish a unified wording for the dream-thoughts which could at the same time be ambiguous, and the two main lines of thought consequently began to diverge even in the manifest content of the dream.

(SE 4, p. 318)

A footnote to the Standard Edition suggests that *You are requested to close the eyes* refers 'to closing the dead man's eyes as a filial duty'.

Freud gives a somewhat different account of the dream and its circumstances in a letter to Fliess (2 November, 1896) written one week after his father's funeral:

> I must tell you about a nice dream I had the night after the funeral. I was in a place where I read a sign:
>
> > *You are requested*
> > *to close the eyes*
>
> I immediately recognized the location as the barbershop I visit every day. On the day of the funeral I was kept waiting and therefore arrived a little late at the house of mourning. At that time my family was displeased with me because I had arranged for the funeral to be quiet and simple, which they later agreed was quite justified. They were also somewhat offended by my lateness. The sentence on the sign has a double meaning: one should do one's duty to the dead (an apology as though I had not done it and were in need of leniency), and the actual duty itself. The dream thus stems from the inclination to self-reproach that regularly sets in among the survivors.
>
> (Freud 1985, p. 202)

Here just one version of the written sign is given, he claims the dream occurred the night after, and not the night before, the funeral and, furthermore, he reveals that he arrived late to his father's funeral! That the family were 'somewhat offended' is surely an understatement.

Yet there is every reason to suppose that Freud was deeply moved by his father's death, and that his dream does not betray, in any simple way, a lack of filial piety. Freud begins the same letter to Fliess in the following fashion:

> I find it so difficult to write just now that I have put off for a long time thanking you for the moving words in your letter. By one of those dark pathways behind the official consciousness the old man's death has affected me deeply. I valued him highly, understood him very well, and with his peculiar mixture of deep wisdom and fantastic light-heartedness he had a significant effect on my life. By the time he died, his life had long been over, but in (my) inner self the whole has been reawakened by this event.
>
> I now feel quite uprooted.
>
> (Freud 1985, p. 202)

And in the 'Preface' to the second edition of *The Interpretation of Dreams*, published nine years after the first edition, in apologising for retaining so much of the original material, he writes that:

this book has a further subjective significance for me personally – a significance which I only grasped after I had completed it. It was, I found, a portion of my own self-analysis, my reaction to my father's death – that is to say, to the most important event, the most poignant loss, of a man's life. Having discovered that this was so, I felt unable to obliterate the traces of the experience.

(SE 4, p. xxvi)

Freud was 40 when his 81-year-old father, who had been terminally ill for several months, finally died. In an earlier letter Freud seems to have been well adjusted to the impending event:

> The old man's condition, by the way, does not depress me. I do not begrudge him the well-deserved rest that he himself desires. He was an interesting human being, very happy within himself; he is suffering very little now, and fading with decency and dignity.
>
> (Freud 1985, p. 195)

Indeed, during his father's final illness Freud left Vienna on several occasions: on a family vacation, to meet Fliess, and on a trip to Northern Italy with his brother Alexander.[1]

Freud's attitude and behaviour displays an ambivalence which biographers and analysts alike have seized upon as an interpretive key with which to decipher the residual personal material which had found its way into *The Interpretation of Dreams*. There is now widespread agreement that the central theme emerging from Freud's self-analysis (which he began directly after the death of his father), and the interpretation of his own dreams, is the significance, not of his childhood relation with his mother, but with his lifelong relation to his father.[2]

The short dream requesting he 'close an/the eye(s)' is best understood in relation to several others he recorded and to which he devoted considerably more attention. The circumstantial detail of 'eyes' and 'being late' immediately connects it with a complex two-part dream, referred to as 'Non Vixit', which occurred some two years later:

> *I had gone to Brücke's laboratory at night, and, in response to a gentle knock on the door, I opened it to* (the late) *Professor Fleischl, who came in with a number of strangers and, after exchanging a few words, sat down at his table.*

This was followed by:

> *My friend Fl. had come to Vienna unobtrusively in July. I met him in the street in conversation with my (deceased) friend P., and went with them to some place where they sat opposite each other as though they were at a small table. I sat in front at its narrow end. Fl. spoke about his sister and said that in three-quarters of an hour she was dead, and added some such words as 'that was the threshold'. As P. failed to understand him, Fl. turned to me and asked*

94

*me how much I had told P. about his affairs. Whereupon, overcome by strange
emotions, I tried to explain to Fl. that P. (could not understand anything at
all, of course, because he) was not alive. But what I actually said – and I
myself noticed the mistake – was* 'Non vixit.' *I then gave P. a piercing look.
Under my gaze he turned pale; his form grew indistinct and his eyes a sickly
blue – and finally melted away. I was highly delighted at this and I now
realised that Ernst Fleischl, too, had been no more than an apparition, a
'revenant'; and it seemed to me quite possible that people of that kind only
existed as long as one liked and could be got rid of if someone else wished it.*

(SE 4, p. 421)

Many lines of thought intersect in this elaborate dream-image and, in the
interest of brevity, most of Freud's intricate elucidatory remarks, together
with a good deal of background information, must simply be stated as
conclusions.

The manifest content of the dream is concerned with Freud's colleagues
at the Physiological Laboratory at the university where he had worked as a
graduate student and as a demonstrator from 1876 to 1882. As a gifted
scientist and a highly cultivated individual, Ernst Brücke, its head, was
Freud's mentor. More than that he was a father-figure, to whose authority
Freud willingly submitted. In his associations to the dream Freud recalls
that:

It came to Brücke's ears that I sometimes reached the students'
laboratory late. One morning he turned up punctually at the hour of
opening and awaited my arrival. His words were brief and to the
point. But it was not they that mattered. What overwhelmed me were
the terrible blue eyes with which he looked at me and by which I was
reduced to nothing – just as P. was in the dream, where, to my relief,
the roles were reversed. No one who can remember the great man's
eyes, which retained their striking beauty even in his old age, and who
has ever seen him in anger, will find it difficult to picture the young
sinner's emotions.

(SE 4, p. 422)

Ernst von Fleischl-Marxov and Josef Paneth, the central characters in the
dream, were Brücke's assistants. The former died in 1891 having become
addicted to cocaine, which Freud, as one of the discoverers of its anaesthetic properties, had urged upon him as a substitute for the morphine to
which he had become dependent during the treatment of an extremely
painful skin condition. Paneth was just one year younger than Freud and
had died of pulmonary tuberculosis in 1890. In the dream they were both
'revenants' (ghosts – literally 'one who returns') who could be 'wished
away' whenever it was convenient. In actuality, at the time when he became
engaged to Martha Bernays, Fleischl stood in his way to a post as Brücke's

assistant; which position would not only have allowed Freud to marry at once but would also have provided a secure foundation for an academic career leading in all probability to his eventually succeeding to his mentor's Chair of Physiology. Paneth, also a lowly laboratory demonstrator, had independent means, often lent money to Freud and, in spite of his illness, seemed to live a carefree existence. So, for different reasons, Freud's friends had aroused in him feelings of envy and jealousy that led to the repressed wish (later realised) that they would dissolve into nothing at a glance.

The dream-thoughts focus on Freud's capacity to survive his colleagues, and are an attempt to calm anxieties over his own health as well as to provide reassurance that he was destined to professional distinction at least comparable to that of Brücke. He had, after all, survived the piercing look which in the dream had wholly destroyed Paneth.

But the omnipotent dream-thought is wrongly expressed as *Non vixit* (he did not live), instead of *Non vivit* (he is not alive). Had he really wished his friends had never been born? With some difficulty Freud traces the immediate source of this error to a quotation on the pedestal of the Kaiser Josef Memorial (a father figure to the nation) which he had seen several days previously at the unveiling of a memorial to Fleischl. Freud quotes, or rather mis-quotes, the inscription as:

Saluti patriae vixit
non diu sed totus.
(For the well-being of his country he lived not long but wholly.)

That is to say, he substituted 'patriae' for the actual 'publica', a word commonly connected in Vienna with 'publica puella', a prostitute or *Freudenmädchen.*[3] From this inscription he had extracted 'just enough to fit in with a hostile train of ideas'.

The Josef II Memorial links a father-figure with a brother-figure. *Josef* Paneth, at one year younger than himself, had been born in the same year as Freud's younger brother Julius, who had died at the age of six months. In the dream Paneth plays the part of a 'revenant' of his dead brother Julius. Freud follows this idea through an additional allusion to the play *Julius Caesar* to further thoughts of ambition and parricide. Freud himself notes that the name Josef plays a significant part, not only in this dream, but in several others, and remarks that 'my own ego finds it very easy to hide itself behind people of that name, since Joseph was the name of a man famous in the Bible as an interpreter of dreams'.[4] The Biblical Joseph was also the first-born son of a Jacob by his second wife, he too was ambitious, and later became a 'revenant' by returning in triumph to his family, as from the dead.

The dream-images, that is to say, play out his own 'family romance' through the currently ambiguous feelings for his deceased colleagues.

Ernst Fleischl and *Ernst* Brücke are father-figures, who, like his own father, no longer have any authority over him. But he was himself involved in the death of Fleischl, and his public honouring of him was not wholly sincere. This duplicity reminds Freud of the character of Brutus, and:

> Strange to say, I really did once play the part of Brutus. I once acted in the scene between Brutus and Caesar from Schiller before an audience of children. I was fourteen years old at the time and was acting with a nephew who was a year my senior. He had come to us on a visit from England; and he, too, was a *revenant*, for it was the playmate of my earliest years who had returned in him. Until the end of my third year we had been inseparable. We had loved each other and fought with each other; and this childhood relationship, as I have already hinted above, had a determining influence on all my subsequent relations with contemporaries. Since that time my nephew John has had many reincarnations which revived now one side and now another of his personality, unalterably fixed as it was in my unconscious memory.

> (SE 5, p. 424)

In the section of *The Interpretation of Dreams* dealing with 'Affects in Dreams', Freud provides further information about the childhood relationships from which the dream had sprung. He and his nephew John had come to blows over their respective rights to some object they both claimed as exclusively their own. Freud, it appeared, carried the day, but notes that, 'on the evidence of the dream, I may myself have been aware that I was in the wrong (*I myself noticed the mistake*)'. John appealed to his grandfather, that is to Freud's father, (the original of the 'piercing glance'?), who later reported to his son that he defended himself with the words 'I hit him 'cos he hit me'.

Freud reports that the mnemic image of this childhood contest, the original of which he claims to have taken place when he was about 2 years old, formed 'an intermediate element in the dream thoughts, which gathered up the emotions raging in them as a well collects the water that flows into it'.

Freud, in an important letter to Fliess, connects his childhood relationship with his nephew John to the death of his brother Julius:

> (I know that) . . . I greeted my one-year-younger brother (who died after a few months) with adverse wishes and genuine childhood jealousy; and that his death left the germ of (self-) reproaches in me. I have also long known the companion of my misdeeds between the ages of one and two years; it is my nephew, a year older than myself, who is now living in Manchester and who visited us in Vienna when I was fourteen years old. The two of us seem occasionally to have

behaved cruelly to my niece, who was a year younger. This nephew and this younger brother have determined, then, what is neurotic, but also what is intense, in all my friendships.

(Freud 1985, p. 268)

Freud's niece, Pauline, and his nephew, John, figure in a further complex dream association which Freud published in disguised form in his paper on 'Screen Memories'. The ostensible subject of the paper is the way in which scenes from early childhood may be used as 'screens' upon which to project *later* emotionally troublesome and therefore suppressed memories. It has been established beyond any question that the 'patient' whose memories Freud reports is himself. He relates a vivid, but disconnected, memory from his third year:

I see a rectangular, rather steeply sloping piece of meadow-land, green and thickly grown; in the green there are a great number of yellow flowers – evidently common dandelions. At the top end of the meadow there is a cottage and in front of the cottage door two women are standing chatting busily, a peasant-woman with a handkerchief on her head and a children's nurse. Three children are playing in the grass. One of them is myself (between the ages of two and three); the two others are my boy cousin, who is a year older than me, and his sister, who is almost exactly the same age as I am. We are picking the yellow flowers and each of us is holding a bunch of flowers we have already picked. The little girl has the best bunch; and, as though by mutual agreement, we – the two boys – fall on her and snatch away her flowers. She runs up the meadow in tears and as a consolation the peasant-woman gives her a big piece of black bread. Hardly have we seen this than we throw the flowers away, hurry to the cottage and ask to be given some bread too. And we are in fact given some; the peasant-woman cuts the loaf with a long knife. In my memory the bread tastes quite delicious – and at that point the scene breaks off.

(SE 3, p. 311)

This 'botanical memory' is explained in turn by its association with a much later event. At the age of 17 Freud visited his home town in Moravia for the first time since leaving it as a child. He stayed with old family friends and fell in love with the 15-year-old Gisela Fluss, also there on holiday from school. Some years later, when he used to holiday in the Alps, he became acquainted with a flower, similar to the dandelion, which was of precisely the colouring of Gisela's summer dress. In fact the dandelion is of the same family, *compositae*, as artichokes, which Freud claimed (in association with the Botanical Monograph) to be his favourite flower.[5]

And when Freud was 20 he visited his relatives in Manchester, an event which stirred those original memories of the meadow and their childhood 'games'. But now he was a dedicated student and so absorbed in study, that, although the family had half planned that he would, he did not, in fact, fall in love (again) with his original playmate. He retained, however, a powerful sense of the first consciousness of the countryside around his home as the most perfect of worlds:

> Of one thing I am certain: deep within me, although overlaid, there continues to live the happy child from Freiberg, the first-born son of a youthful mother, the boy who received from this air, from this soil, the first indelible impressions.

> (SE 21, p. 259)

Freud points out that memories of such early events are almost always a reworking of an original impression in the light of later experience, 'a memory-trace from childhood . . . translated into a plastic and visual form at a later date'. In the recollection, the subject sees themselves as children, and remain outside the events, as privileged observers of a world they cannot wholly enter. This, in fact, is a general condition of passing back beyond the normal threshold of childhood amnesia, and penetrating the experiential world prior to its formation of an ego. There involves, that is to say, a good deal of 'secondary revision', in which the original emotional currents are provided with appropriate images in which they can be addressed to a more mature state of consciousness.

The initial mnemic images may be of quite an innocent kind, and, because of this, are later used as a means of representing memories of a more tendentious sort that, in fact, date from a later period. Freud exemplifies the process with a completely inessential example drawn from a French study of early memories with which he had begun his paper on screen memories. In it an example is given of the memory of a child breaking off a branch from a tree while out on a walk and of his being helped to do so. Freud associates this with the memory of a 'seduction to masturbation', on the flimsy grounds that in German the phrase 'to pull one out' (which seems only remotely connected with 'to break off') is a coarse expression for masturbation. Furthermore he complicates the analysis by drawing attention to the doubtfulness of the linguistic translation and the fact that several other people were supposed to have been present. At the end of the paper the reader is very unclear what is being claimed; it seems that another series of memories are being infiltrated into the text, but their significance remains unexplained.

In the light of his later views, as well as of the Fliess correspondence, it is almost irresistible to read 'screen memories' as 'genuine' memories of highly charged 'real' events.[6] Did Sigmund's games with his nephew and niece in the meadows surrounding their house involve the 'deflowering' of Pauline and mutual masturbation? Were they interrupted by Freud's father at some point with a 'terrible look'? And are the later reworking of these events in the associations to his dreams, and in 'Screen Memories', a kind of hysterical symptom or compromise formation which reveals his secrets through the very mechanism which is designed to conceal them? Speculation abounds, but, certainly, Freud came to remember his first experience of life as an intoxicating freedom, and whatever its value, continuous reinterpretation has stimulated a considerable amount of detailed biographical research which is undoubtedly essential to a proper understanding of Freud's psychological writings.[7]

Sigismund (he did not Germanise his name until he entered the university) spent the first three-and-a-half years of his life (not two-and-a-half as he recalls) in the small Moravian town of Freiberg, now Přibor in the Czech Republic. His father, Jacob Freud, was a wool merchant who spent a good deal of time away from home and was usually short of money. His mother, Amalia Nathansohn, was Jacob's third wife (diligent research has turned up records of a mysterious and short-lived second marriage to a woman named Rebecca about whom virtually nothing is known, and to whom Sigmund and the other members of the family never referred), and twenty years her husband's junior. The Freuds rented a single room in a modest house, a condition of relative impoverishment that Sigmund seems to have obscured by his nostalgia for the freedom of his early childhood. He (mis-)recalls through his 'screen memory' that he 'was the child of people who were originally well-to-do and who, I fancy, lived comfortably enough in that little corner of the provinces'.[8] Two of Jacob's sons from his first marriage lived nearby. Philipp, a bachelor, was just a year younger than Amalia and lived nearby and Emanuel, married and with children of his own, lived directly across the street. Sigismund, who initially treated both families as members of a single household, not surprisingly had a good deal of difficulty in sorting out kinship relations.[9] His step-brothers, whom he saw more often than his father, were of the correct generation to be his father, while his father, appearing intermittently, played the part of a visiting grandfather. His nephew and 'companion in misdeeds' was a year older than the diminutive uncle Sigismund.

Amalia, by all accounts, doted upon her son who remained into adulthood the centre of family attention. But in these early years, and in spite of financial uncertainty, he was also looked after by a 'nanny', in fact a maid, who, in the previously quoted letter to Fliess, the adult Sigmund recalled as playing a fundamental part in his development. Reaching what he took to be a crucial moment of illumination in his self-analysis he writes of the origin of his own hysteria that 'in my case the "prime originator" was an ugly, elderly, but clever woman, who told me a great deal about God Almighty and hell and who instilled in me a high opinion of my own capacities'.[10]

Spontaneous memories, mixed with fantasies, of his nanny played an important part in Freud's self-analysis. In letters to Fliess he records brief passages of dreams and sudden recollections which, 'because I find nothing like this in the chain of my waking memory', he regarded 'as a genuine ancient discovery'.[11] He could recall her encouraging him to steal zehners (ten-kreuzer coins), and (what he apparently feels he could never have invented) that 'she washed me in reddish water in which she had previously washed herself'. That his memories had a basis in fact Freud confirmed by asking his mother about her. He reports her reply to Fliess as direct speech:

> an elderly person, very clever, she was always carrying you off to some church; when you returned home you preached and told us all about God Almighty. During my confinement with Anna (two-and-a-half years younger), it was discovered that she was a thief, and all the shiny new kreuzers and zehners and all the toys that had been given to you were found in her possession. Your brother Philipp himself fetched the policeman; she then was given ten months in prison.
>
> (Freud 1985, p. 271)

On learning this Freud immediately comprehended a scene which:

> in the course of twenty-five years has occasionally emerged in my conscious memory without my understanding it. My mother was nowhere to be found; I was crying in despair. My brother Philipp (twenty years older than I) unlocked a wardrobe (*Kasten*) for me, and when I did not find my mother inside it either, I cried even more until, slender and beautiful, she came in through the door. What can this mean? Why did my brother unlock the wardrobe for me, knowing that my mother was not in it and that thereby he could not calm me down? Now I suddenly understand it. I had asked him to do it. When I missed my mother, I was afraid she had vanished from me, just as the old woman had a short time before. So I must have heard that the old woman had been locked up and therefore must have believed that my mother had been locked up too – or rather, had been 'boxed up' (*eingekastelt*) – for my brother Philipp, who is now sixty-three years old, to this very day is still fond of using such puns. The fact that I turned to him in particular proves that I was well aware of his share in the disappearance of the nurse.
>
> (Freud 1985, pp. 271–2)

It is in this letter that Freud first refers to the Oedipus myth as a general description of the psychological situation of childhood. Noting that 'being totally honest with oneself is a good exercise', he continues:

> A single idea of general value dawned on me. I have found, in my own case too, [the phenomenon of] being in love with my mother and jealous of my father, and I now consider it a universal event in early

childhood, even if not so early as in children who have been made hysterical. . . . If this is so, we can understand the gripping power of *Oedipus Rex*, in spite of all the objections that reason raises against the presupposition of fate . . . the Greek legend seizes upon a compulsion which everyone recognises because he senses its existence within himself.

(Freud 1985, p. 272)

A few months later (February 1898) he is willing to go further. He tells Fliess he has had a 'delightful dream' about being invested with the title of professor; a common theme in the manifest content of his dreams. But he cannot use it in his dreambook

> because its background, its second meaning, shifts back and forth between my nurse (my mother) and my wife and one cannot really publicly subject one's wife to reproaches of this sort (as a reward) for all her labour and toil. Quite generally: the best you know, and so on.
>
> (Freud 1985, p. 299)

The identification in his latent dream-thoughts of his nurse, his mother and his wife is suggestive of another passage from the letter of the previous October. Immediately following the introduction of his nurse as his 'prime originator' he reports that:

> later (between two and two and a half years) my libido toward *matrem* was awakened, namely, on the occasion of a journey with her from Leipzig to Vienna, during which we must have spent the night together and there must have been an opportunity of seeing her *nudam* (you inferred the consequences of this for your son long ago, as a remark revealed to me).
>
> (Freud 1985, p. 268)

Indeed the recollection of his nurse, the train journey and his feelings of hostility at the birth of his brother Julius are all recorded in the same sentence. This condensation, hints at the possibility that it was towards his nurse, rather than his mother, that his libido was awakened.

The precise reason for the family leaving Freiberg is not clear. Freud later adduced the failure of his father's business as the occasion of the break up of the original family 'horde'. However, both Philipp and Emanuel with his family simultaneously departed for England; a somewhat drastic response which hardly seems required by the circumstances. Whether Jacob, as well as Sigismund, sensed a growing closeness between Emanuel/Philipp and Amalia, or the family rearrangement had something to do with Jacob's brother, Joseph, who, it appears, was involved in a counterfeit money operation in which Emanuel may also have played a part, is entirely unclear. His uncle Joseph, like his nurse, was eventually jailed.

The phrase Freud uses in writing to Fliess of his self-analysis, 'Quite generally: the best you know, and so on', refers to one of his favourite lines from Goethe's *Faust*: 'The best you know, you may not tell to boys', which he had the habit of quoting in connection with sensitive and completely analysed material. And, indeed, one can sense the excitement with which Freud communicates these discoveries to Fliess. The hallucinatory exactitude with which he pictures his mother 'slender and beautiful' coming through the door and calming his rage before the empty cupboard requires no further substantiation. But were they discoveries? The incorporation of significant sensory details into memories which, in large measure, are constructed from later reports and then combined into an emotionally charged plastic image is just the process he had described so beautifully in 'Screen Memories'; an essay which the subsequent reception of Freud's work has tended systematically to misread as, exclusively, an authentic personal recollection. It is worth quoting the conclusion to that paper:

It may indeed be questioned whether we have any memories at all *from* our childhood: memories *relating to* our childhood may be all that we possess. Our childhood memories show us our earliest years not as they were but as they appeared at the later periods when the memories were aroused. In these periods of arousal, the childhood memories did not, as people are accustomed to say, *emerge*, they were *formed* at that time. And a number of motives, with no concern for historical accuracy, had a part in forming them, as well as in the selection of the memories themselves.

(SE 3, p. 322)

In fact Freud misplaces all these early 'memories', attributing them to a period up to the age of two-and-a-half when, he claimed, they left Freiberg, briefly for Leipzig and then to Vienna. But the Freuds lived in Freiberg until Sigmund was three-and-a-half, an age which, in fact, fits better with his mnemic image of liberated play.[12]

In Freud's own case it might reasonably be supposed that it was the death of his father which began a process of dreamlike memory construction through which these hallucinatory images were formed. A process which operated, so to speak, in the opposite direction to a normal dreamformation. Rather than the 'indifferent material' of the day-residues forming a lure with which to attract the latent dream-thoughts, the screen memory uses fragments of indifferent material to project a currently intense emotional image into the distant past. The detailed analysis of autobiographical references in Freud's published works and letters is continuing, but a tentative 'synthesis' of those which have a direct bearing on the writing of *The Interpretation of Dreams* might be suggested.

The death of his father is assimilated to the death of his brother Julius, and both with his departure from the paradise of early childhood in the

103

country. Freud's 'family romance' is a complex history of double parenthood. He had two mothers and two fathers. The identification of nurse and mother allowed a progressive separation of the 'bad mother', who was taken away to prison, and the 'good mother', who loved him and stayed with him. But there was no such simple resolution of his ambivalent feelings towards his father. Even though he had defeated his rival (John) in combat, the 'good father' (Emanuel / Philipp) went to live in England while Sigismund was not only left with the 'bad father' (Jacob), he was exiled from paradise. Freud's distaste for Vienna, and devotion to everything English, is understandable in this context.

Was Freud late for his father's funeral as a proof that, finally, he had become independent of both the 'bad' and the 'good' father? And was the dream to 'close an eye' or 'turn a blind eye' less a request to his dead father to overlook his son's faults (masturbation? theft? disobedience?) than a demand placed on the living to absolve the previous generation of their shortcomings? Should he not have loved his father more? The peculiarity of Freud's own early experience in the subsequent elaboration of his psychological theories can hardly be denied, but, equally, the creative forming and reconstruction of his own memory in the light of these developing theories was a phenomenon to which he himself drew attention.

In fact there is no biographical path back to the zero-point of ego-development. Interpretations of Freud's early childhood, including his own, cannot be conceived simply as making good the deficiencies of an adult memory. To seek in 'events' for some determining condition of psychic experience, even though 'events' are themselves formed from these very (malleable) experiences, is to give way to a false objectivism. This is, for a brief period, precisely what Freud did. Prior to, and for sometime after, the announcement to Fliess of his discovery of the universality of the Oedipus complex, and to some extent as a result of the contradictory results of his self-analysis, he maintained the 'seduction theory' of the origin of hysteria.

The ambiguity of 'screen memories' and 'dream analysis' cannot be easily resolved. In modern life, past and present become mixed up. On the Ringstrasse each public building was an imitation of originals taken from different periods. The historicism of architecture was an emblem of the dual process (recollection and dreaming) through which the experience of real duration within the psyche had been destroyed. Every possibility seemed to co-exist with equal validity – and with equal invalidity. Whether through the interpretation of dreams, or through the analysis of spontaneous screen memories and symptoms, the world of intentionality, rationality and continuity gives way to a world of wishing, identification and timeless repetition.

FROM MEMORY TO FANTASY

The transition from the trauma theory to the Oedipus theory involves a transformation from thinking in terms of an 'observing ego' thrust back in time, to an attempt to reconstruct the world in terms of an emerging and hardly formed focus of psychic processes. It thus involves a significant development of Freud's psychological theory.

In fact the development of his ideas from the initial 'seduction theory' of hysteria is governed primarily by considerations of internal consistency. The real difficulty of the seduction theory lay in its adventitious character. If the origin of hysteria was traced to the circumstances of a psychic trauma it was very difficult to link the resulting symptoms logically with other forms of neurotic illness, and, ultimately, to include it within a general psychological theory. The notion of 'psychic trauma' has no essential connection with sexuality, but hysteria was, in Freud's view, non-accidentally linked with sexual development. The idea of 'seduction' (a better term would be 'abuse') is, in fact, only an unstable compromise between a general trauma theory, derived from Charcot's work, and Freud's later fantasy theory; it is a particular, sexual kind of trauma. As sexual development became seen in Freud's theoretical work as the real predisposing condition of hysteria, the precise nature of any 'shock' which might have stimulated the growth of symptoms was viewed as being less significant.[13]

There was, however, no simple line of development in Freud's psychological ideas. The notion of fantasy and the significance of screen memories played an important part in the Dora case, even though it was presented as a confirmation of the seduction theory, and in much later cases Freud not infrequently accounted for specific symptoms in terms of trauma, including sexual abuse, in childhood.

The issues have been widely discussed in recent years, and though the entire development of his psychology, the context of his self-analysis and the relationship of both to the transformation of late nineteenth-century culture in its broadest sense are consonant with such a development, it is worth briefly reviewing the specific reasons Freud himself gave for abandoning his *neurotica*, as he called the seduction theory in discussions with Fliess.[14] Firstly, there was its relative failure in clinical terms. He complained of the 'continual disappointment in my efforts to bring a single analysis to a real conclusion', and his inability fully to account for, far less to treat, his patients' disabling symptoms. Secondly, there was 'the surprise that in all cases, the *father*, not excluding my own, had to be accused of being perverse'. He felt it unlikely that the sexual abuse of children was as widespread as the hysterical symptoms to which his theory suggested this abuse gave rise; indeed, as other predisposing factors had to coincide in the production of symptoms, 'the (incidence) of perversions against children would have to be immeasurably more frequent than the (resulting) hysteria'. Thirdly, and here he introduces a new line of thought which is significant for the entire development of his psychology, there is 'the certain insight that there are no indications of reality in the unconscious, so that one cannot distinguish between truth and fiction that has been cathected with affect'. If, indeed, his patients were describing fantasies rather than recollecting events in the past, then they need not be accused of lying, and the important issue is to understand why 'the sexual fantasy invariably seizes upon the theme of the parents'. And fourthly, in the 'most deep-reaching psychosis' the 'secret of childhood experiences is not disclosed even in the most confused delirium', so that, in these cases at least, the current symptoms cannot refer in a meaningful way to genuine memories of the patient's early years.[15] These are cogent reasons and Freud recognised his change of mind, which was really nothing more than coming to terms with the fundamental tendencies of his thought 'as the result of honest and vigorous intellectual work', and confessed 'I have more the feeling of a victory than a defeat'.

An implication of all this was that, as he had led his patients (the notion of *free*-association is something of a misnomer) towards memories of earlier periods of their childhood, he had, in many instances, encouraged in them the formation of screen memories, the emotional content of which frequently had its origin in later events. From this insight it was a relatively short step to the construction of an alternative and radical theory of fantasy.

This shift in theoretical focus was associated with his own self-analysis, and with a consequential change in perspective; from that of an outside observer concerned primarily with the behaviour of an adult towards a child, to that of the child himself (the fact that he considered the situation exclusively from the male point of view stems from the personal nature of the enquiry as much as from general cultural assumptions and literary conventions).

But what is fantasy, and how is it related to the 'waking' reality of everyday life? There are initial clues to Freud's views on the matter in his essay on screen memories. There he talks of the formation of mnemic images as a consequence of the onset of powerful sexual feelings. This might be seen, literally, as self-abuse replacing abuse by an interfering adult. His patient (himself) is subject to fantasies of 'gross sexual aggression', of 'defloration fantasies', filled with a 'coarsely sensual element'. These fantasies are the work of the conscious mind, presumably (to judge from remarks near the end of the essay) accompanying solitary masturbation. The complex interaction in screen memories between emotionally sensitive recollections projected forward from childhood and those projected backwards on to childhood makes it difficult, even in particular cases, to establish the precise role and significance of fantasy in the construction of those experiences we consider to be spontaneous memories of actual events. Generally Freud seems to argue that, in normal people, fantasy begins as a kind of waking and intentional dream-state, but, on account of their uncensored elements, or, rather, as a result of the censorship acting back upon them, they are projected onto the 'indifferent material' of childhood. As memories they are then transformed into the psychic trace of 'real' events and as such become autonomous contents for which we bear no responsibility. In the case of hysterics, however, he viewed fantasies as the product of wholly unconscious processes, primarily from 'things heard', and according to the rules through which dreams are constructed unconsciously from 'things seen'. For them, fantasies are 'psychic façades produced in order to bar access' to the memory of the earliest events.[16] In either case, spontaneous recollection, as distinct from interpreted dream material, is an unreliable guide to the events of childhood.

In some respects the logic of the trauma theory remains; but rather than the sexual shock of seduction being the instigator of repression, the psychic shock of self-generated fantasy leads to its own repression and disguise as an 'innocent' recollection from the period of early childhood.

The process of forming mnemic images depends upon affects attaching themselves to 'appropriate' sensory images. And where their first and most obvious attachments is inappropriate, for whatever reason, it is displaced according to an associative connection with the original image, and not with the original affect. The resulting screen memory then appears as a spontaneous and disconnected recollection.

Freud's view of screen memories is somewhat inconsistent and at times unclear. He occasionally returned to the issue without finally clarifying whether he considered *all* disconnected spontaneous memories from the age of 2 or 3 to be constructed in that way, or whether some were 'genuine' memories. In any event, his search for *the* originating cause of hysteria gave way to an investigation of the processes through which fantasy was formed.

The most detailed discussion of a reconstructed fantasy is given in the 'Wolf Man' analysis (1918).[17] With Nabakovian precision he described the 'primal scene', apparently witnessed by his patient at the age of 1½, and later displaced into a terrifying dream image of white wolves and to a phobia against looking at pictures of wolves in a book of fairy stories:

> It harmonizes with our assumptions that it was a hot summer's day, if we suppose that his parents had retired, half undressed, for an afternoon *siesta*. When he woke up, he witnessed a coitus *a tergo* (from behind), three times repeated; he was able to see his mother's genitals as well as his father's organ; and he understood the process as well as its significance.
>
> (SE 17, pp. 37–8)

Freud argues that there is 'nothing extraordinary' about this scene; nothing which makes it an incredible, or even an unlikely event. The doubt that the circumstances could have been perceived and understood in just those terms by a child of just one-and-a-half, or that it is inconceivable that it could have remained in his unconscious as a plastic image and revived at a later age is, he claims, simply a prejudice. At first, therefore, Freud is inclined to argue that the 'primal scene' is, indeed, the recollection of an actual event. But he revises this opinion in favour of the view, which is more amenable to generalisation, that the child had projected backwards and applied to his parents the knowledge of copulation he had gained from the observation of animals. The lengthy consideration, in defence of his own view, of a variety of possible interpretations of the 'primal scene' indicates an uncharacteristic hesitancy in his reconstruction of the case.

The difficulty is that, working back from the present ego-consciousness, it seems that fantasy must begin from *some* observation or other, and could not develop as a wholly self-contained domain of significance. The fantasy theory seems ultimately to be as arbitrary as the seduction theory. At best it would require a careful investigation in each case to reveal the specific conditions under which the primal scene was observed. But, as with the seduction theory, it is the regularity with which he comes across almost identical cases which makes Freud look for an explanation beyond that of simply accepting the patient's recollections as empirical descriptions.[18] Furthermore, and in accord with Freud's general intellectual orientation towards the most general levels of explanation, if a mnemic image of the primal scene is at the root of neurosis, it must also play a fundamental part in the formation of normal psychic life. The difficulty with the conclusion in the 'Wolf Man' case is its dependence on a contingent event, and, therefore, the risk of error involved in erecting a general theory upon it. Freud argues that the crucial event, observing animal copulation, is extremely common; much more so, at least, than a direct observation of the primal scene itself. Certainly, the acquisition of sexual knowledge, with anxiety and a resulting phobia, had been related to animal observations in Freud's previously published case history of 'Little Hans' (1909).[19] But the 'high probability' of such incidents could not serve as an automatic explanation for every case presenting similar symptoms, far less as the foundation for a general theory of fantasy in normal psychic life.[20]

FROM FANTASY TO MYTH

The accidents of personal history leads the analyst back to an organised structure of fantasy, rather than to specific and determining events. In terms of our own experience, memory comes up against a barrier beyond which a 'pre-historic' set of structures can be glimpsed; and it is from these obscure psychical formations that the familiar ego emerges in some way which Freud's analytic work on hysteria and on dreams had done little to elucidate. The fundamental processes through which this emergence occurs cannot be understood in terms of the ego itself. Psychical 'development', that is to say, cannot presuppose what issues from it; a difficulty which is openly acknowledged by Freud. He admits, for example, that the 'inner causes' of the successive 'waves of repression and sublimations', fundamental to the construction of the ego, 'are quite unknown to us'.[21] The fundamental structuring principles, which bring the child into contact with the social world through the developments of feelings of shame, disgust and morality, remained mysterious.

The search for the 'primal event' proved to be the pursuit of an illusory reality. The origin of the ego dissolved into fantasies of early life which could only be conceived in terms of the deformations of the consciousness which supplanted them. We are driven, that is to say, to describe experience in terms of the ego, or in terms of abstractions which derive their meaning as inversions or reversals – as deviations – from the ego.

Myth conveys meaning in just this way – it is the fantasy of history. So that, in tracing back the history of western society, we do not discover a decisive originating *event* but, rather, dissolve into a world of strange, but uncannily familiar, experience; a world which is comprehensible only in contrast to an image of modernity which we project back to its putative point of origin. Myth, like the common structures of the neuroses, and the interpreted wishes fulfilled in dreams, reveals a continuously present world in terms of infantile realities.

In writing to Fliess, Freud epitomised the insights he had gained from his self-analysis through a consideration of *Oedipus Rex,* and elaborated on the connection in *The Interpretation of Dreams.* In his view modern audiences, unmoved by the thematic spectacle of an impersonal fate, or of a divine will, working itself out independently of human motives, respond to Sophocles' tragedy in terms of its narrative mechanism. The manifest content of the play, it might be said, corresponds to the latent content of our dreams:

> It is the fate of all of us, perhaps, to direct our first sexual impulse towards our mother and our first hatred and our first murderous wish against our father. Our dreams convince us that is so. King Oedipus, who slew his father Laïus and married his mother Jocasta, merely shows us the fulfilment of our own childhood wishes. But, more fortunate than he, we have meanwhile succeeded, in so far as we have not become psychoneurotics, in detaching our sexual impulses from our mothers and in forgetting our jealousy of our fathers. Here is one in whom these primaeval wishes of our childhood have been fulfilled, and we shrink back from him with the whole force of the repression by which those wishes have since that time been held down within us. While the poet, as he unravels the past, brings to light the guilt of Oedipus, he is at the same time compelling us to recognize our own

inner minds, in which those same impulses, though suppressed, are still to be found.

(SE 4, pp. 262–63)

Interestingly, in spite of his professed interest in archaeology and ancient history, it is the text of the play, and not the tradition from which its content sprang, which is the focus of Freud's attention. He identifies with Sophocles rather than with Oedipus; but Sophocles is responsible for the tragic drama, not the myth. And in some important respects Sophocles transformed the tradition on which his tragedy depended.

Indeed, Sophocles played a central role in intellectual and cultural revolution of the Greek 'axial-age' which saw not only the birth of tragic drama and of comedy, but also of philosophy and science. He was part of the Greek transition from 'mythos' to 'logos', and already looked back on the oral tradition of epic poetry and the oral history of the ancient world from the vantage point of a more individuated and intellectualised standpoint. Freud himself recognises that the Sophoclean drama is a 'secondary revision' of a myth. But, though a new theological purpose is grafted on to the ancient myth, 'in the *Oedipus* the child's wishful phantasy that underlies it is brought into the open and realised as it would be in a dream'.[22]

It has been suggested that Freud dealt with the myth in this indirect manner in part because the Sophoclean version, and in particular its theological elements, fitted best the needs of his self-analysis.[23] Indeed, in some sense, the transformation of the myth effected by Sophocles anticipated his own abandonment of the seduction theory and discovery of the universal significance of fantasy. As compared to the version of the story in Aeschylus and others, Sophocles eliminated the theme of an inherited curse, or any other 'primal event' which rouses Oedipus' lust, and moves the entire drama on to the plane of fate and necessity. By removing the implications of contingency or human failing 'Sophocles transforms the fatal collision of father and son at the crossroads into an ineluctable necessity, and thereby endows the theme of parricide with genuine universality'.[24] Oedipus is unaware of his own situation, and becomes the subject of forces which he cannot wholly conceptualise, far less control. He exactly represents, therefore, the position of the modern individual, dimly aware that archaic processes are continually breaking into and deforming the integrity of the ego.

Furthermore, if the choice of Sophocles betrays a wish to universalise the theme of parricide, and, thus, absolve Sigismund of the guilt he still bore for the final fruit of a terrifyingly destructive omnipotence of thought (Julius, von Fleicshl-Marxow, Josef Paneth – Jacob Freud?), it equally distracts attention from the related cycle of myths from which *Oedipus* is itself a significant deviation. The 'classic' myth of ancient society is a story of royal investiture, which, as recently analysed by Jean-Joseph Goux, involves a sequence of more or less fixed *motifs*. Firstly a king, alerted by an oracle, fears that his position will be usurped by a younger man or person as yet unborn, and takes steps to destroy his presumed rival. Secondly, the future hero escapes, setting in train a sequence of events which leads to a replication of the original situation, and on this occasion the hero is set an impossible task in the expectation that he will perish. Thirdly, a trial ensues in which the hero, aided by a god, wise man or future bride, defeats a monster. Finally, the triumphant hero marries the daughter of the king.

Oedipus is viewed by his father, Laïus, as Jason, Bellerophon and Perseus are by theirs, as a threat to his kingship. And like them he is banished to a distant land. Similarly each later confronts a dangerous (female) monster and emerges as the heroic victor. Perseus overcomes the Gorgon, Bellerophon defeats the Chimaera, Jason vanquishes the guardian of the Golden Fleece, and Oedipus triumphs over the Sphinx. But while Perseus marries Andromeda, Bellerophon marries Philonoë, and Jason marries Medea, Oedipus marries his mother, Jocasta.

This is not the only important anomaly. The attempt on the life of the young hero is not made in the form of setting him a supposedly lethal trial, but is in this case inverted, and Oedipus slays Laïus and confronts the Sphinx of his own free will. Worse, in a singular act of *hubris*, he triumphs, at the first attempt, and unaided by the gods. His victory is assured by a decisive act of linguistic warfare in solving the riddle set him by the Sphinx, who subsequently hurls himself into an abyss. Oedipus, it is worth noting, triumphs by virtue of his native intelligence, rather than by his learning – he is an 'autodidact'.[25]

The 'normal' myth, that is to say, expresses the truth that the young man must free himself from the mother (monstrous female) in order to marry a young woman and take his place in the world. But Freud's approach to the myth is almost exclusively through Sophocles and is, therefore, more properly viewed as part of his literary criticism. This elision is understandable in the context of both his self-analysis and of his developing general psychological theory. His self-analysis was prompted by the realisation of ambivalence towards his dead father. What he discovered was the longing for the death of his father. And as part of an attempt to cope with this unruly passion he recreated it as a timeless and universal wish; as Sophoclean fate. It was, consequently, the requirements of symmetry that led him to discover the originating love for his mother; a love from which, in its vicissitudes, he need never be liberated.

In Goux's interpretation classical antiquity and modernity are linked in their Oedipal inversion; in their radical rejection of the mythic world of initiation through liberation from the mother. The modern subject 'is initially determined by the posture of Oedipus', as a being 'whose identity is not defined by a tradition and a transmission, a hero with whom a new mode of subjectivity emerges'.[26] This self-defining subject, furthermore, expresses itself as insatiable curiosity rather than in the form of love and, thus, develops through knowledge and a growing mastery over the world. Oedipus, a 'metamythical' figure is, thus, directly linked to Freud's other hero-image – Faust.

In this context Freud's Oedipal theory might be viewed as a partially effected transposition *back* into myth of the results of his self-analysis. Freud's ambivalence towards, and at times rejection of, his father can be viewed relatively simply as an aspect of his consuming desire for intellectual independence, creativity and modernity. It is understood by Freud himself initially through his own childhood experience, and then quite generally in terms of fundamental mythic themes. In the process of intellectualisation his feelings reflect, by a kind of mythic reversal, a quite different situation; fear and hatred of the father is transformed into undying love of the mother.

But this tempting simplification would hardly do justice to Freud's insight. His psychology is conceived in the moment of modern disillusionment, and gives subtle expression to the internal collapse of classical ego-psychology and the world it had created. The new (post)modern surface of life is textured by continuous flux, by transience and by the instability of all categorical distinctions. The differentiation of mythos and logos itself gives way to a new 'logomyth' in which ancient and modern are paradoxically conjoined in the rejection of tradition. The distinction between 'mythos' (liberation from the mother) and 'logos' (liberation from the father) is assimilated to a new unstable order of reality: a series of 'logomyths' expressing ambivalence towards *both* the mother *and* the father characterises reflection on contemporary experience.

FROM HISTORY TO ARCHAIC SOCIETY

The search for an originating 'zero-point' in his own personal history initially led Freud to the seduction theory, and beyond that to a general theory of fantasy which was elaborated in terms of an interpretation of *motifs* in ancient mythology. Links between modernity and the ancient world, a tracing back of the *world-line* of the ego, were amplified in a series of extensions to his clinical theories. These anthropological reflections and speculations on the history of ancient civilisations and cultures were conspicuously unsuccessful, in the sense that their fundamental presuppositions have neither been borne out by nor assimilated to subsequent scholarship, nor have they formed the point of departure for a fundamentally new and independent approach to such questions.[27] They are, nonetheless, important in the context of Freud's *psychological* works. They indicate the way in which he hoped to link his self-analysis not only to general philosophical questions, but also to a putative history of human society. They also serve as an indispensable link between his clinical studies and his metapsychological theories.

Freud's intellectual *hubris* did not allow for any resting place. His understanding of modern life, in which the ego tended to dissolve into a series of energetic streams that connected with the entire surface of the past and the present, invited him continually to broaden the scope of his psychology. It is hardly surprising, then, to find him attracted by views about the nature of primitive society and of the archaic world which suggested analogies to his own views about infantile mentality. Anthropologists and psychologists were quite used to drawing parallels between the modes of thought typical of primitive peoples and of children, and between both and the presumed character of archaic human experience. In the 'mental life' of 'those whom we describe as savages' we can view 'a well-preserved picture of an early stage of our own development'.[28] Just as Freud had found in contemporary hysterical symptoms architectural sketches of partially repressed orders of consciousness, so in neurotic obsessions and in phobias he excavated what he took to be the remains of archaic modes of life and thought.

However, just as the phenomenon of childhood amnesia makes it difficult to distinguish between the process of dreaming and the construction of screen memories, so the fact that such an archaic period is not directly observable makes it an ideally receptive surface upon which to project historical fantasies. Freud's vision of the remote past, like the tradition of speculative anthropology which it invoked as its evidential basis, is best viewed, in fact, as an intellectual reconstruction of *modern* experience.

In *Totem and Taboo*, which remained one of his favourite works, Freud used the analysis of obsessional neuroses as a key to the understanding of pre-history. His approach promises nothing less than the conquest of a new field of knowledge:

> Anyone approaching the problem of taboo from the angle of psychoanalysis, that is to say, of the investigation of the unconscious portion of the individual mind, will recognize, after a moment's reflection, that these phenomena are far from unfamiliar to him. He has come across people who have created for themselves individual taboo prohibitions of this very kind and who obey them just as strictly as savages obey the communal taboos of their tribe or society. If he were not already accustomed to describing such people as 'obsessional' patients, he would find 'taboo sickness' a most appropriate name for their condition.
>
> (SE 13, p. 26)

The peculiar character of taboo and of obsessional neurosis is the elaboration of a system of prohibitions 'equally lacking in motive and equally puzzling in their origin'. Appearing at an unspecified moment 'they are forcibly maintained by an irresistible fear'. And the mechanism of compliance is so fully internalised that 'no external threat of punishment is required'. There is 'an internal certainty, a moral conviction, that any violation will lead to intolerable disaster'. And, in obsessional neurosis as in the case of taboo, the fundamental prohibition – 'the nucleus of the neurosis' – is an interdiction against touching some specified object or person; an avoidance of contact which may be extended through any appropriate metaphorical series to include an indefinite number of additional objects.

Like taboos, obsessional prohibitions 'involve extensive restriction on the lives of those who are subject to them', but specific actions may lift some of these and thereafter such actions become compulsive. The obsessive acts are in the nature of 'expiation, penance, defensive measures and purification'.

Freud argues that in the case of obsessional neurotics the first prohibition stems from an original *desire* of the child to touch his own genitals. But this inclination is met by an external prohibition which 'finds support from a powerful *internal* force', that is from 'the child's loving relation to the authors of the prohibition'.[29] As a result, the tendency to touch, which is part of the early psychical organisation, is repressed. But *both* the instinct and the prohibition persist. The conflict cannot be settled, giving rise to the characteristic *ambivalence* of the subject in relation to the specific act of touching. However, as the prohibition originates at such an early age it is subject (as the ceremonial avoidance and defence is not) to an amnesia which renders the motive for the obsessional acts incomprehensible.

Similarly the origin of taboo is unknown to the primitives who observe it. So, arguing by analogy, Freud supposes that taboos:

> are prohibitions of primeaval antiquity which were at some time externally imposed upon a generation of primitive men. . . . These prohibitions must have concerned activities towards which there was a strong inclination. . . . But one thing would certainly follow from the persistence of the taboo, namely that the original desire to do the prohibited thing must also still persist among the tribes concerned. They must therefore have an ambivalent attitude towards their taboos. In their unconscious there is nothing they would like more than to violate them, but they are afraid to do so.
>
> (SE 13, p. 31)

From this Freud argues that 'the most ancient and important taboo prohibitions' are the two fundamental laws of totemism: 'not to kill the totemic animal and to avoid sexual intercourse with members of the totemic clan.' And it follows from this that these must be 'the most powerful of human desires'. He arrives thus at a clear thesis: 'the basis of taboo is a prohibited action, for performing which a strong inclination exists in the unconscious.'[30]

Ambivalence and temptation are highly contagious and this makes taboo easily transmitted from one person to another, or from one object to another. This is particularly associated with transitional states in which people are held to be more vulnerable, though Freud expresses this in an odd fashion which, perhaps, once again displays his feelings towards his deceased father: 'dead men, new-born babies and women menstruating or in labour stimulate desire by their special helplessness.' Any transgression at such times is met with immediate action as otherwise the members of the community would become conscious of their wish to act in the same prohibited way.

Both taboos and obsessional acts stem from self-reproaches, commonly over the death of a close relative who had aroused ambivalent feelings. This ambivalence (Freud once again describes his own situation) is expressed by the primitive on the one hand in mourning, and on the other hand by projecting unconscious hostility towards the deceased; creating, as a result, a detached and malign demon against whom they must protect themselves through rituals of avoidance.

The mechanism of *projection*, however, which is a frequently used neurotic technique of coping with emotional conflict and the fundamental mechanism involved in the construction of taboo, 'was not created for the purpose of defence'. In an important passage Freud argues that projection also plays a significant part in the creation of any normal sense of reality:

> The projection outward of internal perceptions is a primitive mechanism, to which, for instance, our sense perceptions are subject, and which therefore normally plays a very large part in determining the form taken by the external world. Under conditions whose nature has not yet been sufficiently established, internal perceptions of emotional and thought processes can be projected outwards in the same way as sense perceptions; they are thus employed for building up the external world, though they should by rights remain part of the *internal* world.
>
> (SE 13, p. 64)

In more 'civilised' peoples, the development of abstract thought, which has been built upon the prior development of linguistic signs, allows the 'endopsychic processes' to be conceptualised as a specific quality of *feeling*. However:

> Before that, owing to the projection outwards of internal perceptions, primitive men arrived at a picture of the external world which we, with our intensified conscious perceptions, have now to translate back into psychology.
>
> (SE 13, p. 64)

Projection is the basis for understanding primitive thought as 'animism', but 'the prototype of all such systems is what we have termed the "second-ary revision" of the content of dreams'. Dreaming is a kind of primitive mode of experience, and primitive thought is a waking dream, in which the normal barriers to projection are either withdrawn or undeveloped, and a plastic reality freely constructed from processes internal to the psychical mechanism.

Taboo, like 'primal words', has an antithetical double-meaning as both 'sacred' and 'unclean'; its significance, as well as its meaning, is ambivalent. Freud supposes that the process of civilisation effects a gradual but decisive reduction in ambivalence, and thus establishes the autonomy of the external world. But ambivalence cannot be wholly eradicated, and neither the development of new social institutions nor of individuated conscience can win a decisive victory over rejected impulses. Projection, confined to the dream-state or partially liberated in the neuroses, retains a profoundly asocial character which has its 'genetic origin' in the wish 'to take flight from an unsatisfying reality into a more pleasurable world of phantasy'.[31]

Freud goes on to provide a brief outline of the basic notions of animism, as it was presented in the work of Tylor and Frazer. This is, in a sense, the positive side of taboo. Rather than establishing rituals to neutralise the consequence of prohibited acts, animism develops techniques of magical control over the world. Primitive mentality and childhood thought have as their common feature the substitution of the ideal for the real, so that the manipulation of symbols is held to have real effects in the world. The psychic world of the primitive is dominated by the 'omnipotence of thoughts', a phrase Freud had borrowed from one of his patients, the subsequently famous obsessional neurotic 'Rat Man'. Indeed this 'overvaluation' of all emotionally intensified thoughts is characteristic of neurotics, who, in respect to those thoughts at least, 'live in a world apart'. And the 'primary obsessive acts of these neurotics are of an entirely magical character'.[32] For Freud this is more than an analogical relationship. The obsessional neurotic *is* animistic in his thinking, and animistic thinking *is* neurotic. More than that, primitive thinking is still sexualised. The primitive, like the obsessive neurotic, 'cathects' his own ego, and 'the cathexes of objects which he effects are as it were emanations of the libido that still remains in his ego and can be drawn back into it once more'.[33]

And for both the neurotic and the primitive the common 'real event' to which all their projection and ritualisation is related is death; the actualisation of the wished for death of the father. Freud argues that psychoanalytic study of children (whose psychic world, he believed, has much in common with primitives, and thus of archaic humans) shows the ambivalent feelings towards the father are commonly displaced on to animals, and this provides an important clue in the understanding of the origin of totemism. Following Robertson Smith's account of the totemic meal as a festive communion with the spirits, and Darwin's suggestion that the original condition of the human species must have involved dispersal in small isolated bands (confusingly referred to by Freud as a primal *horde*), dominated by a single male, he speculates that the primal meal, in fact, refers to a real situation in which the sons killed and devoured the father:

> Cannibal savages as they were, it goes without saying that they devoured their victim as well as killing him. The violent primal father had doubtless been the feared and envied model of each one of the company of brothers: and in the act of devouring him they accomplished their identification with him, and each one of them acquired a portion of his strength. The totem meal, which is perhaps mankind's earliest festival, would thus be a repetition and a commemoration of this memorable and criminal deed, which was the beginning of so many things – of social organisation, of moral restrictions and of religion.
>
> (SE 13, p. 142)

However, though 'they hated their father, who presented such a formidable obstacle to their craving for power and their sexual desire', they had also loved and admired him. Intense feelings of remorse and guilt set in, with the result that:

> the dead father became stronger than the living one had been. . . . They revoked their deed by forbidding the killing of the totem, the substitute for their father; and they renounced its fruits by resigning their claim to the women who had now been set free.
>
> (SE 13, p. 143)

Hence, according to Freud, originated the two fundamental moral laws of primitive society: the prohibition against eating the totemic animal and the incest taboo – the latter coincidentally having the effect of eliminating the main source of competition and conflict among the men within the group. The patriarchal horde was replaced by the fraternal clan.

Much remains obscure in Freud's exposition. He admits the difficulty, but accepts as necessary the postulate of a group mind, and of the direct inheritance of guilt in the subsequent development of civilisation; conceptions which seem far removed from the atmosphere of Brücke's Physiological Institute where he received his scientific training. Yet, any attempt to represent the pre-conceptual experience of the world through conceptual language makes such obscurities unavoidable and, consequently, *Totem and Taboo*, is best read as a scientific myth, as an extension of the 'logomyth' of Freud's self-analysis.

The ever-broadening sweep of Freud's thought as it moved outwards from his own recollected experience encountered varying levels of 'reality' and 'fantasy'. In his clinical theory he moved from the realism of the seduction theory to the fantasy of the Oedipus complex. In his general theory of hysteria he moved from the interpretation of individual symptoms, as

117

fantasised events to the reconstruction of non-egoistic body images (as realities preserved in fantasy). And in his anthropological speculation he again moved from fantasy to reality; from the inexplicable fact of morality to a macro-historical primal scene. He is himself hesitant over the status of such postulated 'events'. At the end of *Totem and Taboo* he admits that:

> We are justified in believing that, as one of the phenomena of their narcissistic organization they overvalued their psychical acts to an extraordinary degree. Accordingly the mere hostile *impulse* against the father, the mere existence of the wishful *phantasy* of killing and devouring him, would have been enough to produce the moral reaction that created totemism and taboo.
>
> (SE 13, pp. 159–60)

Though he accepts this is a plausible view, he is not wholly convinced by it. Yet his own analysis of the nature and mechanism of projection remain the central theme of the book, and strongly incline the reader to accept the 'powerful argument' he had himself outlined.

What is clear is the confirmation this pre-historic scenario provides for the revised autobiographical reading of *The Interpretation of Dreams*. The psychological core of *Totem and Taboo* is to be found in the theme of ambivalence towards the father, and the intense inner conflict set in train by his death. Freud universalises his own experience in the grandest possible manner:

> The faults of the dead no doubt provide a part of the explanation of the survivors' hostility. . . . (But) the moment of death would certainly seem to be a most inappropriate occasion for recalling any justifiable grounds of complaint that might exist. It is impossible to escape the fact that the true determining factor is invariably *unconscious* hostility. A hostile current of feeling such as this against a person's nearest and dearest relatives may remain latent during their lifetime. . . . But when they die this is no longer possible and the conflict becomes acute.
>
> (SE 13, p. 63)

And what is equally clear, from both his clinical analyses, his theoretical construction and his general historico-cultural speculations, is that the process of repressing disruptive impulses and wishes which arise during the pre-genital/pre-historic phases of human life cannot be solely the work of an outside agency. Repression is a process internal to the psychical mechanism, and it is only as a result of its progressive operation that the consciousness familiar to us can be established. Thus, even if the search for non-contingent sources of fantasy had been wholly successful, it was not clear how these mechanisms could be related to the emergence of the ego.

The search for the primal scene through which wishes were formed into mnemic images is paralleled, therefore, by attempts to explicate the mechanism of repression.

NOTES

1 Schur (1972), p. 106.
2 The work of Schur (1972), Krüll (1979), Balmary (1982), Anzieu (1986), Vitz (1988), Grinstein (1990), and for more general biographical revision and updating Clark (1982), Gay (1988) have done much to revise the 'official' biographical picture found in Jones (1953). McGrath (1986) provides a detailed account of the most significant biographical discussions in a context relevant to the present discussion, and several important contributions to the continuing debate, including otherwise inaccessible work by Swales, are conveniently available in Spurling (1989), Macmillan (1990) and Gelfand and Kerr (1992).
3 Grinstein (1980), p. 285.
4 SE 5, p. 484.
5 Grinstein (1980), p. 60; Clark (1982), pp. 20–7.
6 Isbister (1985), pp. 130–8 as a corrective.
7 See particularly Schur (1972).
8 SE 3, p. 312.
9 Anzieu (1986).
10 Freud (1985), p. 268.
11 Freud (1985), p. 269.
12 Anzieu (1986), p. 13.
13 The issue has been much discussed. Krüll (1979) stimulated biographical accounts, see Balmary (1982), Masson (1985), Anzieu (1986), McGrath (1986).
14 Controversy was stimulated by Masson (1985), but the earlier and equally sensational though less widely known work of Krüll (1979) and Balmary (1982) had made similar suggestions.
15 This account is taken from a letter to Fliess (21 September 1897) in Freud (1985), pp. 264–5.
16 Freud (1985), p. 240.
17 SE 17, pp 3–122. The case history was written in 1914 but not published until four years later. Interesting background material is available in Gardiner (1971), Kanzer and Glenn (1980), Mahony (1984), Hughes (1994), pp. 99–108.
18 SE 17, pp. 48–60.
19 SE 10, pp.5–152.
20 The case of the 'Rat Man's' fantasy (SE 10, pp. 166–7) also has particular and accidental sources, notably a passage from Mirbeau's *Le Jardin des Supplices* (Mirbeau 1986, pp. 216–17) as Mahony (1986) suggests. But this, again, is to explain the meaning of the dream (fantasy) exclusively in terms of the 'day-residues', and leaves unexplained the uncanny power of Mirbeau's text on his reader.
21 SE 7, p. 239.
22 SE 4, p. 264.
23 Rudnytsky (1987), pp. 254–7.
24 Rudnytsky (1987), p. 256.
25 Goux (1993), p. 18. In one of his dreams Freud appeared to himself as an 'autodidact' (SE 4, pp. 298–302).

119

26 Goux (1993), p. 82.
27 For a thoughtful review see Wallace (1983), and examples of the genre, Muensterberger (1969); in this connection the works of Devereaux and Róheim should be considered. This is not to say that Freud's work has not had a more diffuse and important impact on anthropology, which clearly it has.
28 SE 13, p. 1. On the so-called 'biogenetic law' see Gould (1977), Ferguson (1990), pp. 27–46.
29 SE 13, p. 29.
30 SE 13, p. 32.
31 SE 13, p. 74.
32 SE 13, p. 87.
33 SE 13, p. 89.

5

METATEXT
Explaining consciousness

The various elements of experience, spread out across the surface of life, generate a field of forces through which the interconnected ego becomes aware of itself, and represents itself, as a distinctive form. At the same time these energetic flows tend to deform and dissolve the ego, breaking into its precarious inner unity and returning its constituent parts to an elemental primary process. The temporary morphological unity of the ego is not itself the outcome of rational or intentional actions, nor is it the product of reflection and intellectual operations, which, in fact, become possible only as aspects of its emergence. Equally, however, the ego cannot be conceived in terms of a self-generating dynamism; as a Romantic soul. Freud's understanding of the characteristic deformations of the ego, observable in neurotic symptoms and more commonly in dreams, led him towards a general view of psychical functioning in which fantasy played a central role. However, every effort to uncover an 'originating cause' from which sprang the entire process of inner self-development succeeded only in revealing a fantasy which had been carried back to this inconceivable point of indifference as a ready-made explanation of its own subsequent metamorphoses.

Experience is a psychical reality, and nothing else. By definition, 'non-psychical' elements can only be assimilated through a process of representation which itself is wholly psychical. The only reality of which we can become aware is the reality of such representations. In Freud's view, however, it is possible to account for some aspects of the emergence and development of this reality in terms of general and non-trivial considerations about the nature of the mechanism of representation itself rather than, or in addition to, accounts in terms of its content. Dreams, symptoms and a variety of other psychic contents, in other words, can be explained as well as interpreted.

THE *PROJECT*

Freud's understanding of dreams is not only set against the background of his published work on hysteria, it is formulated in the context of his unpublished *Project for a Scientific Psychology* which was composed during September of 1895. It was the culmination of a series of drafts and letters he sent to Wilhelm Fliess in which he attempted to clarify fundamental psychological concepts.

The primary purpose of the *Project* was to 'represent psychical processes as quantitatively determinate states of specifiable material particles, thus making those processes perspicuous and free from contradiction'.[1] The *Project* developed in Freud's mind at the same time as his 'qualitative' understanding of dreams as interpretable contents of experience, and, though never published, many of its basic insights were incorporated into his later writings. And it was in the *Project*, in fact, that he first outlined a systematic account of dreaming.

The *Project* is normally viewed as an initial attempt to provide psychology with a workable model of the brain and nervous system.[2] The 'material particles' of which it is composed can be specified anatomically as neurones which, from an initial state of protoplasmic irritability, become differentiated into two fundamentally different types that are related according to specific principles. What Freud termed ϕ (phi) neurones link the organism to the outside world through the simple transmission of sensory information; they are not altered by their functioning, and they can be identified with the more primitive parts of the brain. Those which he designated as Ψ (psi) neurones discharge excitations of an endogenous origin. They are 'impermeable', are structurally altered by their continued functioning (that is, they possess the basic characteristic of memory) and can be identified with the more developed parts of the brain. Organic needs are transmitted through the system of Ψ neurones, giving rise to what at this point Freud refers to as 'the exigencies of life', which are experienced as 'appetites'.

The differentiation of the nervous tissue had been well established since the pioneering work of Sir Charles Bell in the 1830s and its implications for psychology had been widely discussed.[3] What remained more obscure in Freud's *Project* was the nature of the 'energy' which was conceptualised as being conducted by the neurones. The notion of 'force' was seen as the most primitive assumption of the physical sciences and Freud seems to have assumed that any genuinely systematic psychology would be related systematically to its most general scientific meaning.[4] What was somewhat clearer was the function attributed to both neuronal systems, and to the 'psychical apparatus' as a whole; namely to 'discharge' excitations originating in both the external world and from within the organism. Expressed in the terse language of the *Project*, he asserts that 'the neurones tend to divest themselves of Q', that is, the psychical apparatus tends to reduce the total quantity of excitation to which it is subjected. Ideally the nervous system would maintain itself in a tensionless state or, more realistically, would balance its inputs of excitations with energetically equivalent motor discharges. This Principle of Constancy, which Freud traced back to Fechner was, in various forms, a widely held assumption at the period and one which, particularly as expressed by Simmel and Musil, made sense socially as well as biologically. One of the central psychological problems of the modern age was the 'fending off' of the torrent of stimulation to which the individual was subjected. Freud points out, however, that this fundamental 'law of inertia' of the nervous system is complicated by the structural differentiation of the ϕ and Ψ systems which he had outlined. The tendency of the ϕ system is an evasive 'flight from the stimulus', but this runs counter to the requirement, deriving from the build-up of excitation in the Ψ system, to meet internal needs by acting upon the environment. Consequently the total level of energy cannot be reduced to zero and 'the nervous system is obliged to abandon its original trend to inertia. . . . It must put up with (maintaining) a store of $Q\eta$ sufficient to meet the demand for a specific action'.[5]

The fundamental difficulty of psychology is to account for the transformation of quantity into quality. We are aware only of qualities, 'consciousness knows nothing of what we have so far been assuming – quantities and neurones'.[6] Freud argues that neither the ϕ system nor the Ψ system are adapted to register qualities, and we remain completely unconscious of their operation. The ϕ system conducts excitations from the outside world, but qualities have no meaning in relation to the outside world, which is understood by the natural sciences in terms of a wholly abstract system of forces and masses. At the same time the Ψ system is adapted to register memories, but as this also 'speaking generally, is without quality' Freud feels compelled to assume a third specific neuronal system, the ω (omega) system:

> which is excited along with perception, but not along with reproduction, and whose states of excitation give rise to the various qualities – are, that is to say, *conscious sensations.*
>
> (SE 1, pp. 308–9)

The fundamental gulf between, on the one hand, an understanding of nature as an indifferent system of forces and matter and, on the other, the qualities making up consciousness, had been noted by Müller, whose work had been inspirational for the entire development of scientific medicine in Vienna. But the gulf was either ignored or assumed to be resolved in physiologically subtle investigations of the nervous system, and particularly of the functioning of sensory receptors. Freud, however, was clearly aware that the difficulty had simply been assimilated to a developing scientific language, without ever being resolved. This entire approach owes a great deal to Freud's philosophy teacher, Franz Brentano, who anticipated some of the methodological discussions to which it gave rise.[7] This was by no means a problem unique to psychology; within the physical sciences, too, similar 'gaps' in understanding were appearing, posing the puzzle of 'levels' of organisation of matter in even more intractable forms.

Freud ingeniously suggests that perceptual qualities are transmitted to the ω system as periodic, rather than as energetic, motion. The ω neurones are seen as 'super-conductors' which transmit tiny quantities of energy effortlessly in all directions. The system acts as a sounding board, registering the morphological features of the larger energetic excitations within the ϕ system: 'the ω neurones are incapable of receiving $Q\eta$, but instead they appropriate the *period* of the excitation and that this state of theirs of being affected by period while they are filled with a minimum of $Q\eta$ is the fundamental basis of consciousness'.[8] There are interesting microcosmic resonances here with highly modernist arguments about the 'dematerialisation' of reality within a perspectivist framework.[9] What Freud is striving to define is a coherent scientific approach to the problem of consciousness given the demise, within the context of modernity, of the metaphors of either the mirror or the window. Consciousness does not 'reflect' something outside itself, or provide an internal 'picture' of autonomous objects and events but, rather, represents through its own morphological transformations (qualities) changes within a quite different and inherently unrepresentable order of reality. Furthermore the tiny 'charge' of energy which the ω system requires for its operation has its source, not in the ϕ system which connects with external reality, but with the endogenous Ψ system. The internal state of the organism, in terms of its relative tension in relation to the 'exigencies of life', thus finds its representation as a periodic motion within the ω system; in fact as the sensations of pleasure and unpleasure.

There is much in Freud's exposition which, he admits himself, is 'complicated and far from perspicuous' but the nature of consciousness remained central to Freud's psychology, and it is in relation to his understanding of consciousness that he first outlined a new psychology of dreams. The normal operation of this 'psychic apparatus' results in the construction of 'mnemic objects' charged with 'cathexes' which have their source in the accumulation and discharge of energy within the Ψ system. Then a 'wishful attraction' exerts itself towards the 'friendly mnemic image', while the 'hostile mnemic image' triggers primary defense; the 'fending-off' of potentially painful stimuli.

The *primary process* of the psychical apparatus is preoccupied with the endogenous Ψ system. In the process of discharging its tensions, however, more or less stable 'cathexes' are established through the perceptual system with mnemic images of external objects. The resulting 'ego' has a specific morphological structure, or texture, within the ω system, and this structure has an inhibiting effect on the functioning of the primary process. In adults, however, the primary process reasserts itself during sleep which is characterised by the 'unloading of the ego' and the simultaneous with-drawal of the 'cathexis of attention'. During sleep Ψ processes occur and are experienced as dreams, 'which have many characteristics that are not understood'.[10] Freud then provides an extremely concise, but compre-hensive, account of the major characteristics of dreams that he does believe to be explicable. Several of the fundamental themes of his mature dream theory are clearly introduced at this point. Significantly he draws attention in this brief discussion to the similar 'strangeness' of dreams and hysterical (and other) pathological conditions.

He stresses at this point the 'senselessness and illogicality of dreams' rather than (the *Project* was written prior to his self-analysis) their meaningfulness. The general 'compulsion to associate' characteristic of the dream-state is understood as a consequence of the 'lack of ego-cathexis' and is another illustration of the generally inhibitory character of the ego. The waking state, that is to say, organised in terms of the preferential connections of the ego, excludes a wide range of such possible, but rationally insignificant, associ-ations. At this point what really interests Freud is that, however absurd the connections of the 'dream-thoughts', they are presented with hallucinatory realism. Freud suggests that, in dreams, rather than excitations flowing from the perceptual nerve endings towards motor discharge, motility is withdrawn and the apparatus discharges towards the ϕ neurones, setting up periodic deformations in the ω system. During sleep, in other words, internal process set up conscious images rather as the note produced in a musical instrument sets up harmonic vibrations throughout its structure. He suggests, indeed, that the entire primary process is hallucinatory in character and is only gradually replaced by ego-cathexes.

Significantly Freud seeks to establish a psychology of dreams which is logically related to his view of consciousness; that is as an aspect of the functioning of the psychical apparatus. He concludes a brief listing of dream characteristics with the following note to himself:

> It is interesting, furthermore, that *consciousness* in dreams furnishes quality with as little trouble as in waking life. This shows that con-sciousness does not cling to the ego but can become an addition to any Ψ process. It warns us, too, against possibly identifying primary processes with unconscious ones. *Here are two invaluable hints for the future!*
>
> (SE 1, p. 340)

Dreams are not immediately comprehensible, but an interpretation of their content, rather than an explanation of their occurrence, is possible in terms of the primary process activity to which it is related. Dreams can be understood, thus, as hallucinatory wish fulfillments; and wishes are devoid of ego-characteristics. Dreams take place, as it were, on the same surface as does waking life.

Freud compares dreams, hysterical symptoms and the ego from two distinct perspectives. On the one hand, dreams and hysteria have in common a facility to establish, or rather re-establish, meaningful connections among contents of experience within which the ego has, so to speak, erected an impenetrable barrier of reason and good sense. On the other hand, hysteria and the ego have in common the character of a compulsive and obligatory reality. Emphasising an aspect of hysteria which Janet in particular had stressed, Freud focuses on its involuntary character. For Janet, the hysteric suffers from 'excessively intense ideas'; but, Freud argues, Janet had been wrong to see this compulsiveness as in itself pathological:

> Excessively intense ideas also occur normally. They lend the ego its individuality. We are not surprised at them if we know their genetic development (upbringing, experiences) and their motives. We are accustomed to regarding such *excessively intense* ideas as the product of strong and justifiable motives. Hysterical *excessively intense ideas* strike us, on the contrary, by their oddity; they are *ideas* which in other people have no consequences and of whose importance we can make nothing. They appear to us as intruders and usurpers, and accordingly as ridiculous.
>
> (SE 1, pp. 347–8)

Nor is there anything fundamentally pathological in symbol formation, the result of which strikes us as so odd in the hysteric. What is odd, rather, is the amnesia surrounding the origin of such symbolic connections. The hysteric is unaware of the meaning of the ideas which appear to them involuntarily. At this point Freud's understanding of the process of displacement and repression is in terms of 'ego-defence', but the normal ego remains unaware of its own symbolic origins. The ego is simply the 'normal' form of hysteria; and, in the context of modernity, its 'rationality' has been fatally undermined. The fact that Freud could see the connection between hysteria and the ego is itself indicative of a dissolution of the ego which is characteristic of modern life. And as hysteria and dreams are related as expressions of primary process activity, modern life can be seen as an outbreak of dreaming. The lure of dreams, for the most advanced forms of modernity, is the lure of a new and immediate reality rather than of a flight into transcendence. It is the realism of dreams, therefore, which leads Freud into a more comprehensive treatment of the origin of mnemic symbols.

PLEASURE AND BODY-LOGIC

Dreams proved to be a more effective and realistic guide to the understanding of modern life than did Freud's earlier 'reductionist' general psychological theories. The *Project* proved to be as much of a 'scientific fairy tale' as was the seduction theory. Though its central psychological and functional arguments reappeared in Chapter 7 of *The Interpretation of Dreams* and thereafter in a number of forms, Freud never revived the attempt to ground psychology in a specific physical model of the nervous system. This does not mean, however, that he abandoned his attempt to construct a systematic, scientific psychology. Indeed, the tendencies towards the 'dematerialisation' of the psyche in his work parallels the more general transformation of the natural and cultural sciences during the latter part of the nineteenth century.

The brilliance of Freud's dream interpretations, and his extraordinary understanding of the life histories of his patients, makes it easy to under-estimate the significance and rigour of his systematic thought. But, in fact, the entire development of his psychology was driven by considerations of the most general kind. The real attraction for him of the fantasy-theory over the seduction-theory lay in its greater capacity for generalisation. Although fantasy always involves specific contingent material, related to the personal history of the individual, both its operation within the psychical apparatus and its general content can be understood in terms of the formation of underlying body-images the nature of which is largely independent of environmental conditions. The tracing out of screen memories and dream-images, though concerned primarily with the details of personal histories, did reveal some general principles in the formation of fantasy and mnemic imagery. The transition from the seduction-theory to the fantasy-theory was accompanied by an extension and elaboration of a theoretical framework which Freud regarded as embodying genuinely universal features of human experience.

This is the significance of his developing focus on the role of sexuality in the aetiology of hysteria. Freud initially approached this simply as an empirical question, and only gradually began to grapple with its general theoretical significance. In addressing this issue, however, he developed an understanding of the fundamental processes involved in the psychic life of both normal and neurotic individuals in terms of bodily analogies. General bodily forms and processes provide the *schemata* through which the world (including inner life) is experienced.

The process of theory formation, which moves, so to speak, in the opposite direction from interpretation, seeks the most general level of explanation and ignores the particular meanings and association gener-ated within the psychic apparatus. Bodily schema, however, provide a theoretical point of departure in which genuine psychological 'meaning' inheres. It begins to close the gap between the specific and particular character of the interpretation of dreams, and the 'fiction' of the psychical apparatus through which the function of dreaming could be explained. The body, or, rather, a variety of body-images, thus become a significant level of theoretical elaboration for Freud, and were developed at the same time, and in conjunction with his analytic insights.

In a long letter to Fliess (14 November 1897), Freud makes clear the significance he attaches to this type of theoretical elaboration:

'It was on November 12, 1897; the sun was precisely in the eastern quarter; Mercury and Venus were in conjunction -.' No, birth announcements no longer start like that. It was on November 12, a day dominated by a left-sided migraine, on the afternoon of which Martin sat down to write a poem, on the evening of which Oli lost his second tooth, that, after the frightful labour pains of the last few weeks, I gave birth to a new piece of knowledge.

(Freud 1985, p. 278)

The specific dating and the circumstantial detail links this announcement with the 'flowery' letter written immediately prior to the publication of *The Interpretation of Dreams*. In the very midst of the most exciting period of his self-analysis, in other words, Freud breaks off to impart this piece of 'new knowledge' to Fliess; knowledge, it seems, he believed to be as significant as that contained in his dreambook.

The particular knowledge Freud introduced to Fliess through this elaborate preamble was, in essence, the outline of what was to become *Three Essays on the Theory of Sexuality*, the only work, besides *The Interpretation of Dreams*, which he regularly revised and to which he added new material as subsequent editions were published.

The problem confronting Freud was that, given his understanding of psychic reality, we can have no immediate knowledge of the sexual 'drive' or 'instinct'. We must remain as ignorant of the primary organic character of the instincts as we must of the 'thing in itself' which we assume to be the originating cause of our sensory experience. But just as 'common sense' insists that our sensory experience *is*, and is not simply the sign of, a world of objects independent of the process of perception, so it insists that sexual attraction and gratification is the operation of an elemental instinct which is wholly revealed in the particulars of sexual activity itself. In fact we can be aware of instincts only as 'the psychical representative of an endosomatic, continuously flowing source of stimulation'.[11] The instinct itself is 'without quality', and might be conceptualised as 'lying on the border between the mental and the physical'. But, inasmuch as it is a 'psychical representation', then, like all representations, it is subject to processes of transformation (displacement, condensation, rationalisation) within the psychic apparatus.

Sexuality, like the oneiric image, is riven with the contingent and arbitrary, with a fundamental plasticity which is concealed within conventional forms which have been endowed with the character of 'naturalness'. Freud begins his discussion by pointing to this conventionalisation of sexual behaviour, and to the misunderstanding of the nature of sexuality to which, paradoxically, this has led. The strong prejudice against the choice of any sexual object other than a mature individual of the opposite sex had led the sexologists of the latter part of the nineteenth century to seek to account for 'sexual aberrations' in terms of degeneracy, innate character- istics (mutations) or accidental environmental conditions. However:

> Experiences of the cases that are considered abnormal has shown us that in them the sexual instinct and the sexual object are merely soldered together – a fact which we have been in danger of over- looking in consequence of the uniformity of the normal picture, where the object appears to form part and parcel of the instinct. We are thus warned to loosen the bond that exists in our thoughts between instinct and object. It seems probable that the sexual instinct is in the first instance independent of its object; nor is its origin likely to be due to its object's attraction.
>
> (SE 7, p. 148)

This point is made with equal clarity through a consideration of the very different sexual conventions established in parts of the ancient world:

> The ancients glorified the instinct and were prepared on its account to honour even an inferior object; while we despise the instinctual activity in itself, and find excuses for it only in the merits of the object.
>
> (SE 7, p. 149)

The mobility of the sexual instinct and its readiness for conventionalisation is even more evident in the incidence of the so-called 'perversions'. Freud points out that if the 'aim' of the sexual instinct is genital copulation then a wide range of normal sexual activity must be included within the scope of the perversions. Thus, for example, sexual attraction generally brings about an eroticisation of the entire person, and not just of the genital area (and would be thought abnormal if it did not), and is usually accompanied by an 'intellectual infatuation'; a general overvaluation of all the char- acteristics of the chosen person. Similarly kissing is not merely an accepted but is a highly valued practice. The perversions, indeed, represent the fundamental catalogue of erotic possibilities, and it is in their more ex- treme variants that the most complete 'idealisation' occurs. It is here that a genuine 'omnipotence of love' is evident; and in these abnormalities can be seen 'amalgamations which have been lost to view in the uniform behaviour of normal people'.[12]

Rather than reveal the extremes to which the sexual instinct may go to create possibilities for gratification, the perversions actually demonstrate the extent to which 'normal' sexuality is shaped and directed by internal resistances (shame, disgust and morality) to its absolutely free expression. Indeed, hysteria, which consists in somatic 'transcriptions' of 'emotionally cathected mental processes', may be regarded as 'the negative of per- versions'.[13] That is to say, hysterics do not simply repress impulses which in healthy people find their expression in normal sexual activity, 'they give expression (by conversion) to instincts which would be described as *perverse* in the widest sense of the word if they could be expressed directly in phantasy and action without being diverted from consciousness'.[14]

As it must be assumed 'that an unbroken chain bridges the gap between the neuroses in all their manifestations and normality', this approach allows Freud to transpose the analysis of individual cases to a much more general level. In letters to Fliess he had talked of discovering an 'architecture of hysteria', and of finding the general meaning of its symptomology. In linking hysteria to the perversions Freud was able to introduce the logical model, and the somatic structure, of this architecture and place the personal meaning of the symptoms within a general and impersonal framework.

The sexual instinct receives its qualitative character from the interaction between a specific form of excitation and the texture of the organic surface which receives its innervation. In hysteria, as in the perversions, 'erotogenic zones' superseded in the normal case by the genitalia once again become active:

> The part played by the erotogenic zones is immediately obvious in the case of those perversions which assign a sexual significance to the oral and anal orifices. These behave in every respect like a portion of the sexual apparatus. In hysteria these parts of the body and the neighbouring tracts of mucous membrane become the seat of new sensations and changes in innervation – indeed, of processes that can be compared to erection – in just the same way as do the actual genitalia under the excitations of the normal sexual process.
>
> (SE 7, p. 169)

The continuous surface of the body, modified at places into sense organs and mucous membrane, is 'the erotogenic zone *par excellence*'. The body, that is to say, is first of all a continuous surface upon which a process of excitation has inscribed a series of differentiations. The sensory surface and the erotic surface coincide anatomically but receive a different pattern of innervation and undergo separate processes of differentiation. The architectural models, or body-images, which might thus be formed are limited in number and are constructed according to a few basic principles. There is, that is to say, a body-logic to which the psychic apparatus progressively adapts itself, and which imposes its own principles of structure on inner experience in much the same manner as Kant had argued that sensory impressions were perceived through *a priori* categories of the mind. However, in the case of the sexual instinct at least (which is just one of the 'component instincts' which have their source in internal and unknowable organic processes), rather than there being one schema, there are a number of such, internally meaningful, structuring principles.

These alternatives, first glimpsed as the more general framework for the interpretation of hysteria and other neuroses, can be confirmed more directly by the observation of young children. The phenomenon of childhood amnesia, which is itself an unresolved problem for psychological theory, and 'which turns everyone's childhood into something like a prehistoric epoch', is responsible, in Freud's view, 'for the fact that in general no importance is attached to childhood in the development of sexual life'.[15] But simple observations, known to all mothers and nannies, make it obvious not only that sexuality is present from earliest infancy and is expressed openly around the third or fourth year of life, but that it is organised into a number of 'perverse' patterns.

Freud notes that it is also during the period of childhood amnesia, and extending beyond it throughout the 'latency period' prior to puberty, that are 'built up the mental forces which are later to impede the course of the sexual instinct and, like dams, restrict its flow – disgust, feelings of shame and the claims of aesthetic and moral ideals'.[16] Importantly he adds that although we might easily imagine 'the construction of these dams is a product of education', the appeal to an external restraint of this kind cannot fully explain the course of psychosexual development. The 'energy' required for this construction must itself be derived from the instinct which is being diverted, and the entire process must come under the control of an unconscious organic agency. He has already argued, in discussing the perversions, that disgust and shame are in those cases overcome by the sexual instinct. At this stage Freud merely hints at a general solution by suggesting that the auto-erotic character of childhood sexuality itself arouses feelings of unpleasure, as well as of pleasure, and it is upon the former which are built the peculiar quality of feeling and the mnemic images associated with disgust and shame.

The most striking feature of the 'original configuration' of the sexual instinct is that it has no object outside the body, but establishes paths of gratification in the auto-erotic stimulation of widely dispersed areas across its surface. Freud takes sucking to be the original form of sexual gratification. 'Sensual sucking', he points out, 'involves a complete absorption of the attention and leads either to sleep or even to a motor reaction in the nature of an orgasm'.[17] It is spontaneously accompanied by holding and rhythmic stroking so that it is reasonable to suppose that 'many children proceed by this path from sucking to masturbation'. A mnemic image of pleasure is thus built up and later becomes available as an additional source of pleasure. And while this structural link is made without the intervention of outside agencies, he points out – in a footnote that it has been conjectured refers to experiences in his own infancy – that it may, in fact, be reinforced by contingent events, as 'it is well known that unscrupulous nurses put crying children to sleep by stroking their genitals'.[18]

But sensual sucking already involves a complex displacement and

131

substitution, and thus the establishment of some form of memory; typically the thumb comes to represent the nipple. That is, meaning is established and transformed across body surfaces, and this is possible because pleasure in the stimulation of the erotogenic zone, the lips and inside of the mouth, is originally linked with the need for nourishment:

> No one who has seen a baby sinking back satiated from the breast and falling asleep with flushed cheeks and a blissful smile can escape the reflection that this picture persists as a prototype of the expression of sexual satisfaction in later life.
>
> (SE 7, p. 182)

But the need for repeating sexual satisfaction detaches itself from the purpose of self-preservation, and:

> reveals itself in two ways: by a peculiar feeling of tension, possessing, rather, the character of unpleasure, and by a sensation of itching or stimulation which is centrally conditioned and projected on to the peripheral erotogenic zone.
>
> (SE 7, p. 184)

This repetition effects a general ordering of sexuality into an oral, or cannibalistic 'pre-genital sexual organisation', traces of which survive into later forms:

> Here sexual activity has not yet been separated from the ingestion of food; nor are opposite currents within the activity differentiated. The *object* of both activities is the same; the sexual *aim* consists in the incorporation of the object – the prototype of a process which, in the form of identification, is later to play such an important psychological part. A relic of this constructed phase of organization, which is forced upon our notice by pathology, may be seen in thumb-sucking, in which the sexual activity, detached from the nutritive activity, has substituted for the extraneous object one situated in the subject's own body.
>
> (SE 7, p. 198)

This initial differentiation of the body-surface into zones of feeling does not, then, simply disappear, but is assimilated to later levels of organisation.

The anal zone, similarly, undergoes eroticisation through the stimulation of the mucous membrane which occurs during defecation. The pleasure in intense stimulation and the satisfaction in its removal can be controlled by 'the retention of the faecal mass, which is thus carried out intentionally by the child to begin with, in order to serve, as it were, as a masturbatory stimulus upon the anal zone'. At the same time defecation brings the child into contact 'with an environment hostile to his instinctual impulses', and, as a result, faeces become the first concrete and detachable, but ambivalent, symbol expressing antithetical values – as a 'gift' of part of the child's own body and as worthless 'dirt'. The anal organisation encompasses two opposed currents 'which runs through all sexual life'; an *active* aim of mastery, which is exercised first in relation to muscular self-control, and a *passive* aim of pleasure in the erotogenic mucous membrane. This organisation too has far-reaching implications as it is subsequently transformed into the psychologically meaningful imagery of 'masculine' and 'feminine'.

The sexual stimulation of the genital zone appears briefly in early infancy, reappears at about the fourth year, only to disappear again until puberty. Freud does not attempt a complete explanation of this typical history, but repeats his modified view that seduction is a widespread, but by no means universal, means by which infantile masturbation and other childhood sexual practices are revived.

The period of childhood is a veritable storehouse of every possible means of procuring sexual satisfaction. Indeed, it is not only in relation to self-defining erotogenic zones that childhood sexuality can be observed, but practices of scopophilia, exhibitionism and cruelty, which require other beings as sexual objects, also appear spontaneously and reveal a polymorphously perverse disposition as the origin of all more developed sexual tendencies.

The development of adult sexuality out of the pre-genital organisation is by no means straightforward. On the anatomical completion of the sexual apparatus three distinct source of stimulation have become available to set it in motion: the direct stimulation of the erotogenic zones by external means; internal organic processes; and mental life, 'which itself is a storehouse for external impressions and a receiving-post for internal excitations'.[19] Infantile sexuality is fundamentally different in that it seeks a pleasure continuous with the fore-pleasure of adult sexuality, and is distinct from the end-pleasure, which is the pleasure connected exclusively with the complete discharge of tension. And it is in the possibility of fore-pleasure that earlier eroticised body-images are assimilated, and subordinated, to the genital organisation.

Indeed, Freud argues, the narcissistic character of 'ego-libido', which is realised in early childhood, 'is merely covered by the later extrusions of libido, but in essentials persists behind it'.[20] The vicissitudes of puberty which are characterised by the development of libidinal 'object-choice' are only further and partial differentiation of the 'narcissistic or ego-libido' which is 'the great reservoir from which the object-cathexes are sent out and into which they are withdrawn once more'. Freud's use of terms here is somewhat misleading. He calls the 'original state of things' both 'narcissistic libido' and 'ego-libido', but the notion of the 'ego' already involves a particular level of differentiation in which the 'self' is cathected as an object. The ego, that is, has a certain stability and objectivity which is sustained by a continuous libidinal investment through which it is distinguished from the primary body-images that exist intermittently in erotogenic excitement. And direct experience of narcissistic libido involves a transformation and distortion of normal experience, which is viewed in terms of the 'body-logic' of the ego as an idealised point-mass. The entire architectural structure of narcissistic body-images, from which the ego emerges through a process of differentiation, is known indirectly through imaginative reconstruction. It is only 'from the vantage point of psycho-analysis [that] we can look across a frontier which we may not pass, at the activities of narcissistic libido, and may form some idea of the relation between it and object-libido'.[21]

This understanding of 'the original state of things' also allows Freud to find a non-accidental basis for the Oedipal relationship. The original 'object-choice' is made in terms of narcissistic libido. The primal satis-faction of the breast defines a sexual object outside the infant's body, and it is only later that object is lost. But this, Freud points out, is probably 'just at the time when the child is able to form a total idea of the person to whom the organ that is giving him satisfaction belongs'.[22] And in terms of the earliest of body-images it hardly makes sense to speak of the breast as an external 'object' at all.

Later object-choice is modelled on this original relation, which is not only the focus of the first quasi object-choice, but is the normal route through which erotogenic excitation of various sorts is aroused:

> A child's intercourse with anyone responsible for his care affords him an unending source of sexual excitation and satisfaction from his erotogenic zones. This is especially so since the person in charge of him, who, after all, is as a rule his mother, herself regards him with feelings that are derived from her own sexual life: she strokes him, kisses him, rocks him and quite clearly treats him as a substitute for a complete sexual object.
>
> (SE 7, p. 223)

METAPSYCHOLOGY AND ITS VICISSITUDES

The complications in Freud's theorising is related in part to his difficult personal relations with his followers and more particularly with Jung. Theoretical differences had become clear in their separate approaches to the Schreber case and, more obviously, in Freud's ambitious *Totem and Taboo*, which had been written simultaneously with, and in distinction to, Jung's *Transformations and Symbols of Libido*. The difference between them can be summed up in the observation that Jung's work was a continuation of the Romantic tradition in German cultural life, while Freud's approach was rigorously modern.[23] Thus, where Jung interpreted symbols in terms of presumed archetypes lodged in the soul, Freud developed a distinctively new body-logic to account for the origin and form of mnemic symbols in general.

Freud's metapsychology is an attempt to develop the distinctiveness of his own viewpoint and reassert his superiority over the rebellious son. Yet Jung's influence is not simply rejected, or even repressed. Freud struggled to assimilate what he took to be an important and partially valid point of view which his one-time chosen successor had been guilty of over-extending. Jung had counterposed a non-sexualised psyche to Freud's sexual theory of libido. The metapsychology, though rejecting Jung's view as the basis for a general psychology, nonetheless acknowledged the approach on equal terms with his own. The emerging dualism represents a significant but not a wholly unprecedented development in Freud's views. Freud continued to vacillate over the seduction theory, over the connection between the actual neuroses and the psychoneuroses, and these suppressed dualisms found a more open and complete expression in his metapsychology.

An unmistakable ambivalence, thus, marks Freud's more general theoretical writing. He expressed considerable distaste for the task which, he claims, was made necessary by Jung's defection. And he did not publish the metapsychology in the form of a book, as he had planned, but allowed under half to appear as separate essays, and seems to have destroyed the others.[24] Yet he wrote the series of papers which were to constitute the complete metapsychology quickly and with intense concentration. Whatever personal conflicts might have stimulated their composition, the metapsychology was not just a means of settling accounts with his followers. The continuous extension of the dream theory and of his clinical analysis to a broad range of cultural and historical phenomenon threw up new issues and yielded insights which had then to be assimilated to a general psychological theory. By 1915 the revisions and extensions demanded a more systematic treatment and it was towards a fresh synthesis and clarification that Freud wrote the series of essays on fundamental psychological concepts. Though never published in full, the views which he formulated at that time became the point of departure for all his subsequent theoretical work and through it the general outline and intention of his metapsychology has become clear.

The starting point for this reassessment of his fundamental ideas was clearly stated in an important discussion of narcissism which was published in 1914, and which might be regarded as a general introduction to the major themes of the metapsychology. It marked an attempt, begun several years earlier, and stimulated by his initial collaboration with Jung who was at that time Bleuler's assistant at the Burghölzli psychiatric clinic in Zurich, to include an account of the psychoses within his general psychology. Patients who suffered from what was generally known as dementia praecox, the nomenclature used by the psychiatric authority Kraepelin ('schizophrenia' was introduced by Bleuler in 1911, and quickly established itself in preference to either the older term, or to Freud's brief usage of 'paraphrenia'), were characterised by 'megalomania and diversion of their interest from the external world'.[25] Freud devoted a full length study, based on Schreber's memoirs, to such a case, and the paper on narcissism which followed this discussed the whole issue at a more general level.[26]

Hysterical and obsessional neuroses also displayed a 'turning away' from the world, but in those cases 'erotic relations to people and things' had not been completely abandoned. They had been retained, rather, in a distorted form as fantasy. The neurotic has:

> substituted for real objects imaginary ones from his memory, or has mixed the latter with the former; and . . . he has renounced the initiation of motor activities for the attainment of his aims in connection with these objects.
>
> (SE 14, p. 74)

In the case of schizophrenia, however, 'he seems really to have withdrawn his libido from people and things in the external world, without replacing them by others in phantasy'. And it is just this total withdrawal of object-libido which accounts for their characteristic megalomania:

> The libido that has been withdrawn from the external world has been directed to the ego and thus gives rise to an attitude which may be called narcissism. But the megalomania itself is no new creation; on the contrary, it is, as we know, a magnification and plainer manifestation of a condition which had already existed previously.
>
> (SE 14, p. 75)

These ideas are consistent with the development of his notions about the similarities between the mental life of children and of primitive people. They too are characterised by;

> an over-estimation of the power of their wishes and mental acts, the 'omnipotence of thoughts', a belief in the thaumaturgic force of words, and a technique for dealing with the external world – 'magic' – which appears to be a logical application of those grandiose premises.
>
> (SE 14, p. 75)

Freud hypothesises that 'original libidinal cathexis of the ego' takes place, creating a fundamental division and relation between 'ego-libido' and 'object-libido'. The term 'ego-libido' is somewhat confusing here, and does not refer to the conscious 'self-identity' of waking life, but rather to the whole force of the organically founded drive for self-preservation. The distinction has an obvious parallel with the felt difference between hunger (ego-libido) and love (object-libido). More significantly for Freud, it reflects a double perspective within which human sexual behaviour becomes meaningful:

> The individual does actually carry on a twofold existence: one to serve his own purposes and the other as a link in a chain, which he serves against his wishes, or at least involuntarily. The individual himself regards sexuality as one of his own ends; whereas from another point of view he is an appendage to his germ-plasm, at whose disposal he puts his energies in return for a bonus of pleasure. He is the mortal vehicle of a (possibly) immortal substance – like the inheritor of an entailed property, who is only the temporary holder of an estate which survives him.
>
> (SE 14, p. 78)

It is, thus, considerations of a general biological kind, rather than clinical psychological material, which argue most powerfully for the importance of this distinction. But it is not without psychological significance. In normal people, illness and sleep implies a narcissistic withdrawal of the libido and a loss of interest in the outside world.

In hysteria the relative strengths of these interests vary from the normal, but in the schizophrenic 'end of the world' the object-cathexis is completely swallowed up in the ego, while in the normal state of being in love, the ego-cathexis is reduced to a minimum and 'the subject seems to give up his own personality in favour of an object-cathexis'. It is, in fact, only with the differentiation of object-cathexis from an original state of narcissism that the specific quality of sexual energy as distinct from the energy of the ego-instincts becomes observable.

Where, for whatever reason, object-cathexes are withdrawn, the 'internal working-over' of ego-libido within the psychical apparatus, which, as always, seeks to discharge the unpleasure of over-excitation, sustains a sense of reality attached to imaginary rather than to real objects. And where sexual-libido may be sublimated and displaced, so ego-libido is transformed and projected as an idealisation to which the ego aspires:

> The subject's narcissism makes its appearance displaced on to this new ideal ego, which, like the infantile ego, finds itself possessed of every perfection that is of value . . . . What he projects before him as his ideal is the substitute for the lost narcissism of his childhood in which he was his own ideal.
>
> (SE 14, p. 94)

The schizophrenic experiences this idealisation in a regressive, fantasised form, as delusions of being watched and persecuted. Both ego-libido and sexual-libido are at first narcissistic in nature, but are turned outward in object-cathexes which are at the same time related to the displacement of libido on to an ego ideal 'imposed from without'.

This broader conception of narcissism, and the dualism to which it was (temporarily) related, forms an important part of Freud's metapsychology. The difficulty of 'growing up' in the face of the insistent undertow of narcissism becomes one of its central themes, and one which is given the broadest possible biological interpretation.

Recurrent sources of stimulation originating from within the psychical apparatus are now termed 'instincts' and provide, by their unresponsiveness to muscular movement and avoidance behaviour, a general basis for distinguishing between the 'inside' and the 'outside' of the body.[27] Reflex action is powerless to remove the build-up of internal stimuli, which thus:

> make far higher demands on the nervous system and cause it to undertake involved and interconnected activities by which the external world is so changed as to afford satisfaction to the internal source of stimulation. Above all, they oblige the nervous system to renounce its ideal intention of keeping off stimulation. We may therefore well conclude that instincts and not external stimuli are the true motive forces behind the advances that have led the nervous system, with its unlimited capacities, to its present high level of development.
>
> (SE 14, p. 120)

This view, of course, goes back to the unpublished *Project for a Scientific Psychology*, but, rather than attempt to anchor psychology in a physiological model of brain function, Freud now proposes to interpret it within the context of a general evolutionary biology. He continues:

> There is naturally nothing to prevent our supposing that the instincts themselves are, at least in part, precipitates of the effects of external stimulation, which in the course of phylogensis have brought about modifications in the living substance.
>
> (SE 14, p. 120)

This was not, to be sure, an entirely novel theme in Freud's work, and he had elaborated on various aspects of the connection between psychology and a phylogenetic history of the species in letters to Fliess as early as 1897. But in his metapsychology these considerations became a central theme. The postulate of a 'biological purpose' for the mental apparatus is more basic than the division of instincts (for descriptive psychological purposes) into ego (self-preservative) and libido (sexual), which is now treated as no more than a 'working hypothesis'. And in this framework there can be no question of any simple relationship between 'inside' and 'outside', or between a 'pleasure principle' and a 'reality principle'. The situation, in fact, is highly complex, whether described phylogenetically (in terms of the evolutionary development of the species) or ontogenetically (in terms of the development of the individual).

Generally speaking Freud viewed the emergence of 'reality' as dependent on the manner in which the instincts are distributed between three polarities which operate within mental life. The distinction of subject (ego)/object (external world) is complicated by its relationship to the differentiation of pleasure/unpleasure, and of active/passive. In the 'primal psychical situation . . . at the very beginning of mental life, the ego is cathected with instincts and is to some extent capable of satisfying them on itself'.[28] Here there is a coincidence of 'narcissism' (in terms of ego-instincts) and 'auto-erotism' (in terms of sexual-instincts), and, therefore, 'the external world is not cathected with interest . . . and is indifferent for purposes of satisfaction'. The 'ego-subject' coincides with pleasurable sensations and the external world, if it forces itself upon the subject at all as a source of unwanted stimuli, is identified with unpleasure. However, in relation to instincts of self-preservation the ego comes to 'acquire objects' from the world which have become sources of pleasure (introjection), and expels whatever within itself has become a cause of unpleasure (projection). Thus emerges a pure 'pleasure-ego' which defines reality inclusively in terms of the sources of pleasure:

> For the pleasure-ego the external world is divided into a part that is pleasurable, which it has incorporated into itself, and a remainder that is extraneous to it. It has separated off a part of its own self, which it projects into the external world and feels as hostile. After this new arrangement, the two polarities coincide once more: the ego-subject coincides with pleasure, and the external world with unpleasure (with what was earlier indifference).
>
> (SE 14, p. 136)

The earlier distinction between love and indifference is replaced by the antithesis between love and hate. Whereas 'love' is connected directly with the sexual instincts, 'hate' covers the relation of 'unpleasure' of any sort:

> The ego hates, abhors and pursues with intent to destroy all objects which are a source of unpleasurable feeling for it, without taking into account whether they mean a frustration of sexual satisfaction or of the satisfaction of self-preservative needs. Indeed, it may be asserted that the true prototypes of the relation of hate are derived not from sexual life, but from the ego's struggle to preserve and maintain itself.
>
> (SE 14, p. 138)

This is significant, particularly in the development of social relations in which ego-instincts and their frustration play a decisive part.

The metapsychology, however, after introducing this dualism concentrates its discussion of repression and the unconscious primarily on an elaboration of the psychical mechanism in relation to the vicissitudes of the sexual instinct. This involves not only a restatement of the 'topographical' distinction between the 'systems' Unconscious, Conscious and Preconscious, and a confirmation of the 'dynamic' aspect of all mental contents, but the emergence of a distinctive 'economic point of view'. Repression is not a singular act, but the continuous 'turning away' from consciousness of unwanted elements. Both 'primal repression' in which the original 'psychic representative' of the instinct is repressed, and its chains of mental derivatives which suffer the same fate through its 'after pressure', requires a continuous expenditure of psychical energy, and the effects of this expenditure can be traced in both normal and pathological processes.

It is in terms of a careful consideration, from both a topographical and an economic point of view, of some of the linguistic features of the onset of schizophrenia that Freud establishes his most fruitful point of contact with the psychotic world. Going back to remarks in the 1895 *Project*, and even earlier to his pre-analytic study *On Aphasia*,[29] Freud points out that the characteristic transformation in schizophrenia is towards '*organ-speech*'; that is the whole content of the patient's thought and experience is represented in relation to bodily states and organs. A patient, for example, who felt she had been treated with insufficient refinement by her lover, described a feeling of 'being put into a certain position', that is of being 'put in a false position'. And the same patient complained that her lover's eyes 'were not right, they were twisted', which is to say he was a hypocrite and 'looked different' each time she saw him. More generally Freud refers to Bleuler's extensive material and concludes that:

> In schizophrenia *words* are subjected to the same process as that which makes the dream-images out of latent dream thoughts – to what we have called the primary psychical process. They undergo condensation, and by means of displacement transfer their cathexes to one another in their entirety. The process may go so far that a single word, if it is specially suitable on account of its numerous connections, takes over the representation of a whole train of thought.
>
> (SE 14, p. 199)

The entire 'strangeness' of schizophrenic substitute-formation as compared, for example, to hysterical symptom-formation or everyday parapraxes is derived from 'the predominance of what has to do with words over what has to do with things'. In schizophrenia object-cathexes are given up, that is to say the patient is withdrawn from all interest in the world, but 'the cathexis of the *word*-presentations of objects is retained'.[30] It is just this distinction, and the peculiarity associated with treating a word as a thing, which is suggestive of the distinction between conscious and unconscious presentations:

> The two are not, as we supposed, different registrations of the same content in different psychical localities, nor yet different functional states of cathexis in the same locality; but the conscious presentation

comprises the presentation of the thing plus the presentation of the word belonging to it, while the unconscious presentations is the presentation of the thing alone.

(SE 14, p. 201)

The process of repression splits words from things and thus effectively removes them from consciousness and linguistic modes of mental functioning.

These considerations lead Freud naturally to a reconsideration and amplification of certain elements of his dream theory. In the context of a more generalised biological framework, sleep rather than dreams becomes the central issue, and while 'dreams only show us the dreamer in so far as he is *not* sleeping; nevertheless they are bound to reveal at the same time characteristics of sleep itself'.[31] Sleep involves a temporal regression, in relation both to the ego, which is 'carried to the point of restoring primitive narcissism', and of the libido, 'which goes back to the stage of hallucinatory satisfaction of wishes'.

The egoism of dreams is now understandable in terms of a regression to narcissism. Hence also the magnification of all bodily processes, and the diagnostic value of dreaming in detecting incipient bodily changes which mark the onset of illness, both of which depend on the withdrawal of cathexes from the external world. But this withdrawal is rarely complete, and dreams may take as their starting point 'day residues' which have not wholly submitted to this process of regression. This persistence may be a result of its having already served as a point of contact with an unconscious wish which can be expressed through it. The dream-wish:

must be sharply distinguished from the day's residues; it need not have existed in waking life and it may already display the irrational character possessed by everything that is unconscious when it is translated into the conscious.

(SE 14, p. 225)

Dreams involve a *topographical* as well as a temporal regression. During sleep, the dream-wish formed in the preconscious cannot be discharged in motor activity, or gain access to an intentional and rational consciousness, but, rather, undergoes a reversal and is discharged as hallucinatory images. Here thoughts are transformed into images, or, as the studies of schizophrenia had revealed, 'word-presentations are taken back to the thing-presentations which correspond to them'. The dream process seems, from a metapsychological standpoint, more dominated by 'considerations of representability' than by considerations of censorship. This allows Freud to distinguish between the dream-work and the strange deformations of schizophrenia:

In the latter, what becomes the subject of modification by the primary process are the words themselves in which the preconscious thought

141

was expressed; in dreams, what are subject to this modification are not the words, but the thing-presentations to which the words have been taken back. In dreams there is a topographical regression; in schizophrenia there is not.

(SE 14, p. 229)

Interestingly the process of interpreting dreams illuminates the process of dream-construction but tends to divert attention from the finished dream which, for the dreamer, is experienced immediately and as a hallucinated plastic image. The metapsychology, as distinct from the interpretation of dreams, focuses directly on this striking characteristic.

These considerations make clear the fact that dreaming establishes two quite distinct and separable conditions: 'it not only brings hidden or repressed wishes into consciousness; it also represents them, with the subject's entire belief, as fulfilled'.[32] Freud points out that there is no necessary connection between these two states. When awake we can readily distinguish reality from wishes, and, on the other hand, belief in reality normally seems to be bound up with perception through the senses. If there was nothing more to hallucination than regression then every regression would carry with it an internal sense of reality:

But we are quite familiar with situations in which a process of regressive reflection brings to consciousness very clear mnemic images, though we do not on that account for a single moment take them for real perceptions. Again, we could very well imagine the dream-work penetrating to mnemic images of this kind, making conscious to us what was previously unconscious, and holding up to us a wishful phantasy which rouses our longing, but which we should not regard as a real fulfilment of the wish.

(SE 14, p. 231)

The realism of our dreams indicates that in a state of sleep the 'reality-testing' function of consciousness, which hinges on whether muscular action can remove a stimulus, is completely withdrawn. That this also can occur in the waking state is revealed in Bleuler's descriptions of what had been termed 'amentia', which is a reaction to a severe loss, in which the insupportable aspects of the external world are simply replaced by a directly hallucinated and preferable alternative.

In the context of the metapsychology, rather than of interpretation, all the fundamental characteristics of dreams can be deduced from a proper understanding of the condition of sleep. The background to this 'supplement' to his dream theory, and to the metapsychology as a whole, has become more prominent in recent years as part of a general reassessment of Freud's work in the context of post-Darwinian biology.[33] This is a valuable perspective within which to interpret some, though by no means all, of

Freud's psychological insights. The speculative character of his own bio-logical views, which remained influenced by Fliess and embraced Lamarckian ideas, has become more evident since the publication of a draft of one of the previously unpublished papers on metapsychology. The 'Overview of the Transference Neuroses', which he accurately calls 'a phylogenetic fantasy', was the final paper of the series and indicates the way in which Freud envisaged his psychology might be developed on a systematic basis. His central concern is to link together the various pathologies in a signifi-cant way. He returned to the issue at various times as the problem of 'the choice of illness'; what determined that one person should become a hysteric, another an obsessive, a third schizophrenic, and so on.

According to Freud, the various neuroses and psychoses formed a syste-matic series in relation to the temporal regression which they displayed. The 'age of onset' varied systematically; anxiety hysteria is the oldest, followed by conversion hysteria (which dates from the fourth year), while obsessional neuroses do not appear until between the ages of 9 and 10. The narcissistic neuroses are absent from childhood, schizophrenia is classically a disturbance of puberty, while paranoia and melancholia/mania appear only in maturity. Thus, rather than separate the neuroses (regression of sexual libido) from psychoses (regression of ego libido) a unified series emerges:

anxiety hysteria – conversion hysteria – obsessional neurosis – dementia praecox – paranoia – melancholia/mania

Furthermore, if the matter is considered in terms of phylogenetic re-gression (rather than ontogenetic temporal regression), then a similar series emerges. Influenced by Ferenczi's phylogenetic speculations, Freud is tempted to see in 'the dispositions to anxiety hysteria, conversion hysteria, and obsessional neurosis regressions to phases that the whole human race had to go through at some time from the beginning to the end of the Ice Age'.[34] The speculative history of *Totem and Taboo* seems almost tame in comparison with the boldness of this hypothesis. He argues that it was the privations of the early Ice Age that first created a state of anxiety. Prior to the Ice Age he seems to regard environmental conditions for the species as so benign that they remained cocooned in a kind of natural paradise. But as 'the hitherto predominantly friendly outside world, which bestowed every satisfaction, transformed itself into a mass of threatening perils', it is conceivable that the threatened ego abandoned its object-cathexes and retained its energy as anxiety. As external reality kept up an unrelenting pressure primal humans had to reduce their needs by limiting their ca-pacity for reproduction. This resulted both in the onset of guilt (over infanticide) and in the practice of pre-genital 'perverse' sexuality, giving rise to an epoch of conversion hysteria. This primal regression of sexuality released psychic energies which allowed the males to develop their intelligence and mastery of the world. Language, the animistic world view and the social situation analysed in *Totem and Taboo* emerged. Obsessional neurosis 'recapitulates' this period. The generation of the sons, fearful of the father, are driven out when they become sexual competitors. Thus, the onset of schizophrenia is a living through of phylogenetic castration, and 'the speech alterations and hallucinatory storms . . . represent restitutive attempts'.[35] The replacement of the horde with a band of brothers could be sustained only by the development of pacified social bonds based on homosexual affection. Paranoia emerges as an attempt to ward off this phylogenetic inheritance. Finally melancholy/mania, the successive waves of ecstasy and depression which characterise the mature psychosis, recalls the oscillation between triumph and mourning following upon the primal patricide as it is embodied in religious festival and folklore.

These phylogenetic speculations go further than the contextual assumptions of *Totem and Taboo,* and are continuous not only with them, but more significantly with the background to *Three Essays on the Theory of Sexuality,* and to arguments he had first made in letters to Fliess. The pursuit of 'non-accidental factors' in accounting for the neurosis led ultimately to the phylogenetic fantasy. Certainly, though he did not publish 'Overview of the Transference Neuroses', its implications for his dream theory were given some consideration in *Introductory Lectures on Psycho-Analysis,* which were written at the same period. There the *regressive* character of the dream-work is emphasised:

> it harks back to states of our intellectual development which have long since been superseded – to picture-language, to symbolic connections, to conditions, perhaps, which existed before our thought-language had developed.
>
> (SE 15, p. 199)

Dreams, which had proved to be 'the royal road' to the unconscious, might also reveal the features of archaic forms of psychic life:

> The prehistory into which the dream-work leads us back is of two kinds – on the one hand, into the individual's prehistory, his childhood, and on the other, in so far as each individual somehow recapitulates in an abbreviated form the entire development of the human race, into phylogenetic prehistory too.
>
> (SE 15, p. 199)

Indeed, 'the symbolic connections, which the individual has never acquired by learning', to which Freud had devoted much more space in the second and subsequent editions of *The Interpretation of Dreams,* 'may justly claim to be regarded as a phylogenetic heritage'.

The nature of the wishes revealed in dreams, 'actively evil and extravagantly sexual' are comprehensible as aspects of this double regression:

It is children, and precisely in those earliest years which are later veiled by amnesia, who often exhibit this egoism to an extremely marked degree Children love themselves first, and it is only later that they learn to love others and to sacrifice something of their own ego to others.

(SE 15, p. 204)

In fact 'it is literally true that *his egoism has taught him to love*'.

In dreams, the individual has access to fantasies and to symbolic modes of expression which reappear in the body-imagery of hysteria. All these *primal fantasies* are conceived as part of our phylogenetic endowment:

In them the individual reaches beyond his own experience into primaeval experience at points where his own experience has been too rudimentary. It seems to me quite possible that all the things that are told to us in analysis as phantasy – the seduction of children, the inflaming of sexual excitement by observing parental intercourse, the threat of castration (or rather castration itself) – were once real occurrences in the primaeval times of the human family, and that children in their phantasies are simply filling in the gaps in individual truth with prehistoric truth.

(SE 16, p. 371)

Does the metapsychology amount to a new synthesis of Freudian insights?[36] His stress throughout these papers on general biological principles is not intended to 'explain' the psychological processes he is describing by reducing their difference to a conceptual unity, but, rather, offers to each a common context in which their particular and irreducible significance can be highlighted. Freud, in fact, defines 'metapsychological' in terms of a comprehensive description of a psychical process in terms of three distinct points of view: dynamic, topographic and economic. Significantly he does not argue that the resulting 'presentation' can be regarded as a theoretical unity or totality of some kind. And in the future the phylogenetic perspective (should it be established on a credible basis) will not provide a synthesis of these different and irreconcilable modes analysis, but is likely, rather, to further complicate the picture by adding to them a fourth essential and distinctive approach. Each of these 'points of view' retains their distinctive and elemental character. Psychological descriptions are points of view from which we can 'make sense' of processes which, in reality, are simple, but to which we have no direct access in experience. Both experience and the conceptual language of the mind are highly differentiated sectors of the inclusive surface of life, and our efforts to represent this more inclusive reality are limited by the means at our disposal. We are constrained always to represent the whole by a part.

145

DETACHMENT AND ANXIETY

The mechanism of representation is a limiting condition of experience. We become aware of these limits as feelings which are oddly detached and unconnected with the rest of psychic life. Joking and parapraxes, for example and in a minor way, illustrate that a certain level of detachment is characteristic of modern life. Most social encounters are neither so demanding nor so absorbing that we are wholly engaged in the interaction they require. Conformity to everyday conventions does not exhaust our supply of psychic energy so that, to varying degrees, we can observe and as it were inwardly comment on our every action. And through slips of the tongue, amnesias and other symptomatic acts, or in joking word-plays, we regularly accuse ourselves of hypocrisy, cynicism and scepticism. Hardly any conversation remains free of subtle innuendo or, consequently, of its quota of self-mockery.

But there is a more radical sense in which this detachment from the surface of life takes place. The disjunction between the polite forms of public life and the inward reality of our thoughts and feelings is far more pronounced in relation to the connection (or, rather, disconnection) between our own most primitive 'feelings' and the 'mnemic-images' through which we experience them. This can be illustrated by a condition which is best understood as a logical and psychological negation of play; that is, anxiety.

No concept or term in Freud's vocabulary remains wholly constant and consistent. In a manner which is quite typical of the modern life he sought to describe, his analytic vocabulary was continually revised and, from time to time, completely overhauled. The 'vicissitudes' of his theoretical language is illustrated by the convoluted history of his use of the term 'anxiety'.[37] But throughout the changes in meaning and context, the characteristic directionality of his thought is again evident. This is a movement from the classical bourgeois 'egoism' of the 'point-mass' in intentional movement through empty space, to a 'dispersed' and decentred subjectivity absorbed in and by the fluid transformations of the surface to which it clings.

In 1895 Freud had proposed distinguishing 'anxiety neurosis' from 'neurasthenia'. Both belonged to the group of so-called 'actual neuroses' which, unlike the psychoneuroses, originated not from an unpredictable shock, but from a definite and repeated physical cause, which includes excessive masturbation, all states of 'unconsummated excitation' and 'coitus reservatus by means of condoms'. The clinical picture of anxiety neurosis consists in general irritability, anxious expectation (hypochondria, moral anxiety, excessive scrupulousness, doubting mania, etc.), anxiety attacks (involving various combination of a large number of physiological irregularities), pavor nocturnus of adults (waking up at night in a fright), vertigo, 'protective' phobias, digestive disturbances and 'para-sthesias' which, like the hysterical aura, accompany vertigo.[38]

Now, although no 'psychical origin' can be detected in such conditions, which result directly from the accumulation of undischarged excitation, Freud does recognise the peculiar nature of the symptoms themselves. Thus of anxiousness in general, or what he terms a 'quantum of anxiety in a freely floating state', which is 'constantly lurking in the background', he remarks that:

> it can suddenly break through into consciousness without being aroused by a train of ideas, and thus provokes an anxiety attack. An anxiety attack of this sort may consist of the feeling of anxiety, alone, without any associated idea, or accompanied by the interpretation that is nearest to hand, such as ideas of the extinction of life, or of a stroke, or of a threat of madness.
>
> (SE 3, pp. 93–4)

Thus, although caused by specific 'sexual *noxae*', anxiety gives rise to a curiously detached state, in which an internal sense of fear or fright is not immediately linked to any obvious threat. A host of somatic disturbances may thus become associated with anxious states, and 'from this combin-ation the patient picks out in particular now one, now another, factor'.

Freud retained this non-psychic theory of anxiety states in relation to the 'actual neuroses' even after he had abandoned the seduction theory in favour of a fantasy theory of the aetiology of the psychoneuroses. But he became increasingly interested in the role of anxiety within the psycho-neuroses where, though not as central to the clinical picture, it frequently played a significant part in the symptomology. In the 'Little Hans' case history he discussed the origin of infantile anxiety in relation to the onset of repression of powerful longings for the mother. In his case, increased affection for his mother 'turned suddenly into anxiety'. It 'succumbed to repression' and 'like every infantile anxiety, without an object to begin with: it was still anxiety and not yet fear'.[39] It seems that anxiety as 'object-less fear' is an extension and a generalisation of an original fear of losing the mother, which is well founded in his experience of the onset of repression. Inasmuch as repression succeeds, Little Hans is left with un-satisfied longing as well as fear of loss, neither of which can be consciously attached to its 'real' object. The resulting anxiety is an indefinite state of fear which is displaced on to more or less appropriate substitute objects; in the case of Hans to a fear of horses, then to a fear of going out into the street, then on to his father. Little Hans experienced anxiety attacks in the street, and developed phobias and obsessional thoughts which were moti-vated by the specific gain in falling ill; that he would be able to remain with his mother.

Such 'anxiety-hysterias' are 'the most common of all psychoneurotic

147

disorders' and are '*par excellence* the neuroses of childhood'.[40] They do not depend upon peculiar constitutional predispositions, or specific accidental causes, and thus are widespread. The development of phobias is almost inevitable:

> From the outset in anxiety-hysteria the mind is constantly at work in the direction of once more psychically binding the anxiety which has become liberated; but this work can neither bring about a retransformation of the anxiety into libido, nor can it establish any contact with the complexes which were the source of the libido. Nothing is left for it but to cut off access to every possible occasion that might lead to the development of anxiety, by erecting mental barriers in the nature of precautions, inhibitions, or prohibitions; and it is these defensive structures that appear to us in the form of phobias and that constitute to our eyes the essence of the disease.
>
> (SE 10, p. 117)

Soon Freud included anxiety within the psychoneuroses. The model of tension reduction within the psychical apparatus allowed him to argue that 'accumulated excitation', from whatever source, might remain 'unbound' as anxiety rather than undergo 'conversion' into somatic symptoms. Indeed, the notion of anxiety as the 'transformation of accumulated tension' goes back to his correspondence with Fliess and is repeated in the metapsychology of 1915.[41] However, accepting that a psychical trauma, as well as a physical cause, might be an originating factor allowed anxiety to be interpreted, as in the case of Little Hans, in terms of loss, or fear of loss; of the mother, of the penis, etc. And, given the general shift in his analytic stance from explanation in terms of sexual attack to fantasy, anxiety can also be assimilated to infantile fantasy. Thus, he claims, that children witnessing, or overhearing, the 'primal scene' of intercourse between their parents 'divine something uncanny', which arouses anxiety.[42]

In fact, the close connection between repression and the arousal of anxiety is brought out by Freud in his essay 'The Uncanny', one of his most successful pieces of literary criticism. Examining stories by E.T.A. Hoffman, who Freud regarded as the literary master of the uncanny, particularly in 'The Sand-Man' and 'The Devil's Elixir', he argues that the uncanny is aroused by the unconscious recognition of something once familiar that has been repressed. Hoffman invokes the omnipotence of thoughts, the phenomenon of 'doubles' and the entire vanished world of infantile thought and feeling.

There is, clearly, a connection between the notion of a traumatic loss and the idea of repression as the loss of the infantile as a valued period of life. And, whatever the precise mechanism involved, anxiety can be viewed as transformed libido, which, unbound to psychic contents, is subsequently attached to some more or less appropriate mnemic symbol, giving rise to characteristic rationalisations, phobic avoidance and compulsive ritualisation of behaviour.

Freud seems never to have been wholly satisfied with this account of anxiety. As early as the 1895 *Project* he speculated over the development of 'signals' of unpleasure that would act automatically to inhibit the aversive source. And in the metapsychology this idea is revived and shortly afterwards in the *Introductory Lectures* is linked to the specific 'feeling' of anxiety. In that more general treatment Freud begins by connecting anxiety with 'rational fears' of threatening objects and situations in the external world. Anxiety is aroused with the perception of such situations, and 'may be regarded as a manifestation of the self-preservative instinct'.[43] Anxiety would then seem to be directly linked to our knowledge of the external world and to our ability to master its threats. Again this is related to the idea of a signal. Knowledge allows us to anticipate and take evasive or other action before a threatening situation becomes overwhelmingly dangerous.

But, Freud points out, this view of 'realistic anxiety' is hardly adequate. Anxiety is clearly 'inexpedient' in a situation of danger, and indeed, when excessive it paralyses action. Freud argues, rather, that anxiety, like other affects, is best understood as 'the repetition of some particular significant experience'. And given the generality of realistic anxiety 'this experience could only be a very early impression of a very general nature, placed in the prehistory not of the individual but of the species'.[44] Anxiety, that is to say, can be understood in the same way as hysteria, as the unconscious repetition of a consciously forgotten, primal experience. In this context, he suggests that:

> it is in the *act of birth* that there comes about the combination of unpleasurable feelings, impulses of discharge and bodily sensations which has become the prototype of the effects of a mortal danger and has ever since been repeated by us as the state of anxiety.
>
> (SE 16, p. 396)

The birth trauma is prototypical both in terms of its form – restriction in breathing, heightened attention – and in terms of it relation – separation from the mother. The ubiquity of anxiety is accounted for in terms of this origin together with a universal 'disposition to repeat'.

Freud argues that the process of repression is the fundamental intermediary in relations between anxiety and neurosis. Anxiety replaces any affect whose 'ideational content' is subject to repression, irrespective of its specific quality. Freud refers to anxiety as the 'current coinage' of repression and it is, therefore, the prelude to symptom formation for all neuroses. It is clear in the case of compulsive behaviour that any voluntary surrender of the symptom, which is in many cases recognised by the patient as absurd, results in an immediate increase in anxiety. The result of the process of repression is:

149

either a generating of anxiety pure and simple, or anxiety accompanied by the formation of a symptom, or a more complete formation of a symptom without anxiety. It would thus seem not to be wrong in an abstract sense to assert that in general symptoms are only formed to escape an otherwise unavoidable generating of anxiety.

(SE 16, p. 404)

Freud also argues that the relation between realistic and neurotic anxiety can be understood on the basis of the distinction he had formalised in his metapsychology between the ego instincts and the libido. Realistic anxiety is a response to external threats to the ego, while neurotic anxiety develops in relation to libidinal dangers which are subsequently projected into the external world. Thus:

Just as the attempt at flight from an external danger is replaced by standing firm and the adoption of expedient measures of defence, so too the generation of neurotic anxiety gives place to the formation of symptoms, which results in the anxiety being bound.

(SE 16, p. 405)

And just as a careful examination of sexual perversions had revealed their normality for children, so observations of children demonstrate that it is neurotic anxiety, rather than the quite different realistic anxiety, which is the normal condition of childhood (and therefore of primitive and archaic) experience. Children show very little inclination to fear external dangers. Freud had shown, after all, that they have quite a different assessment, compared to adults, of their significance in relation to external reality. Young children typically alarm their parents by their dangerous games and show no fear in many situations which 'ought' to arouse realistic anxiety. On the other hand obsessive and compulsive behaviour is common in childhood, as are phobias of all sorts.

It is not, that is to say, just their weakness or helplessness (which goes unnoticed by them) which is the condition of generating anxiety in children. General apprehensiveness is common in children and, Freud argues, is a result of the onset of repression within a world of megalomaniac narcissism. The first phobias, Freud points out, are connected with the fearful loss of the mother. Separated from the mother the child's libido is transformed by disappointment and longing into anxiety, and thence into fear of anything associated with the loss, such as the dark. Now, in fact, Freud can argue that anxiety is not so much the consequence but rather an aspect of repression: 'Repression corresponds to an attempt at flight by the ego from libido which is felt as a danger.'[45]

The more systematic presentation attempted in the *Introductory Lectures*, which might be read as a version of the missing metapsychological paper on anxiety, underwent further development, along with Freud's general theoretical framework, in the direction of an 'ego psychology'. His most extensive discussion of anxiety appears in his 'revisionist' work *Inhibition, Symptom and Anxiety*, which, written in 1925, recast his most basic ideas in the light of his new topological categories of ego, id and super-ego. Anxiety is here viewed 'realistically' as emanating from the ego, which goes back, as in the case of Little Hans or the Wolf Man, to fear of castration. Anxiety produces repression, not the other way around. And while the repeated experience of separation might seem to prepare the ego, and, so to speak, lead it towards the fear of castration, the birth trauma theory does not seem to be essentially connected to either separation, loss or castration. The shock of birth cannot be experienced as a separation because there is, for the new-born, not yet any perceivable boundary to its own body. And even if there were, why should anxiety, rather than grief, follow upon this primal separation?

Freud admits that 'anxiety is not so simple a matter', and concedes that 'up till now we have arrived at nothing but contradictory views about it'.[46] The peculiar character of unpleasure in anxiety, and the extent to which it seems to be definitely bound up with particular physiological processes, encouraged Freud in the view (derived ultimately from Darwin) that, along with other affective states, it is the reproduction of an early 'perhaps even pre-individual, experience[s] of vital importance'. Affects, he goes on:

> I should be inclined to regard as universal, typical and innate hysterical attacks, as compared to the recently and individually acquired attacks which occur in hysterical neuroses and whose origin and significance as mnemic symbols have been revealed by analysis.
>
> (SE 20, p. 133)

Anxiety is objectless fear, and the specific feeling tone which we recognise in anxiety is a literally objectless representation; a 'feeling' which has not yet been projected onto the outside world and attached to a suitable object. Anxiety, and other affects, is a kind of perception of instinctual impulses without accompanying images drawn from the external world. It is often inexpedient because it repeats, in any situation of danger, a physiological reaction which, at one point (possibly at birth), was appropriate. And this mechanism might have been retained because, although inexpedient in real situations of danger, it is an effective warning, or signalling device, prompting us to take realistic action as a means to reduce anxiety and, thus, avoid whatever danger threatened. These varied points of view, and the exceptional indecisiveness of Freud's discussion, alerts the reader to the difficulties of the issue. Freud finally attempted to resolve the complications by arguing that loss, separation and the form of anxiety are comprehensible in the light of the *helplessness* of the infant in the face of its own instinctual demands. Birth and the increasing tension of unsatisfied needs must be experienced as an overwhelming disturbance in the economy of the narcissistic libido, and as a repetition of the situation of danger. The reaction of anxiety is still expedient for the infant because it results automatically in its crying out and attracting its mother's attention. It is only as the infant associates the presence of the mother with the removal of internally generated tensions that anxiety shifts to the situation of being separated. In both cases anxiety is a response to the physiological and mental helplessness of the infant. Anxiety, like sexual pleasure, has a tendency to excite a prefigured body-image which in this instance is focused on the respiratory system. But unlike sexuality, this structure is not capable of a series of transformations into new structures but retains its original form. There is no variety of *anxio-genic* zones, because anxiety cannot be harnessed and directed to some purpose beyond that of signalling a danger. What does undergo 'development' is the conception of the situation which arouses anxiety, which changes from separation anxiety, to castration anxiety, to moral anxiety.[47]

Though Freud's later theory views anxiety in terms of ego-defence, his efforts to trace it back to an originating cause or situation are no more successful than were his efforts to bring to light the originating trauma of hysteria. In effect he describes a psychic world in which affects appear mysteriously, as if from nowhere, and literally leave people breathless. Much of our inner life is consumed with the effort of 'secondary revision'; of hastily attaching 'appropriate' mnemic-images to the affective states which incomprehensibly sweep over us. What does emerge from his tortured discussions of anxiety is that, in the case of aversive affects, as much as with pleasure, the fundamental rule of metapsychology is repetition.

REPETITION

Following Groos, who had drawn attention in a general biological context to an 'instinct' to practise given capacities, Freud argues that *play* in childhood is a preliminary stage of joking. Play discovers certain pleasurable effects:

> which arise from a repetition of what is similar, a rediscovery of what is familiar, similarity of sound, etc., and which are to be explained as unsuspected economies in psychical expenditure.

(SE 8, p. 128)

Initially, play is an unmotivated activity organised by an underlying tendency towards and 'peculiar pleasure in constant repetition'.[48] But this repetition becomes 'rationalised' (as does the repetition of anxiety) in terms of an emerging 'economic rationality' which operates within the psychic apparatus:

> This play is brought to an end by the strengthening of a factor that deserves to be described as the critical faculty or reasonableness. The

play is now rejected as being meaningless or actually absurd; as a result of criticism it becomes impossible.

(SE 8, p. 128)

Play is simple repetition of freely practised movements, a process which establishes certain elementary preferences for bodily action. The 'economy' of effort gained through repetition has no other 'utilitarian' purpose. Play (again like anxiety), is not immediately harnessed to the developing ego-instincts, in the way in which the flow of sexuality is progressively directed into erotogenic zones and becomes integrated with purposive and intentional action, but remains free and purposeless.

Play 'belongs' to childhood, therefore, in just the way that sexuality (genitality) does not and, consequently, nothing serves so well to liberate the adult from cares of the ego. The subversiveness of play, its lack of integration with the other instincts and, therefore, its independence from their civilising 'vicissitudes', means that play, more than sexuality, is subversive of 'reality' and consequently is repressed. It becomes available only in 'moods' of frivolity and intoxication and, even then, persists primarily as a delight in verbal nonsense rather than in physical movement. The joke is a sublimated and rationalised form of play; it is what the psychical mechanism exchanges for the absolute liberty of its original condition, and a means of concealing the nonsense which the joke liberates. It is:

a question of prolonging the yield of pleasure from play, but at the same time of silencing the objections raised by criticism which would not allow the pleasurable feeling to emerge. There is only one way of reaching this end: the meaningless combination of words or the absurd putting together of thoughts must nevertheless have a meaning. The whole ingenuity of the joke-work is summoned up in order to find words and aggregations of thoughts in which this condition is fulfilled.

(SE 8, p. 129)

Thus, while the technique of jokes allows access to the inhibited pleasure of play, their purpose (when they have a purpose) lies in disguising expressions of hostility or sexual interest. But, though first claiming that the tendentious joke yields the greater pleasure, Freud progressively came to view the release of what might be termed 'primary playfulness' as a fertile source of enjoyment. In a 'jest' the pleasure:

is derived from play with words or from the liberation of nonsense, and . . . the meaning of the joke is merely intended to protect that pleasure from being done away with by criticism.

(SE 8, p. 131)

A good thought 'bribes our powers of criticism and confuses them', making

153

us more susceptible to the regression of the joke-work. The joke-work fills in, as it were, the distance between the ego and an original source of pleasure. And, just as with sexuality, the mechanism works by an arousal of 'fore-pleasure' through some intellectually refined technique, the more important function of which is to lift internal inhibitions, criticisms and repressions on primal sources of instinctual gratification. It is worth noting here two further aspects of the joke-work. Firstly, like eroticism and dreams, it makes *pleasure* (i.e. a developed 'quality' of the ego) rather than the 'primary process' available. The indifferent 'energy', economies upon which is the energetic source of pleasure, is never directly experienced but must always remain unconscious. Thus the 'refinement' of joking does not simply remove obstacles to the enjoyment of normally forbidden pleasures, but should be thought of as a mechanism through which 'feelings without quality' are translated into 'pleasurable feelings'. Secondly, joking, unlike other pleasure producing mechanisms, is able to connect the ego both with its own primal sources of gratification (play) and also with other instinctual sources of satisfaction (aggression, sensuality).

Repetition is the simple organising principle of play; it is its only rule. Once this is understood the entire 'economic' aspect of psychic life is seen in a new light. It is all too easy to understand repetition as the *consequence* of pleasure, as if, making associations on the basis of utility, only satisfactory actions are repeated. But, after some hesitations, Freud came to grasp the more important truth that pleasure is only gradually experienced through repeatable mnemic-symbols and that its repetition must initially hinge on some non-utilitarian and non-purposive impulse. The play impulse, that is to say, underlies *both* the repetition of pleasure *and* the persistence of anxiety. There is a sense in which pleasure is only accidentally (or at least only distantly) linked with mnemic-symbols associated with the satisfaction of needs and anxiety linked with mnemic-symbols associated with danger. Both sets of symbols are fundamentally 'secondary-revisions' of an underlying tendency to repeat which is, in itself, psychically meaningless.[49]

Pleasure and unpleasure can only be felt as such by the ego, so instinctual impulses and excitations which undergo a series of vicissitudes can give rise to varied 'feelings'. Neurotic unpleasure is, in fact, just 'pleasure that cannot be felt as such'.[50] What seems strange is the extent to which unpleasure is repeated in an involuntary fashion. The example of traumas during wartime provided Freud with much new material. These patients were very frequently troubled by recurrent dreams of their traumatic experiences. Yet such patients seemed not to be much disturbed by conscious memories of these events in their waking lives. Our 'rational' expectation would be quite the reverse; as dreams are wish-fulfilments they would have obliterated the trauma, while the conscious memory would be tormented by the difficulty of forgetting impressive and horrifying experiences.

The 'compulsion to repeat', then, which is so evident in children's play and in psychotherapy where the repressed material is commonly 'transferred' to the analytic situation itself, is by no means limited itself to the repetition of pleasure, but:

also recalls from the past experiences which include no possibility of pleasure, and which can never, even long ago, have brought satisfaction even to instinctual impulses which have since been repressed.

(SE 18, p. 20)

Both neurotic and normal people, not content with memories or dreams, strive with great ingenuity to revive the most painful experiences of their childhood. We repeat all the tragedies of our earlier years. Freud eloquently catalogues the events and circumstances which provide a rich foundation for the repetition of painful experiences:

The early efflorescence of infantile sexual life is doomed to extinction because its wishes are incompatible with reality and with the inadequate stage of development which the child has reached. That efflorescence comes to an end in the most distressing circumstances and to the accompaniment of the most painful feelings. Loss of love and failure leave behind them a permanent injury to self-regard in the form of a narcissistic scar. . . . The tie of affection, which binds the child as a rule to the parent of the opposite sex, succumbs to disappointment, to a vain expectation of satisfaction or to jealousy over the birth of a new baby – unmistakable proof of the infidelity of the object of the child's affections. His own attempts to make a baby himself, carried out with tragic seriousness, fails shamefully. The lessening amount of affection he receives, the increasing demands of education, hard words and occasional punishment – these show him at last the full extent to which he has been scorned.

(SE 18, pp. 20–1)

The pattern of adult life tends to be set by these experiences, which are repeated, as it were, for their own sake. Taking account of the impressive evidence of transference neurosis and the varied life histories which he had examined, Freud finds no alternative but 'to assume that there really does exist in the mind a compulsion to repeat which over-rides the pleasure principle'.[51]

This urge to repeat is a kind of 'organic elasticity', or 'the expression of inertia inherent in organic life', through which the organism tends to restore itself to an earlier state. And if indeed all instincts are fundamentally conservative in nature, it follows that 'organic development must be attributed to external disturbing and diverting influences'.[52] The aim of all living things is to return to their original condition, to the endless and undisturbed repetition of death. The life instincts are merely:

component instincts whose function it is to assure that the organism shall follow its own path to death, and to ward off any possible ways of returning to inorganic existence other than those which are immanent in the organism itself.

(SE 18, p. 39)

But not all instincts conform to the same patterning of death. The dualism, which had been a central element in Freud's thinking, certainly since the *Three Essays on the Theory of Sexuality*, was redefined yet again; this time as the distinction between the death instinct and the life or sexual instinct. Both are fundamentally conservative, but the latter conserves the germplasm of the species and aims at uniting and forming larger aggregates, where the former seeks to return to an inorganic state. And it must be remembered that:

the death instinct is discovered, not in connection with the destructive tendencies, not in connection with aggressivity, but as a result of a direct consideration of repetition phenomena.

(Deleuze 1994, p. 16)

Though introducing this idea in the context of a speculative essay on biological theory, Freud quickly began to work out its implications for aspects of his psychology. Thus in his paper on 'The Economic Problem of Masochism' he revised an earlier view and argued that the compulsion to repeat can take the form of a primary masochism which is quite independent of the pleasure principle. And in a brief paper on 'Negation' he viewed aggression, in the intellectualised form of negative judgement, as a component part of aggression which was no longer assumed to be an attempt to master the world, and thus establish a safe position within it, but as an independent wish for destruction.[53]

The flexibility of Freud's interpretive and analytic psychology is matched by the multiplicity of its explanatory models. The metapsychology makes no attempt to reduce this diversity or to harmonise its differences. Freud's psychology, like the most advanced of the physical sciences, extracts from, and applies to, the 'simplest' of data several distinctive and even incompatible explanatory frameworks. The fragmentation of modern life is not reintegrated in some 'other' theoretical and non-existent realm, but is itself consecrated to the task of explanation. His theoretical writings, therefore, like his descriptive psychology, sketches a number of *schemata*, which, themselves bound up with the given conditions of experience, provide a limited number of irreducibly distinct viewpoints, each of which carries a certain explanatory weight, and none of which accounts wholly for those conditions.

For Freud 'theory' is not the 'ego' of science; it does not gather together and arrange into a systematic unity; it is, rather, the 'dream' of science, a mode of representation which, unrestricted by the exigencies of life, is sensitive to the multiplicity of meaningful perspectives immanent in experience.

NOTES

1 SE 1, p. 295.
2 For reformulations along these lines Gill, Merton M. and Pribram, Karl H. (1976), Holt (1989).
3 Bell (1830). For the development of the research tradition see Spillane (1981), Brazier (1987), and for critical studies Young (1970), Clarke and Jacyna (1987), Harrington (1987).
4 An idea of such conceptions can be gained from Büchner (1884), and Helmholtz (1884).
5 SE 1, p. 297. Q is the total energy 'bound' to the neuronal system, as distinct from Q, which is the quantity of energy in the external world.
6 SE 1, p. 308.
7 Brentano (1973). Freud's earlier work on aphasia, following Hughlings Jackson, took a somewhat more 'epiphenomenal' standpoint, though here also the characterisitc tendency of his thought towards an autonomous psychology is discernible. See Forrester (1980), pp. 14–29, Harrington (1987), pp. 235–47.
8 SE 1, p. 310.
9 Lockwood (1989).
10 SE 1, p. 337.
11 SE 7, p. 168.
12 SE 7, p. 161–2.
13 SE 7, pp. 163–4. He had used this expression in a letter to Fliess as early as January, 1897.
14 SE 7, p. 165.
15 SE 7, p. 176.
16 SE 7, p. 177.
17 SE 7, 180.
18 Vitz (1988).
19 SE 7, p. 208.
20 SE 7, p. 218.
21 SE 7, p. 218.
22 SE 7, p. 222.
23 As revealed by their letters, Freud and Jung (1974), Ellenberger (1970), pp. 657–748, Roazen (1976), pp. 235–303, Kerr (1994), pp. 129–57.
24 Stepansky (1986).
25 SE 14, p. 74.
26 SE 12, pp. 1–84, published in 1911; SE 14, pp. 67–104, published in 1914.
27 SE 14, p. 119.
28 SE 14, p. 134.
29 Freud (1953), Forrester (1980).
30 SE 14, p. 201.
31 SE 14, p. 223.
32 SE 14, p. 230.
33 Particularly Sulloway (1980).
34 Freud (1987), p. 13).

35 Ibid., p. 17.
36 Holt (1989) for a suggestive discussion.
37 SE 20, pp. 77–86; Laplanch and Pontalis (1988).
38 SE 3, pp. 90–115.
39 SE 10, p. 25.
40 SE 10, p. 116.
41 SE 20, p. 79.
42 e.g. in the 'Dora' case, SE 7, p. 80; and the 'Wolf Man' case, SE 17, pp. 36–8.
43 SE 16, p. 394.
44 SE 16, p. 396.
45 SE 16, p. 410.
46 SE 20, p. 132.
47 SE 20, pp. 145–6.
48 SE 8, p. 226.
49 Deleuze (1994), pp. 16–17, is a clear statement of this principle. Repression is a consequence of repetition.
50 SE 18, p. 11.
51 SE 18, p. 22.
52 SE 18, p. 38.
53 SE 19, pp. 157–72 and SE 19, pp. 235–42.

6

INTERTEXT
Pre-modern and postmodern dream images

It was in the conflicting contexts of, on the one hand, a scientific culture which treated them as meaningless and, on the other, a literary tradition for which they were highly significant, that Freud first became interested in dreams. In re-invigorating the study of dreams Freud was, in some respects, rediscovering the roots of modernity; but he was also connecting modernity with some of the oldest traditions within western society. His texts, therefore, should be read not only in the context of social and intellectual traditions impinging on *fin-de-siècle* culture, but more generally in relation to a broader framework of changing western conceptions of the nature and significance of dreams.

In fact it was only for a relatively brief period that the dream was held to be an essentially individual, private and incommunicable state of inwardness. Both in terms of its meaning and, just as significantly, in terms of the range of experience designated by the term, the dream was understood as opening on to the world of divinity, or the world of the future, in rather the same way that the waking senses opened on to the immediate world of the present. Modernity excluded the dream from forms of rational discourse so that the dream became withdrawn from life, closed in on itself, and hermetically inaccessible. Freud opened out the dream once again and, so to speak, spread it across the surface of waking life. Once anatomised in this way, the dream slipped effortlessly back into existence, and, rather than being defined through its radical difference from the waking world, became that world's most appropriate emblem. Freud's psychology, then, contrary both to a common view and to his own mode of presentation, is fundamentally historical in orientation. His writings provide an ideal psychology of *modern* life, and this becomes clearer if they are viewed in the context of the major transformations in the understanding of dreams which have characterised different periods in the development of western society.

DREAMS IN ANCIENT SOCIETY

Among the oldest of literary remains are inscriptions recording dreams and their interpretations. Many of these are strangely dull. The repetitive structure of an Assyrian dreambook lacks all the specific personal references which we now assume to be central to dreams:

> If one gives him an empty goblet: the poor will become poorer.
> If one gives him a full goblet: he will have a name and offspring.
> If one gives him wine: a friendly word; his days will be long.
> If one gives him beer: his (personal) god will remove his 'heart' from him; they will speak to him but he will forget.
> If one gives him an unknown kind of beer: he will worry.
> If one gives him honey: in his family (there will be) cases of death.
> If one gives him mountain-honey: he will obtain his heart's desire.
> If one gives him oil: sweet word(s), friendliness.
> If one gives him scented oils: ditto.
> If one gives him beef 'oil': profits are in store for him.
> If one gives him mutton 'oil': prosperity in his term (of office).
> If one gives him bird 'oil': they will shout: 'Watch out, watch out!'
> If one gives him fish oil: there will be steady expenses for him.
> If one gives him lion 'oil': he will reach perfection.
>
> (Oppenheim 1956, p. 279)

Such inscriptions testify to the remoteness of ancient ideas from any modern conception of the dream as a personal and essentially incommunicable experience. For the ancients a private and inward dream is only a tiny segment of a much more extensive and significant range of phenomena. Interestingly:

> the Egyptian word for 'dream' (*rswt*) is not only etymologically connected with the root meaning 'to be awake', but is also written with the determinative representing an opened eye.
>
> (Oppenheim 1956, p. 190)

Recorded dreams in ancient societies fall into several different categories, but each type was concerned with the regulation of public affairs and referred to oneiric experiences of important individuals or functionaries. Many dreams, for example, record revelations of divinity. These may be transparent or require interpretation, but in any event they are dreamed only by kings or priests. Similarly 'mantic dreams', in which forthcoming events are prognosticated, are the monopoly of religious professionals who play a central role in the organisation of social life. And dreams which reflect, symptomatically, the state of mind, the spiritual and bodily health of even the most illustrious dreamer are rarer and are not recorded in detail. There is nothing personal and inward in such dreams.

The stylised 'message dream', even when it is used as a literary device, describes the setting, and identifies the dreamer and the circumstances before recording the content of the dream itself. The public character of dreams is further emphasised by the ritualised transition from a normal waking state to the dream state. Frequently this channel of communication with divinities is initiated by the dreamer.[1] 'Incubation dreams', thus, are controlled by sacred setting and imagery:

> The sleeper in the cella, lying at the foot of an image, conditioned by appropriate ritual preparations which nourish his apprehensions and by reports which channel his imagination, distorts this image in his dream into a towering size and hears his name called in the stillness of the night.
>
> (Oppenheim 1956, p. 190)

The dreamer then abruptly awakes. There is no reference here to the typically modern association of dreaming with an intermediary twilight zone, rich in hypnagogic experience, between waking and sleeping.[2] This is simply because the altered state of consciousness known as dreaming is not the private experience of a sleeper but is, rather, the medium of divine communication with the rulers of society. In the Ancient Near East, as opposed to Classical Greece, the central figure is always either the deity or more usually a specially constructed messenger, who, even when disguised as a known person, is of towering appearance. The dream, thus, lends authority to statements and even in purely literary examples this remains its central significance. In principle, if not in practice, the dreamer is the passive recipient of oneiric images which bear directly on important current events.

Ancient Near Eastern civilisations were, generally, theocratic states in which the legitimating role of deities played an important part. Where, however, as in Ancient Judaism, strong independent traditions of law and community were established, dreams, as privileged communications, were less commonly invoked as the legitimating grounds of commands.[3] Indeed, they were more likely to figure in the context of subversive prophecies, though even in that context they were less important than the interpretive ambiguity initiated with the tradition of law itself. Although Freud occasionally identified himself with the dream interpreters of the Old Testament, dreams, in fact, do not appear to play such a fundamental role in Ancient Judaism as they do in the ancient epics from neighbouring cultures. The codification of the law and the tradition of commentary upon it replaced any direct interrogation of divinities through the medium of dreams, or in any other way.

Important Old Testament dreams, thus, date from an early period, and help to establish the religious significance of Moses and the patriarchs. Genuine prophets are distinguished by, among other characteristics, the ease with which they can receive vivid dreams:

Moses and more generally the patriarchs experience visions in which Yahweh speaks clearly, as opposed to the kings and prophets who experience more enigmatic dreams and visions and, finally, the pagan kings, recipients of obscure messages.

(Le Goff 1988, p. 194)

For a later period, characterised by religious conflict and factionalism, dreams are more often denounced as illusory; the dangerous ravings of false and deceitful prophets. In the Old Testament dreams are generally not recounted by the dreamer and their significance depends to a large extent on a 'polemical, apologetic or ideological' context.[4] But where they are genuine, dreams put the dreamer in touch with God.

Pagan dreams within ancient Greco-Roman culture also, though vaguely, originated with the gods, but in this case were regarded as persisting in an autonomous domain to which the dreamer was granted temporary access. Since Nietzsche drew attention to the ecstatic elements in classical Greek culture, and Rohde charted the progressive 'spiritualisation' of the concept of *psyche* from the Homeric myths to Platonic philosophy, many classicists have analysed the development of notions of 'shadow', 'soul', 'ghost' and other concepts in classical antiquity, all of which have a bearing on the meaning and interpretation of dreams during the period and subsequently. Freud was himself superbly educated in classical culture, and read Greek and Latin texts directly under the influence of this revival of classical learning. Just as the Renaissance had anticipated modernity by a return to antiquity, so, towards the end of the nineteenth century, the end of the bourgeois era and the premonition of a postmodern age was announced by a repetition of this recovery of classical scholarship. But now, rather than see in Greece a model of calmness and measured harmony, an appreciation of Dionysian spiritual fervour, suppressed during the development of ascetic bourgeois culture, broke through with renewed vigour.

In the Homeric epics dreams usually visit a sleeping man or woman and are 'seen' as independent of the dreamer. The Greeks of the period 'saw' dreams rather than 'had' them; and the fact that they were asleep was often announced by the dream-image itself. Thus, for example, 'You are asleep, Penelope' announces the 'shadowy image' in the *Odyssey*.

This dream-image is closely associated with the notion of *psyche*. Originally, according to Rohde, whose classic study inaugurated a long and distinguished research tradition, the *psyche* goes 'unnoticed during the lifetime of the body' and is observable only when separated by death from the body to which it belongs. The term is associated with 'breath' and, on death, escaping through the mouth, or a gaping wound, it forms itself into an image (*eidolon*), 'withdrawing from the grasp of the living, like smoke, or a shadow'. Rohde claims that the relationship between *psyche* and living body can be conceptualised as follows:

162

it is not the psyche which communicates its own faculties to man and gives him capacity for life together with consciousness, will and knowledge. It is rather that *during the union* of the psyche and the body all the faculties of living and acting lie within the empire of the body, of which they are functions. Without the presence of the psyche, the body cannot perceive, feel, or will, but it does not use these or any of its faculties through or by means of the psyche.

(Rohde 1925, pp. 5–6)

Disunited through death the *psyche* is without feeling; 'a shadowy double of mankind', it persists as a morphological reminiscence of the living person. The Homeric notion of the human 'does not sever the corporeal from what we call spiritual or psychic, but always sees the one in the other'.[5] And in neither aspect, it might be added, did human unity belong to the individual. The body as much as the 'mind' or 'will' was a loose aggregation rather than a functioning unity.[6] Thus terms such as *thumos* and *phren* refer both to specific bodily organs or organic functions and to particular psychological or emotional states.[7] Thus 'A man's *thumos* tells him that he must now eat or drink or slay an enemy. . . . He can converse with his "heart" or his "belly" almost as man to man.'[8]

Progressively, and particularly during what is sometimes known as the 'axial-age', from the fifth to the fourth centuries BCE, which is associated with the dominance of the city-state, the emergence of a money economy, and extraordinary intellectual and cultural fertility, *psyche* came to represent the integration of human experience within the individual; a personality. This was, simultaneously a 'spiritualisation' of emotional and intellectual life:

Instead of the individual being intimately bound to a living body and a *psyche* presented like the *eidolon* of the body that is no longer here, its phantom or double, it is now the immortal *psyche* that constitutes one's real being in the interior recesses of each and every individual during the period of one's life. The living body therefore changes its status: it now becomes a simple appearance, an illusory, insubstantial, fugitive, and transitory image of what we ourselves truly and always are. . . . We have thus passed from the soul, ghostly double of the body, to the body as a ghostly reflection of the soul.

(Vernant 1991, p. 190)

This is also the transformation, it should be noted, which is the background to the Sophoclean version of the *Oedipus* myth.[9] And as a result of this process of individuation, dreams became associated with the 'shadow' of the personality, rather than with the identifying form of the body.

In this intellectual context Plato, in *The Republic*, originates a profound interpretation of the connection between oneiric and waking experience;

163

linking dreams with unwelcome desires in a way which was to be lastingly influential. Dreams are prompted by desires:

> that wake while we sleep, when the reasonable and humane part of us is asleep and its control is relaxed, and our fierce bestial nature, full of food and drink, rouses itself and has its fling and tries to secure its own kind of satisfaction. As you know, there's nothing too bad for it and it's completely lost to all sense and shame. It doesn't shrink from attempting intercourse (as it supposes) with a mother or anyone else, man, beast or god, or from murder or eating forbidden food. There is, in fact, no folly nor shamelessness it will not commit.
>
> (Plato 1955, p. 392)

The most complete and subtle Platonic theory of dreams dates from a much later period (around 400 CE) and was due to Synesius of Cyrene, whose short treatise *Concerning Dreams* proposed an influential *pneumatic* theory. Dreams, he argues, like all other forms of human knowledge, 'are signs' which share a common nature as 'brothers in a single living creature, the cosmos'.[10] And the obscurity of some dreams is not essentially different to the enigma of many natural signs. Forming an image which was to become a recurrent theme in the western discourse on perception in general, as well as on dreams, he argues that, while in existing things form and matter are coalesced, the cosmos is also filled with free-floating images:

> From all that nature possesses, all things that are, that have come into being and that shall be (since this too is a phase of existence), from all these things, I say, images flow and rebound from their substance.
>
> (Synesius 1930, p. 328)

It is the character of human beings to possess an 'imaginative *pneuma*' which is 'a powerful reflecting mirror of all the images that flow off in this way'. Dreams, as the temporary reflection of these images deprived of natural substance, exist on 'the borderland between unreason and reason, between the bodiless and the body'.[11] Dreams are a natural process of receiving the 'efflorescences of unfulfilled natures', and it is through these images that 'divine elements are brought into contact with those furthest removed from them'. The enigmatic character of some dreams arises not only from the nature of the images received by the imagination, but depends on the character of the reflecting *pneuma*. Where it is 'pure and well-defined', then the individual 'whether he is waking or sleeping receives true impressions of things'.[12] And as for almost all people the *pneuma* is imperfect, there is a continuing need for dream interpretation.

A sceptical tradition in relation to dreams also developed. Aristotle suggested there was nothing divine in dreams, which arose through the continuing stimulation of the senses during sleep, both from external sources and, more particularly, from within the body. Dreams might, because of this, serve a useful cathartic function; an idea which seems hardly to have been developed further before Freud.[13] The apparently premonitory character of some dreams depends simply on their being intermediary between an initial and poorly formed intention, and its realisation in action:

> impulses in sleep must often be the first cause of actions in the daytime, because the way has been paved for the intention to do those actions in dreams at night.
>
> (Aristotle 1935, p. 377)

In the context of both popular religious practices and of Platonism the art of oneiromancy flourished and became highly developed. Dreams became significant to a wider range of dreamers who required them to be interpreted so that they might benefit from the knowledge which, obscurely, they seemed to contain. The *Oneirocritica* of Artemidorus, a native of Daldis in Lydia, a region noted for its wealth and civilisation, comes at the end of a long period of such development (second century CE), and, though earlier handbooks had all but disappeared, its author explicitly acknowledges the tradition within which it was conceived and written.[14] Indeed, he is writing in part to reclaim this tradition from sceptical attacks inspired by Aristotle. To this end he claims not only to have 'taken special pains to procure every book on the interpretation of dreams', but to have 'consorted for many years with the much despised diviners of the marketplace'.[15]

What is at once evident from his text is the extent to which dream interpretation had become a popular art which hinged on accurate knowledge of both the circumstances and personality of the dreamer. Books IV and V of the *Oneirocritica* were written primarily as a training manual for the author's son, and are full of highly practical advice:

> You should learn local customs and the peculiarities of every place if you are not already acquainted with them. Travelling and extensive reading will provide you with the best information on the subject. For books on dream interpretation are not sufficient in themselves to assist you, but you need other sources of information as well.
>
> (Artemidorus 1975, p. 189)

Dreams can only be interpreted when precisely recounted and when the interpreter is acquainted with the detailed circumstances of the dreamer's life. But not all dreams are meaningful. Artemidorus formalises a number of distinctions fundamental to the practice of dream interpretation. Most significantly he draws a distinction between *enhypnion* which is directly linked to the present state of the body and mind of the dreamer and acts as its irritating cause, and *oneiros* which indicates a future state of affairs. The *enhypnion* is the common type of dream and is understood in terms which had become familiar through brief works on the subject by Aristotle and the writers of the Hippocratic Corpus.[16] It is 'close to the mind' of the dreamer, and continues only during sleep. Thus, 'it is natural for a lover to seem to be with his beloved in a dream and for a frightened man to see what he fears, or for a hungry man to eat and a thirsty man to drink'.[17] Bodily needs, appetites or superfluities, fears or hopes are represented in terms of immediately understandable but, in terms of wider considerations, insignificant dream images. The *oneiros*, on the other hand, persists in wakefulness and 'signifies good or bad things that will occur in the future'.[18] However, incorporating Aristotle's criticism into his own divinatory practice, he sees nothing magical in this, for 'it is the nature of the *oneiros* to awaken and excite the soul by inducing an active undertaking'.[19] Such dreams, thus, when properly understood, have predictive power because they reveal an intention not yet fully conscious to the mind of the dreamer. Of course, the precise interpretation of such dreams depends on detailed knowledge of the client's circumstances; they may, for example, indicate that the dreamer will be disappointed, rather than that some nascent plan of action will be accomplished.

Some *oneira* are theorematic (direct), while others are allegorical, and 'through them, the soul is conveying something obscurely by physical means'.[20] There is no simple correspondence between the dream symbols appearing in allegorical dreams and their significance for the dreamer. Not only do 'some dreams proclaim many things through many images' while some indicate 'a few things through many images', there is no fixed 'dictionary' through which such images can be understood. Thus:

> The penis corresponds to one's parents, on the one hand, because it has a relationship with the seed. It resembles children, on the other hand, in that it is itself the cause of children. It signifies a wife or a mistress, since it is made for sexual intercourse. It indicates brothers and all blood relatives, since the interrelationship of the entire house depends upon the penis. It is a symbol of strength and physical vigour, because it is itself the cause of these qualities. That is why some people call the penis 'one's manhood'. It corresponds to speech and education because the penis (like speech) is very fertile. . . . Furthermore the penis is also a sign of wealth and possession because it alternately expands and contracts and because it is able to produce and to eliminate.
>
> (Artemidorus 1975, pp. 105–6)

It is hardly surprising, therefore, that Artemidorus counsels his son that 'the interpretation of dreams is nothing other than the juxtaposition of similarities'.[21]

The practical distinctions offered by Artemidorus coexisted with typologies of a more theoretical sort. Cicero, for example, drawing together several different strands of thought within the ancient world, distinguishes dreams by their sources; they might originate with man, or rather with his own spirit, with immortal spirits or with gods. Premonitory dreams fell into one of three groupings: *oneiros* (*somnium*) or enigmatic; *horama* (*visio*) or clear vision; and *chrematismos* (*oraculum*) or divinely inspired though often also enigmatic. Non-premonitory dreams were of two types: *enupnion* (*insomnium*), a dream, symbolic or direct, that referred to ordinary events and particularly bodily states during sleep; and *phantasma* (*visum*) or pure illusion.[22]

This multiplication of types, in which learned and popular traditions were merged, serves to emphasise the wide range of phenomena falling within what a more modern and general terminology would designate as the 'dream'. In fact the most influential such scheme, and one which, written around the end of the fourth century CE, forms a bridge from antiquity to medieval Christendom, was the *Commentary* by Macrobius on Cicero's *Dream of Scipio*.[23] Indeed, Cicero's original outlasted the commentary, and was to be revived as the inspiration for Kepler's lunar dream, as well as Burton's 'Digression on the Air' and a number of other early modern cosmological voyages.

Macrobius tried to accommodate a variety of theoretical and practical views within a fivefold dream typology, and it was in terms of his definitions that the Latin west inherited the rich literary and oral dream traditions of antiquity. He distinguishes:

chrematisma / oraculum: oracular dream
horama / visio: prophetic vision
oneiros / somnium: the enigmatic dream
phantasma / visum: apparition
enhypnion / insomnium: nightmare

As Kruger points out, this scheme, which is fundamentally neo Platonic in structure, involves both opposition and hierarchy.[24] There is a basic contrast between true and false, opaque or revealing, which goes back to Homer. Thus, reliable dreams (*oraculum, visio, somnium*) issue from the gate of horn 'the nature of which is such that, when thinned, it becomes transparent'. While, from the gate of ivory, 'the composition of which is so dense that no matter how thin a layer of it may be, it remains opaque', issue false dreams (*visum, insomnium*) of no prophetic significance. However, within each type a hierarchy is established, creating a continuum from the mundane to the transcendent.

The *insomnium* is completely mundane, caused by 'mental or physical distress', and 'vanish[es] into thin air' when the dreamer awakes. The *visium* similarly does not involve any contact with a higher realm, and is characteristic of 'the moment between wakefulness and slumber'. The higher forms of dream, however, reveal truths otherwise inaccessible to the waking intelligence. The *oraculum* is more impressive than the *visio*, and

167

reveals a truth directly through the words of an authoritative figure. The *visio* is the representation of some everyday event, but the event is realised in the life of the dreamer. It is a higher form by virtue of anticipating, rather than transcending, the everyday.

The *somnium* stands mid-way between mundane and transcendent dreams. It reveals nothing directly, but, rather, 'conceals with strange shapes and veils with ambiguity' the true meaning of the information being offered, and thus 'requires an interpretation for its understanding'.[25] The *somnium* can be seen as 'the perfect middle term between revelation and deception'.[26]

CHRISTIANITY AND DREAMS

The Platonic schema was a major influence on Augustine, whose authority assured its broad dispersal throughout the Latin west. Yet, though significant in Augustine's understanding of his own religious development, Christianity, generally and over a long period, subjected dreams to suspicion and devaluation. The omnipresence of the divine will ensured that all dreams, and not just a particular category of oneiric phenomena, were meaningful. Moreover, for Christians, God had revealed himself in a unique and 'once-and-for-all' manner, so that dreams ceased to be regarded as a privileged mode of contact with the divine will, which was understood and interpreted in terms of a sacred history and of a contemporary theology. It was important to distinguish this condescension from pagan 'visions' or historically unimportant 'dreams'.[27]

Le Goff has suggested a number of additional reasons for the growing Christian suspicion of dreams.[28] Pagan practice centred on the divinatory function of dreams, but for Christians the future was exclusively God's concern. Moreover, dreams were associated with the dangers of sexuality, heresy and the devil.[29] From the fourth century onward Christians hypostasised all demons and other diabolical agencies into a singular spiritual enemy; Satan. And as Satan was empowered to affect the human soul, he could send false dreams to confuse and misguide the individual. In particular he inspired a concupiscent soul to lustful dreams and entire groups of people with false beliefs.

It was, perhaps, the growth of Gnosticism which did most to encourage Christian distrust of dreams. It was only gradually that Christian orthodoxy, in terms of specific beliefs, was established and this process was effected primarily through the identification and suppression of a number of what were ultimately declared to be heretical doctrines.[30] Gnosticism was a widespread belief in ontological dualism. Creation, including the social and cultural products of human activity, were interpreted as the works of a powerful and evil god which had trapped the authentic divine spirit within a world of material objects; more particularly within the human body.

Salvation was conceptualised as a spiritual release and reunion with the divine which depended on ascetic practices and the withdrawal from the world of sensuous appetites.[31] It also depended on special knowledge of the divine, which was secretly communicated to the spiritually perfect. Dreams, for the Gnostic, thus took on added significance as the secret messages upon which salvation depended. Christianity, insistent on maintaining a clear distinction between its monotheistic tradition and Gnostic specu- lation, consequently devalued all dreams.

Officially condemned, oneiromancy nonetheless flourished as a popular art throughout the medieval west. Medieval dreambooks, influenced directly by the ancient literature, and indirectly through Islamic examples which were themselves based on ancient sources, were extremely wide- spread. Many of these were unsophisticated; dream chancebooks and alphabets were commonplace and operated by drawing a letter at random from the Psalter and then consulting the corresponding letter in the dreambook where the 'meaning' of the dream was recorded. Dream inter- pretation also became associated with astrological and medical theories, and interpretations were linked to the phases of the moon, to birth signs and so on. There were also physiological dreambooks based on Aristotelian principles. And the most popular of dream handbooks, the *Somnia Danielis*, though based on Greek originals, consisted of nothing more than a 'library of dream topoi', in which no attention was paid to the circumstantial details such as the age, sex, occupation, social position and location of the dreamer, which had been so significant for Artemidorus.[32]

It would be misleading, however, to regard the medieval period as deficient in either the capacity to dream, or the ability to interpret them. During the medieval period dreams became an important literary motif, particularly in love poetry and epic.[33] Most significantly the romance, which Cervantes was later to revive in order to parody, can be seen as an extended dream. Here too conventionalisation predominates. Interpret- ation in terms of a relatively fixed meaning assigned to each of the symbolic elements within a dream was the approved model.

And just as Freud's dream interpretation continually establishes contact with the world of everyday events, so the history of dream interpretation continually makes reference beyond itself to the larger context of a chang- ing culture. Thus, while Christianity had devalued the dream as a revelatory experience, it had deployed the most elaborate of hermeneutic techniques in its 'reading' of nature and of human history. Empirical phenomena were conceived as merely the edge of a vast reality, the greater part of which remained inaccessible to the senses. The quest for knowledge, through contemplation of the divine ordering of creation into a natural hierarchy, was driven by a desire to 'see through' the particular phen- omena; beyond and beneath the fleeting changes affecting the senses, to the realm of permanent being upon which everything depended for its existence. In this context the entire world of physical experience was transformed into a dream whose meaning was deciphered by theology, philosophy and other religiously inspired legitimate arts. All knowledge was interpretation, and all of creation was fundamentally enigmatic. Creation, after all, was God's 'dream' as much as it was His 'act' and could be understood only in terms of a continuous process of interpretation.

For a world which was conceived as 'a vast reservoir of symbols', the capacity to comprehend the inner meaning of the natural and social order was founded on the assumption that the human being was formed as a *microcosm* of creation. The human form, as a synthesis of body, soul and spirit, was both a miniaturised replica and an element within a *macrocosmic* structure. Thus, uniquely, 'all created things exist for us as a book, a picture, and a mirror'.[34] For medieval writers it is evident that 'the world is a book written by the hand of God in which every creature is a word charged with meaning'.[35] God's being was inscribed in creation, and the human soul was capable of both reading and reflecting these divine images.

Generally it was mirror imagery which provided the dominant metaphor for human knowledge. And if man was a mirror of nature, then, in its turn, nature was 'a mirror in which man can contemplate the image of God'.[36] Indeed, from the twelfth century on 'the mirror can be said to constitute the central image for a particular world-view'.[37]

The human being, the *microcosm*, was a symbol within the larger order of signification, and, sharing in God's rational spirit, was capable of comprehending this order, in its elements and in its magnificent totality. Drawn to some particular object or event, the intellect mirrors not simply its appearance but immediately connects it with the immaterial presence which it symbolises. The intellect, thus, is continually led away from superficial reflection upon the physical world, soaring, as do cathedral walls, beyond material existence in search of its authentic transcendental archetype.

Indeed, so much was the sensory world taken for granted to be a realm of symbolism that throughout the medieval period there was no general term for 'symbol' or 'symbolic'. *Symbolum* was used in a limited clerical sense, as in *symbolum Nicea*, as an abbreviated statement of the faith, a kind of mnemonic code for the vast edifice of the Christian tradition. As variants of *signum*, Augustine distinguished *figura, imago* and *allegoria*, each adapted to mirror some particular type of correspondence between the human mind and the real nature of things. These correspondences became formalised in terms of four distinctive relations of similitude: at an *analogical* level the *microcosmic* structure reveals its meaning, for example the head is above and in control of the limbs as God is above his creation; at an *allegorical* level a specific connection with the Church or its teaching is established; the *topological* level refers to the Christian soul; a final *anagogical* level mirrors the organised structure of dependence in which these various symbolic levels are held.[38]

The world was open to an 'interminable' process of interpretation which operated, in practice, in terms of associative chains of reasoning through which the intellect's likeness to God was partially revealed. Far from devaluing the dream, therefore, medieval culture succeeded in 'converting' all experience into an exemplary dream. And if, for modernity, the dream has raised fundamental problems of memory, the continuity of an inner self and the experience of duration, there was, for medieval culture, an intimate link between the dream of reality as a symbolic structure and the 'art of memory'.[39] In largely pre-literate societies memory assumes a more central significance in the organisation of public life than it does in modern society. In the ancient world considerable attention had been given to developing techniques of memorising public speeches, and these methods were further developed within the context of Christian reflection.

The art of memory involved two fundamental techniques. Firstly, the forming of 'mnemic-symbols', in relation to which rhetorical figures and a number of literary devices were used. Such formalisms divided the discourse into specific sections which were linked according to a fixed set of rules. Each section could then be associated with a particular visual image, again according to conventions developed within the discipline of poetics. Secondly, these associated images were then projected and located in a place-sequence; typically at the best known landmarks on an imaginary walk through the city, or, like a vast imaginary frieze set between the supporting pillars of the arena. It was then, with practice, a simple matter to 'read-off' an intricate discourse with the aid of these visualised *topoi*.

Memory systems were most effective when they could be seen as utilising 'natural' associations and connections. The formulation of literary figures and their association with visual images became increasingly the province of logic, which, revealing the given mechanisms of the mind, defined those associative connections which were most readily recalled. And as the mind, and language, within the Christian tradition was viewed as part of the creation it mirrored, place-logic was, simultaneously, an outline of structure of created being. The art of memory, thus, progressively developed into a comprehensive science of the order of things.

It is also worth noting a further connection between the modern experience of dreaming and medieval culture. Since Mikhail Bakhtin's remarkable work on Rabelais, increasing attention has been paid to the carnival tradition in the medieval west.[40] From the present point of view what is striking in his account of the 'popular-festive forms' of the medieval west is not just that they operate as a comprehensive symbolic inversion of the 'official' order of things, but that the distinction between carnival and everyday life bears a certain resemblance to the modern distinction between dreaming and waking experience.

The carnival amounted to a periodic 'transvaluation of all values', and:

celebrated temporary liberation from the prevailing truth and from the established order; it marked the suspension of all hierarchical rank, privileges, norms, and prohibitions. Carnival was the true feast of time, the feast of becoming, change, and renewal. It was hostile to all that was immortalized and completed.

(Bakhtin 1968, p. 10)

This radical transformation involved a thorough re-ordering of experience in terms of festive laughter, the degradation of all sacred and serious categories and, even more significantly, in its 'materialisation' as immediate bodily functions and appetites. In a society which defined the human in terms of an image of the divine and the world through a complex symbolic hierarchy, the carnival reunited all with nature as a collective human body; continually fecund and unbounded. The carnival body is focused on the 'lower bodily stratum' and its functions, and on its dynamic interplay with the world. Bakhtin describes the carnival as a 'regression' towards the primary process, towards a reality of such compelling immediacy that it constituted a world of its own; another world, rather than a division within the official order of things.

Medieval culture, however, rather than oscillating between dreaming and waking, is better viewed as lurching between two dreams; the dream of religious transcendence, and the carnival dream. Each provides a model of de-individuated experience which is conditioned by faith or by appetite and, constructed through participatory processes of identification, gives rise to a corresponding picture of the world as a symbolic order or as an organic process.

The breakdown of these dream-worlds, associated with the collapse of feudalism, was consequential on the reaffirmation of the wholly transcendental character of God and, therefore, on a recognition of the abysmal gulf separating the divine from the merely human being. Adrift in the cosmos human reason fell back on itself and sought to comprehend the connections among *things*, as an indwelling order. The Reformation, following immediately upon the collapse of feudalism, and similarly rejecting all hierarchical notions, pre-adapted European culture to both the emergence of capitalism and the rise of modern science. The nature of God was the concern of faith, and not of knowledge; so that, conversely, a proper understanding of the natural world, and a just ordering of society, became (gradually, but ultimately exclusively) a matter for waking deliberation and for reflection fully aware of itself as an autonomous human capacity.

Through the Renaissance an irreversible process of separation between a world of objects and an inner world of the human subject was established. The world existed independently of the human capacity to observe it, but pleasure in observation and investigation of nature became a legitimate, and even an exalted, activity. Before the worlds of object and subject completely withdrew from each other, their residual interpenetration fuelled the revival of Platonism, sophisticated theories of magic and Hermetic dreams of cosmological flight. Utopianism flourished everywhere, and a new era of human self-assertion seemed imminent.

FICTION

Modern philosophical consciousness, or the philosophical consciousness of modernity, begins with dreaming; it literally takes shape as a dream in the mind of Descartes. And not in his mind alone. Not only as philosophy, but as literature and as science, modernity was announced in dreams. The dream, rather than being an integral part of an entire hierarchically ordered world of experience, split apart, as did every other aspect of reality, and represented through its own incoherence and incommunicability the solitariness of each observing ego and the contingent and adventitious character of all our pictures of the world.

The characteristic modern literary form, the novel, is similarly linked to the exemplary power of dreams. Cervantes introduces his fictional master-piece (the exemplary modern novel), as did Proust three centuries later, with the uncertainty of an intermediate state between waking and sleeping.

The author of the 'Prologue' to *Don Quixote*, which the reader at first assumes to be Cervantes, recounts the exceptional difficulties he experienced in composing these opening remarks. It is not difficult to believe that he had habitually nodded off over the incomplete text:

> Many times I took up my pen to write it, and many times I put it down, with the paper before me, my pen in my ear, my elbow on the desk and my hand on my cheek, thinking what to write.
>
> (Cervantes 1950, p. 26)

Indeed, it was only the fortuitous interruption of 'a lively and very intelligent friend' that roused him from this slumbering posture, and, providing the occasion for an explanation, prompted the completion of his self-imposed task. But the reader must wonder whether this interruption is real or imagined; has he, in fact, just fallen asleep and dreamt the facilitating encounter? And did that dream in turn unlock the entire labyrinth of imagined events which is the substance of the novel?

Many stylistic features of the book, *Don Quixote*, are dreamlike. The narrative complexity, the difficulty of keeping track of time and space, the matter-of-fact tone to which many absurd details are alluded, and above all its intense visualisation all belong to the clarity of dreams. After all, there is generally nothing imprecise and dull in dreams. And quite beyond its rich sensory quality there is much in its structure, plot and theme which remain inextricably bound up with enigmatic dream-states. The reader, addressed in the opening line of the 'Prologue' as 'idle reader', and

173

presumably also given to dreaming, conspires with its several authors to create a plastic reality which, at once natural and full of surprises, is never wholly under the control of a single narrator.

The reader, in fact, becomes lost in narrative complexity. It is not clear that the author of the 'Prologue' continues as the narrator of Don Quixote's adventures; 'though in appearance Don Quixote's father', the author at that point claims to be 'really his step-father'. In any event, a secondary author (or one of a series of such authors) intrudes at various points and takes over the narrative at Chapter ix of Book I. The narrative is interrupted at this point, a critical point at that, in which the Don and a Basque are engaged in combat:

> with naked swords aloft, on the point of dealing two such furious downward strokes as, had they struck true, would have cleft both knights asunder from head to foot, and split them like pomegranates.
>
> (Cervantes 1950, p. 75)

At this very point 'our delightful history stopped short and remained mutilated, our author failing to inform us where to find the missing part'. But as in all interrupted dreams, it was begun again, by chance. The last commentator, annoyed at the loss of such an entertaining text (we are informed he was in the habit of reading 'torn papers lying in the street'), was alert to an offer to purchase some parchment on which he recognised Arabic inscriptions. He had the text translated. He claims it to be a 'true history' of Don Quixote, based on the original lost text, by an Arabic scholar, Cide Benengali. The text we read is part translation of the supposed original, part report by the narrator on his reading of this text, part commentary by both Benengali and the narrator. The author disappears before our eyes, and the book we were about to read dissolves into nothing. Part II, which followed several years after the publication of Part I, and spreads fresh doubt on the authenticity of what has already been read. Indeed, Part I appears within it as another false book of chivalry, a scandalous misrepresentation of events which, 'mingling a thousand lies with one truth', Don Quixote recalls in a different way. In a very real sense, therefore, Cervantes allows, in fact requires, that the reader assist in the creation of a narrative which continually subverts itself.[41]

These devices, which draw the reader, so to speak, into the space vacated by the single author with an authoritative and unified point of view, transforms the story into a dreamlike spectacle. Like the viewer of Velazquez' *Las Meninas*, and the spectator of our own dreams, the reader exists both inside and outside of the given text.[42] The reader lacks all conscious control over the production of the images connected in his or her mind. The 'authentic history' emerges as a 'thread' which being 'carded, twisted and reeled' leads the reader unsuspectingly into a series of diversionary scenes. But the reader alone is the connecting consciousness

174

among these many partial views and entertaining diversions. In an obscure and troublesome way the reader becomes responsible for the story, which can exist only as an act of synthesis in his or her imagination, and which lacks all external reality as a deliberately constructed unity; it is not a 'book', and, in spite of being printed and furnished with a dedication, if not dedicatory sonnets and learned footnotes, it is, in itself, nothing.

If these formal considerations were not themselves sufficient, at various points the narrative itself touches on the nature of dreams; and, of course, a good deal of the plot revolves around the difficulty of distinguishing reality from appearance; a distinction reduplicated and exemplified in the difference between dreaming and waking experience. Don Quixote is trapped in a waking dream. With hallucinatory fervour he lives out his destiny as a questing knight. He cannot be wakened to reality, 'for everything which he saw he adapted with great facility to his wild, chivalrous and errant fancies'. His infatuation with old romances – a defunct literary form at the time of Cervantes' composition – predisposes him to interpret reality in an idiosyncratic fashion. He is aware that his quest 'appears mad' to others, but assimilates this to his imaginary world. Wicked enchanters transform mounted knights into windmills and deceive his companions and enemies alike into a false and degrading reality. But enchantment, like dreams, cannot be easily undone. Don Quixote repeatedly explains the deceptive root of other people's false experience though he cannot comprehend his own. Immediately after the innkeeper's daughter reports a falling dream he admits the difficulty of combating enchantment:

> there is no point in taking any notice of matters of enchantment, nor in getting angry and enraged about them. For, as these magicians are invisible and supernatural, we shall find no one to take vengeance on, however hard we try.
>
> (Cervantes 1950, p. 127)

The reader, of course, sees through all this, believes in Don Quixote's madness and, with the priest, condemns the literary sources of his fascination.[43] Chivalry, we know, 'is all fiction, fable and lies – dreams told by men awake', or rather half asleep. At one point, on mistaking a troupe of costumed actors for 'some of the strangest shapes imaginable' Don Quixote himself admits that 'appearances are not always to be trusted'.[44] Typically, in fact, Don Quixote's delusions are not permanent, but where the reader and his companions resort to the hypothesis of a deranged imagination to account for these wild oscillations, he has recourse to the hypothesis of sorcery to account for his periodic disillusionment from the adventures he is convinced are real.

These oscillations include the movement from dreaming to waking experience. While asleep at an inn Don Quixote continues the combat he has been anticipating with a giant. The innkeeper and Sancho observe him, slashing the air with his sword, but:

> his eyes were not open, because he was asleep, and dreaming that he was battling with the giant. For his imagination was so bent on the adventure which he was going to achieve, that it made him dream he had got to the kingdom of Micomicon and was already at grips with his enemy.
>
> (Cervantes 1950, p. 317)

In his frenzy he slashes open some wine-skins and floods the room. Don Quixote is partially awakened by having a pitcher of cold water thrown over him. He handles the momentary break in his experience with the typical cunning of a 'secondary revision'. 'Now I know that everything about this house is enchanted', he observes, for, 'the head isn't to be found, though I saw it cut off with my own eyes, and the blood pouring from the body like a fountain.'[45]

Don Quixote seems perverse because he refuses to fully awaken, and sees the world continually through dream images. Within this enchanted circle even the distinction between dreaming and waking can be reproduced in a counterfeit form. Thus, he relates, when in the deep caves of Montesinos, bewildered by his surroundings and in 'perplexed meditation':

> suddenly and involuntarily I was overcome by a deep sleep, and when I least expected it, not knowing how or why, I woke up to find myself in the middle of the most beautiful, pleasant and delightful meadow nature could create or the liveliest human imagination could conceive. I opened and rubbed my eyes, and saw that I was not asleep but really awake. For all that, I felt my head and my bosom to make certain whether it was my very self who was there, or some empty and counterfeit phantom; but touch, feeling and the coherent argument I held with myself assured me that I was then just as I am here now.
>
> (Cervantes 1950, p. 615)

This, of course, is no test of wakefulness, and the reader's suspicion is immediately confirmed by the fantastic appearance from out of the depths of Montesinos himself, who addresses him: 'It is many centuries', he informs Don Quixote, 'that we who dwell in these enchanted solitudes have been waiting to see you.'[46]

When asleep, that is to say, the distinction between waking and sleeping is as unreal as every other imagined distinction. Only when really awake does the difference between dreaming and waking experience bear a genuine ontological value. Cervantes' entire book fleshes out this fundamental truth of modernity. The distinctions which the reader brings to the text work at first to establish Don Quixote's madness, and the unreality of his adventures, but the formal complexity and ingenuity of the narrative gradually absorb the reader into another world; not, it is true, a world in which Don Quixote's dreams become realised and Sancho appears as the dupe of a wicked sorcerer (Descartes' Demon), but a world in which the distinction between these different realms of representation has no more validity than Don Quixote's specious 'proof' that he is awake. The reader is lulled into accepting as 'really' distinct, levels of reality which have a meaning only within the text. *Don Quixote* is a book over which the ideal reader should fall asleep.

For the dreamer all reality is given an oneiric form, so that the dreamer's conviction that he is awake remains a purely internal 'proof'. Cervantes returned to this paradigmatic form of self-deception in *Exemplary Stories*, in which, as for Descartes, it is the apparently logical coherence of the dream, rather than or in addition to its sensory intensity, which most irresistibly counterfeits the character of waking experience. The narrator of 'The Dog's Colloquy' admits that an overheard conversation between two dog's might appear to be a misreported dream, but argues that:

> The things they discussed were many and varied, and more suitable for discussion by wise men than to be in the mouths of dogs; so that, since I could not have invented them off my own bat, in spite of myself and against my better judgement I have come to believe that I was not dreaming and that the dogs were talking.
>
> (Cervantes 1950, p. 192)

Cervantes' fiction, like the most convincing of dreams, reproduces within it all the characteristics of the world of waking experience, including the distinction between waking and sleeping. Indeed, this difference is given added significance as a general characteristic of his own novel in comparison to the hundreds of degraded romances which was the material of Don Quixote's diseased reading. In this Cervantes was carrying through the programme of humanism which, taking its point of departure from Petrarch, attacked romantic literature as unconvincing, aesthetically failed 'dreams'.[47] Juan Luis Vives, and others, sobered by the collapse of feudal forms of restraint and order, criticised the tradition of the romance for its fantastic elements, and its evident lack of realism. Literature of all kinds must be conditioned by the needs of a new age in which the most pressing need was for educational reform so that the individual, liberated from the compulsory order of closed and hierarchical communities, would learn through reason the art of self-mastery.

The rediscovery of Aristotle's works, however, and particularly the influence of his *Poetics*, had persuaded others, notably Tasso, that marvels, in being correctly linked and ordered, could be a proper means of aesthetic, and even of moral, refinement. For this tradition the romance, revived by the discovery of Heliodorus' *Ethiopian History* during the sack of Buda by the Turks in 1526, remained the ideal form of literature. And the key to becoming the 'Homer of the *roman*' was to engage the *admiratio* of the reader through the judicious use of fabulous elements. Within *Don Quixote* the lengthy discourse by the Canon of Toledo provides a more sophisticated Aristotelian criticism of the romance, which had by that time degenerated into formulaic storytelling. While defending the worth of literature 'whose purpose is only to delight and not to instruct', he argues that, for the contemporary reader at least, *admiratio* depends upon 'verisimilitude' rather than upon the marvellous.

Cervantes brilliantly incorporates these varied perspectives into his complex narrative, and then subverts them all with his own astonishing novelties. In *Don Quixote* the fabulous, as dream images, becomes a new species of 'verisimilitude' and arouses *admiratio*. This method has the initial effect of flattering the reader, who accepts the marvellous elements as symptoms of Don Quixote's derangement. It seems the narrative has no purpose other than to delight and entertain. But such is the reticence of its original author that, absorbed into the fiction and given a creative role as the point of narrative synthesis, the reader increasingly finds it difficult to clarify the distinction between dreams and waking experience, between appearance and reality, between the fictional world of the book and the mundane existence of everyday life, or between the author and the reader.

Fiction, like the dream, is an inclusive rather than an oppositional category. It is not defined, so to speak, by drawing a line upon a continuous and unmarked sheet of paper. The dream is another world, and not a particular place, or definite area, within a common reality. The book is a circumscribed object, which exists along side innumerable other similar and unlike objects, but once opened, the act of reading unfolds a limitless world for which the reader exists as its invisible medium. Cervantes' invention of the novel recognises the potential within the post-medieval period for experiencing the world in terms of an individuated ego; and more than that, he frees the ego to experience, through reading, all possible and impossible worlds. *Don Quixote*, written for an age which discovered silent, inward reading, offered an example that was eagerly followed; indeed, 'every novel embeds the *Quixote* within itself like a secret masterwork, just as every epic poem encases the *Iliad*'.[48]

The novel, thus, is the literary form of modernity. And as every silent reader could enter in his or her own way into the imaginary terrain of the story, an essential complicity links the fictional world and the dream: 'to depict a dreamer, therefore, is to depict an authorial figure'.[49] The novel, that is to say, is an essentially private form of literature, an enigmatic dream, which 'begins out of an erosion of belief in the authority of the written word'.[50]

When he was 17 Freud and his friend Eduard Silberstein taught themselves Spanish so that they could enjoy Cervantes in the original. For several years they corresponded with each other as the two members of 'the Spanish Society'. What is evident from these letters is not only Freud's maturity as a psychologist, but his talent as a writer. If his interest in dreams was not directly instigated by reading Cervantes, then, certainly, it was encouraged by it. It is also reasonable to suppose that, at the same period, he became aware of other literary classics of the Spanish Golden Age, in a number of which the dream is a significant motif in the exploration of an emergent new world.[51]

Francisco de Quevedo, even more directly than had Cervantes, exploited the dream as a subversive literary device. The dream, for him, is not simply an illusion of reality, but a mechanism which exposes and undeceives the hypocrisy of the waking world. His *Dreams and Discourses* reverses what was to become the orthodox dismissal of the dream as 'merely' a personal fiction and exploits its power to demystify conventional reality by exposing its corruption. The chapter titled 'The World from the Inside' reveals with brutal clarity the deceptions of conventional and polite society; the dream is more truthful than a reality which is composed of nothing but hypocritical masks:

> Everything about man is deception and falsehood, examine it how you will, and thus it is that those who are as ignorant as yourself are taken in by appearances. Consider the case of sin, for instance. All sins stem from falsehood. It is there that they have both their beginning and their end, and from whence a thousand others – anger, gluttony, pride, avarice, luxury, sloth, murder – all spring and draw their nourishment.
>
> (Quevedo 1989, p. 193)

Hypocrisy is a waking deception so that 'not only are things not what they seem, they are not even what they are called!'. The dream, on the other hand, reveals the unvarnished truth of an inner reality, exposing (at least to the dreamer) the genuine, but disreputable, motives behind conventional behaviour. For Quevedo's dreamer the waking world is made up of a series of deceptions; 'everything you see is window dressing and nothing is as nature made it.'[52]

Coming at the end of the Golden Age of Spanish literature, Calderón de la Barca's *Life is a Dream* is one of the most sustained and paradoxical reflections on the oneiric theme in the early modern period, and was later to become known in Vienna through Hugo von Hoffmansthal's free translation.[53] An amazingly prolific and popular dramatist, Calderón uses dream imagery to convey, among other things, the artificiality of a social world conscious of having awakened from its period of imperial splendour. It is a play which, along with Cervantes' great novel, is a fitting point of departure for Freud's lifelong fascination with dreams. A central character, named Segismund, is held captive in a tower by his father, who hopes thereby to save his people from the dangerous passions which stir his son to violence. Confined for many years he cannot recall his origins and, on gaining his liberty, only gradually, as if awaking from a long dream, becomes aware of his true identity as a prince.[54] But his conviction is undermined, and he is persuaded that this waking self-recognition is, in its turn, just another dream. He becomes as doubtful as Descartes or, in another way, as uncertain as the reader of *Quixote*:

> Can it be I'm only dreaming
> though I think myself awake?
> I am not dreaming, for I know
> and feel what I have been
> and what I am

Indeed, the dream may recreate a complete sense of waking reality. By the third act Segismundo's questioning has become purely rhetorical:

> Can it be possible that such
> A similarity exists between
> Our dreams and all the things we took
> Such pleasure in that what we held
> Was true proves false, and false proves true?
> Must we believe that what we see
> And touch and hear with clarity
> Is in the end in constant doubt,
> An object of uncertainty;
> And thus conclude that what we thought
> Must be the true original
> Is nothing more and nothing less
> Than some pale imitation of
> Reality?

Equally, waking life can often appear as absurd and insubstantial as a dream:

> . . . for the world
> we live in is so curious
> that to live is but to dream

The most bizarre characteristics of the dream are no stranger than the phantasmagoria of modern life:

> What is life? A frenzy.
> What is life? An illusion,
> fiction, passing shadow

So strange has life become:

> The world, in short, is where men dream
> The different parts that they are playing
> And no one stops to know their meaning.

He fittingly concludes:

> I think that life is but a dream,
> And even dreams not what they seem

(Calderón 1991, Act 3)

KNOWLEDGE

If dreams can recreate a complete sense of reality – including the doubt we discover at its core – then might they not serve a genuinely investigative function? They reveal, as well as the truth concealed behind the deceitful mask of social life, the inner harmonic structure of nature. Early modern science is the dream of cosmological knowledge. And we should not be surprised that Galileo's methodological novelty was to take seriously the task of analysing idealised and imaginary situations, or that Johannes Kepler, whose role in the transformation of astronomy can hardly be underestimated, measured his hard won knowledge against the truth of dreams.

Written originally in 1609, but not published in his lifetime, the revised and heavily annotated text of Kepler's *Somnium* which his son issued in 1634 seems in retrospect to be a bizarre mixture of fiction, scientific theory and utopian philosophy.

Its opening is as bold and deceitful as Cervantes' novel:

> It happened then on a certain night that after watching the stars and moon, I stretched out on my bed and fell sound asleep. In my sleep I seemed to be reading a book I had got from the market. This was how it went:

(Lear 1965, p. 87)

Kepler's expository technique is to relate the dream while simultaneously commenting upon its imagery through elaborate and detailed footnotes. Indeed, in some respects anticipating Freud, it is not so much a commentary as the outline of another discourse which replaces, in its claims to rationality, coherence and order, the immediate reality of the dream itself.[55]

Kepler's dreamer, to whom he gives the name Duracotus (which 'came to me from a recollection of names of a similar sound in the history of Scotland'), is forced to undergo his first voyage as a result of his mother, Fiolxhilde, selling him to a sea captain. She does this to make good the loss of a sale of herbs and embroidered cloth which resulted from her son's unrestrained curiosity in cutting open the pouch which contained them, thus allowing them to be 'scattered all about'. He is taken to the observatory of Tycho Brahe who, recognising the child's talent, teaches him all he knows of modern astronomy. On his return, after five years, he is

181

reunited with his mother, and discovers that she has come to know by her own esoteric means all that he himself has learned.

There are clear autobiographical references in this part of the dream. Kepler's own mother was an uneducated peasant with the potentially lethal reputation for being 'wise' and bad tempered. She was accused of witchcraft and saved from execution only by her son's strenuous efforts over a period of five years. Kepler himself served as Tycho Brahe's assistant at Helsinborg, and on his mentor's death in 1601 came into possession of a large quantity of important unpublished material and observations.

The second and more daring journey is to the moon; a distance traversed either through initial transformation into a daemon, or, for a persisting human traveller, during sleep. In a note Kepler associates the word 'daemon' with 'knowledge of the phenomena of the stars'; dreams and knowledge thus become part of a single transformation in which the human subject becomes intimate with the cosmos. Kepler's dream, unlike the genre which his work inspires, does not dwell on the technical difficulties of the journey itself. Hurrying along 'by willpower' the journey is accomplished in four hours. Reliance on emotional energy links the *Somnium* with the spiritual expansiveness of the Renaissance revival of magic, and particularly with the writings of Ficino and Bruno.[56] At the same time, in describing this 'ascent' into a strange region inhabited by intelligent but inhuman creatures, Kepler provides an unprecedented and unrepeated 'scientific' commentary on a host of physical and dynamic questions.

Kepler's short book, circulating in manuscript form, was influential even before it was published.[57] It was the '*fons et origo*' of the new genre, a chief source of cosmic voyages for three centuries'.[58] Other scientists, notably John Wilkins, as well as a host of writers stimulated by the 'New Astronomy' were to use the dream-journey as the frame for a rational discourse, but none tied the dream so closely to the ideal of knowledge. What is significant here is the care with which he reconstructs the lunar view of the universe. Lunar inhabitants imagine themselves to be at the centre of the cosmos and worship the earth as a celestial god. The change in perspective, even more the arbitrariness of any perspective which is implied in this wilful inversion of the 'natural' point of view, reveals a fundamental affinity linking science with the dream.

His description of the moon and its creatures also connects the *Somnium* with the Renaissance explosion of utopian literature. Kepler himself mentions Campanella's *City of the Sun* in this regard.[59] But Kepler was too good a scientist to use the moon as a setting for an ideal community. His moon is pock-marked, irregular and as corrupted as the earth; it is the moon revealed through Galileo's telescope. In fact, in Kepler's text the moon is an anti-utopia; primitive and unattractive it 'represents a defective here' rather than a perfected 'no-place' (*ou-topos*). But a genuinely utopian element is transferred from the dream itself to the scientific discourse which it inspires: 'The new positive science negates a positive fiction and does so with the methods of fictional discourse.'[60]

In Kepler's work what links science, utopia and dream imagery is not the hope of creating a better world, but the intuition of a *harmony* immanent in creation. His need to go beyond Copernicus was based on a demand for *decorum*; on the unity of form and function. The cosmos could no longer be conceived as a divine hierarchical order, composed of qualitatively distinct places and substances, linked through an unbroken chain of sub-ordination and dependence. It had, rather, to be conceivable as a structure of indifferent matter distributed throughout uniform space. Given such a fundamental shift – which was associated with the decline of feudal social relationship, the Reformation, the emergence of national states and cultures, and the development of commodity exchange and monetary relations – Kepler sought tirelessly to uncover the proportional relations which governed this distribution.

Kepler's dream, thus, is not so much a deviation from, as a point of transition to a new scientific discourse. But it is a strange discourse, and Kepler, it is true to say, is 'one of the founders of modern science whom it is nonetheless strictly impossible to reduce to the norms of our modernity'.[61] His science, indeed, is more dreamlike than the *Somnium*. His thought is presented, unlike modern scientific works, as a narrative of discovery, as an imaginative journey through the fierce hardship of error, false pathways, and laborious endeavours which come to nothing before the true 'poetic structure of the universe' is revealed.[62] The finally revealed structural model is conditioned first of all by aesthetic considerations: 'Nature likes simplicity and unity,' he asserts, in his first book, *Mysterium Cosmographicum*.[63] And this underlying unity and simplicity is apparent in the design of creation; a central motionless body, the sun, around which move six planetary bodies in orbits so arranged that each can be inscribed both within and without imaginary regular solids placed between the orbit of each. This dream of Pythagorean unity is, simultaneously, a Christian image:

> The mobile Universe is to be related to the regular solid bodies, of which there are five. If they be regarded as the boundaries or walls . . . they cannot give rise to more than six things. Consequently, there are six bodies in motion round the Sun. Therefore, the Sun which keeps its place, motionless, in the midst of the planets, and which is never-theless the source of all motion, provides the image of God the Father, the Creator, for the creation is to God, as motion is to the Sun. As the Father creates through the Son, so the Sun gives motion in the midst of the fixed stars. . . . But the Sun diffuses and bestows motive power across the *intermedium*, in which the planets are placed, in the same way that God the Father, considered as Creator, acts

through the Holy Ghost, or in virtue of the Holy Ghost. Consequently, it necessarily follows that motion is proportional to the distances.

(Koyré 1973, p. 154)

Using Tycho Brahe's precise observational data, Kepler tried to show that this picture of the cosmos was physically true as well as mathematically accurate, aesthetically appealing and religiously necessary. After years of labour, particularly in relation to calculating the orbit of Mars, he was forced to admit there were minor inaccuracies. The difficulty was triumphantly overcome, however, by admitting the planetary orbits were ellipses rather than perfect circles. This provided not only a simpler mathematical expression for their observed paths but an opportunity for a deeper understanding of the harmonic structure which they expressed. Using these slight eccentricities he was able to compare the angular velocities of the planets at aphelion and perihelion and show that their proportions could be expressed as simple harmonic ratios. Planetary motions, that is to say, united geometric and musical harmonies, so that in describing a real but invisible architectonic structure they sounded the equally real but inaudible notes of a music of the spheres.

Harmony is revealed, as if in a dream – which had once been the privileged medium of communication with the divine – but the dream is now composed of rational thought. The entire structure exists, in fact, so that human contemplation can realise itself in a rational form. This is why the earth cannot occupy a fixed central point in the cosmos but, through its own motion, reveals to the enquiring mind with dreamlike clarity the beautiful structure which has been created for its contemplation:

If the earth, our home, did not measure the annual orbit of the other planets – changing from place to place and station to station – human reason would never have arrived at knowledge of the precise intervals of the planets and other things that depend on those intervals; it would never have invented astronomy.

(Hallyn 1990, p. 245)

This structure is revealed, moreover, only when man imagines himself to be elsewhere; in order to appreciate the divine plan, he must reconstruct the relative motions of the planets as if viewing them from the sun. Man, in truth, is an eccentric being. Born of the ellipse, he dreams of fantastic journeys which lead him, in the end, to the truth. This spatial dislocation was an inversion and ultimately a more powerful device than the construction of pictorial space which had preceded it. There, demonstrated by Alberti and Brunelleschi, the painter's perspective represented a privileged viewpoint, occupied in turn by the artist and the viewer, from which could be seen first one and then another artificially created 'scenes'.[64] The position remained fixed and different worlds appeared in succession through the fecundity of the artist's imagination. For Kepler the privileged position required an imaginative act of distancing, so that the human observer could incorporate into a larger structure a true vision of the place where he actually existed.

For Kepler, as for Cervantes, dreams are realised in the true structure of the world. His science operated by 'an application of the schemas of analogical thought to the field of quantity'.[65] Thus, where ancient astronomy had contented itself with 'saving the appearance' – with a dream of rational, perfect circular motion from whose complexities observable events could be recovered by geometric manipulation – Kepler transformed idealised geometry into a precise physical description of the planetary system.

THE BAROQUE IMAGINATION

The ellipse, which distinguishes Kepler's astronomy both from the ancient and medieval vision of perfect circularity and the Cartesian insistence on the straight line of rectilinear motion and categorical distinction, characterises the baroque in much the same way as the rounded arch does the Romanesque, or the pointed arch does the gothic. It is possible to view both Kepler and Cervantes as exemplars of baroque culture. Certainly, Freud's initial interest in dreams was stimulated by baroque models, and in particular by the work of Cervantes. But the full implication of this original identification can only be gauged by a more comprehensive view of the baroque imagination.

Stylistic elements, such as the ellipse, while significant as indicators of a particular period, do not immediately convey the complex inner unity of the baroque, which exists as 'the embodiment of certain widely held ideas, attitudes and assumptions'.[66] And baroque ideas can now be seen, after a long period of neglect, to have been as fundamental to the character of modernity as was the Enlightenment from which, more generally, cultural historians have taken their point of departure.[67] The establishment of science and the control of nature, including human nature, by reason seems remote from the spectacular and voluptuous forms of the baroque which immediately preceded it. But a contemporary disillusionment with the many aspects of the scientific world view and its implications encourages the reinvestigation of an age rich in anticipations of cultural discoveries we thought peculiarly our own. The baroque, that is to say, might be viewed as simultaneously 'pre-modern' and 'postmodern'.

Developing first and most completely in Spain, the baroque is a culture incubated outside the main lines of historical development which, since the writings of Max Weber, have provided the basic points of reference for sociological investigations of the emergence of modern society. Without a legacy of feudalism, Spain during the first half of the seventeenth century was remote from those forces which, in northern and western Europe, were bringing capitalism and its bourgeois sobriety into prominence by sweeping aside the surviving forms. The baroque is not there identified, as it was throughout the rest of Europe, with the counter-Reformation, because there the Reformation had no meaning. The baroque was formed, in other words, within a decaying empire; it reflected upon a society responsible for the discovery and naming of a new world, but one whose period of growth and world domination had been over for some time. Its aristocratic ruling class was no longer insulated from criticism, and the prevention of popular insurrection became the major preoccupation of the state. The baroque is an era of crisis; Philip IV, recognising the intensification of the social struggle, remarked that 'today we are all on the verge of being lost'.[68]

The growth of a rootless population, together with the marked decline in Spain's political and cultural pre-eminence, gave a new urgency to the control of public opinion. But, while for northern and western Europe new mechanisms of self-control were institutionalised through religious and educational reforms (a culture within which science and humanism were identified as progressive elements), baroque culture tried to establish direct techniques of mass control. 'Everything that belongs to the baroque', argues its most competent contemporary guide, 'emerges from the necessities of manipulating opinion and feelings on a broad public scale.'[69]

The maintenance of public order was essentially an urban problem. A large and growing population of beggars was controlled by force and the threat of force. The presence of authority was everywhere made manifest, particularly in military establishments, public buildings and palaces. The grandeur of baroque building was designed to intimidate; it was part of the violence which constituted the 'baroque pedagogy of the sentiments'.[70] It was, above all, a society of the spectacle.[71] And its most significant and characteristic cultural form was the theatre.[72] Indeed, the theatricality of everyday life, the intimate connection and easy identification of one with the other, was far more than a literary or dramatic conceit. In Spain, theatres, often temporary *corrales* adapted for the occasion from the internal courtyards of existing domestic buildings, were an intimate part of everyday life. The reversible identity of theatrical and public order, of art and life, became the 'major vehicle for expressing the radical baroque conviction that the phenomenal world is illusion'.[73] And the play, as its most accessible cultural form, became 'an ambivalent celebration and critique of illusion'.[74]

Almost every aspect of baroque culture can be understood in the context of an ideological struggle between the court and an impoverished urban mass. The 'baroque aesthetic of exaggeration and surprise', it has been claimed, was 'invented to evoke wonder in the public'.[75] This is nowhere more evident than in the dramatic power and melodic richness of the vast and colourful operatic entertainments provided for its luxury-loving audiences by Monteverdi and Cavalli.

(Skrine 1978, p.12)

While baroque refers to an epoch rather than to a style, its many variations nonetheless exhibit common themes and forms, as well as a uniform purpose:

> What distinguishes baroque from neo-classical unity in much of literary as well as plastic art . . . is the employment of multiple perspectives, fluidity of form, oblique and sensuous movement, delight in effects, deliberate illusioning and disillusioning, all-embracing theatricality, artistic wit.
>
> (Hoffmeister 1983, p. 6)

The immediately experienced world, condensed, as it were, from the symbolic unreality of late medieval categories which were secularised but not wholly abandoned in the Renaissance, is valued both for itself and as a bearer of spiritual powers:

> The whole art of the baroque expresses an acceptance of the material world, through the realistic representation of man and nature, through the affirmation of the senses and the emotions and through a new perception of space and infinity.
>
> (Martin 1977, p. 39)

It is just this 'baroque sensualisation of experience' which links Kepler and Cervantes; and distinguishes them both from Descartes. It is a world in which no absolute distinctions exist, in which forms flow continually into one another, where outside and inside interpenetrate, and where every boundary remains sensuously indefinite and whose hidden structure is defined by the scale and proportion of the human body.[76] The 'verisimilitude' which is central to the art of Cervantes is just as fundamental to Kepler's search for the physically real, yet transcendental, structure of the cosmos; a structure revealed only 'by sensuous means'. And while the body provides a measure of social and cosmological harmony and order, it also represents in its own unavoidable corruption and decay the irreversible tendency towards chaos. The closed and idealised body form of the Renaissance Vitruvian figure gave way to an altogether more disturbing identification with disease:[77]

> The baroque sensibility of the artists of the first quarter of the seventeenth century, deeply affected by anatomical knowledge and ever-present doctors, scientists, and barber-surgeons, produced like-nesses that departed more and more from Renaissance canons of proportion. The macabre and monstrous theatricality of anatomical

investigation pervaded seventeenth-century body imagery. The open cadaver, a dualistic image of perfection and decay, became the most genuine *momento mori* of the time; the body symbolized semidivine humanity and its inevitable destiny of corruption.

(Calvi 1989, p. 217)

The 'nightmare of universal putrefaction' was a terrifying vision of a life-long struggle against the forces of nature, rather than an image of death.[78] It was a form of sensuousness associated with catastrophic instability rather than with slow, vegetative decay. And, since this dizziness affected all the senses, it was more terrifying and immediate than the most apocalyptic *picture* of reality. Not simply a vision, the overwhelming sense of chaos was also a 'sublime olfactory deliria'.[79] Wrenched from the stability (or imagined stability) of pre-modern social life, everything became infected with turbulence. Kepler's universe, especially for less mathematically gifted observers, was a physical drama that seemed only remotely to be the realisation of an inner harmony. More commonly the heavens were suggestive of cosmic vertigo:

The heavenly vault, hitherto site of blissful contemplation and stillness, was now transformed into an acrobatic gymnasium, a whirling torch of precipitous journeys.

(Camporesi 1988, p. 29)

Yet, simultaneously and without contradiction, the baroque world is permeated by metaphysical tensions. The 'illusionism' central to many of its characteristic artistic expressions is an 'integration of real and fictive space'.[80] The 'paradoxical and the phantasmagoria' was everywhere in evidence, its poetry was rich in 'hallucinatory, nightmarish, theatrical or playful' elements.[81] The favourite *trompe l'oeil* in ceiling decoration was a playing with perspective techniques that could just as easily be used to create a false as a true impression. This too has a persuasive purpose, 'that of transferring the mind of the viewer from material to eternal things'.[82]

This kind of illusionism also highlights the baroque fascination with infinity. Gilles Deleuze has characterised the baroque imagination at its most metaphysical, in the writing of Leibniz, as an 'operative function' which 'endlessly produces folds . . . pushing them to infinity'.[83] Matter and soul are differentiated, but not as Descartes had indicated by the rectilinear logic of a clear distinction between two types of substance; rather they are distinguished by the characteristic morphology, by the style of convolution, in which a singular substance is differently inflected.

The infinitely folded 'muscular' continuity of matter, which can be likened to human flesh, has a distinctive 'inside' as well as texture, extension and mass. Matter is a 'continuous labyrinth' which;

offers an infinitely porous, spongy, or cavernous texture without

188

emptiness . . . each body contains a world pierced with irregular passages, surrounded and penetrated by increasingly vaporous 'fluid'.

(Deleuze 1993, p. 5)

The baroque soul – 'tangled in the pleats of matter' – cannot be separated from this labyrinth, in which it is endlessly implicated.

Modernity so 'soldered itself' to the Enlightenment, and to a particular vision of science, reason and progress, that it is difficult now to conceive of the contemporary disenchantment with that world as anything other than the catastrophic liberation of *post*modernity. But the baroque anticipates all those characteristics of the modern age which we take to be most decisively postmodern: perspectivism, sensuousness, the interpenetration of soul and body, the merging of spatial and temporal categories, the superficiality and theatricality of social life and the 'feminisation' of philosophy, art and religion with all that it entails for the reorientation of the subject towards reality in terms of immediacy rather than of reflection. The interrupted tradition of modernity, linking the culture of the baroque with contemporary fashion, not only contextualises the otherwise incomprehensible fragmentation of the present, it redefines the rationality of the classical bourgeois world as a deviation from *its* normative pluralism. In a recent discussion, Buci-Glucksmann forcefully expresses this much needed corrective to contemporary short-sightedness:

> 'baroque Reason': the term may appear provocative, so greatly has the explaining (*rendre raison*) of reason obliterated the *plurality* of classical reasons and obscured the baroque as a paradigm of thought and writing which overflows conventional models of identity, essence and substantiality. For those who identify reason with the 'long chains', Cartesian or other, it seems impossible that a *ratio* should be stylistic and rhetorical, that it should be permanently at grips with its theatricization and dramatization, that it should act itself out in 'bodies'. But in the baroque, the reason of the unconscious and the reason of utopia present themselves to be interpreted. The baroque signifier proliferates beyond everything signified, placing language in excess of corporality.

(Buci-Glucksmann 1994, p.139)

Though rejecting the general aims of Leibniz's philosophy, both contemporary science and philosophical psychology have rediscovered the value of these conceptions of continuity, implication and relativism.[84] The fusion of matter and space in infinite labyrinthine complexity, rather than their separation as isolated bodies in the infinite extension of formally distinct and empty dimensions of space and time, are indicative of a partial recovery of, if not a full-blown return to, the baroque. And, making a significant contribution to this recovery, Freud's theory of dreams,

189

whatever it owes in detail to the inspiration of Cervantes, elaborates in a bold new way the elements of a baroque psychology.

Contemporary society, however, is not simply a resurgence of the baroque. To parody Max Weber it might be said that while the baroque masses were forced to be distracted, the modern public want to be.[85] The difference lies essentially with the triumph of a distinctively bourgeois principle of self-regulation. For the baroque era it was not yet clear that modern society *would* become self-regulating. The liberation from feudal forms of constraint, and the consequential mobility of the populace on a hitherto unknown scale, posed a genuine threat to social stability. It was only gradually that the inefficiency of baroque techniques of constraint gave way to the institutionalisation of the market and to powerful new means of social control through rational self-regulation. Once deprived of all means of self-preservation other than through the exchange of commodities, the populace could gradually be released from external forms of mass constraint, and progressively integrated into modern society through the contract of work. Free to act as they willed, reason dictated that everyone willed to work. This fundamental, and ingeniously concealed, mode of domination rendered obsolete the baroque's more spectacular techniques of coercion and the manipulation of public opinion.[86]

This was by no means a simple and painless transition; its history, as the history of any transition, is written in violence and suffering. But the force of 'reason' prevailed so that now we go to work (when we can) without even willing it. The problem of social control is no longer that of exacting a foundational act of compliance with the underlying logic of modernity, but is (merely!) one of satisfying the expectations aroused by this historic surrender.

Thus, whereas the public magnificence and spectacle of the baroque era was a state policy predicated on fear and distrust of the masses, the contemporary 'culture of excess' is predicated on the dynamic (and presumed beneficial) consequences of private consumption. The difficulties of understanding the contemporary social world consequently appears to be an inversion of the problem of explaining nature. For the natural sciences the level of phenomena can be readily accounted for in terms of a coherent and systematic science, but at a 'deep' level of unobservable events no systematisation seems possible, causality appears to break down; and the scientist despairs of constructing a rational model of fundamental processes. In the social world, on the other hand, the 'deep' level of reality is now taken for granted and has, so to speak, been forgotten. The fundamental 'mechanisms' of commodity production and exchange have become invisible in the sense of being regarded as matters of contingency, and we are oriented towards these processes as a 'second nature'. But at the 'superficial' level, of consciousness, consumption, culture and dreams, everything is in a state of flux; and the sociologist despairs of being able to describe and analyse the commonest phenomena in a coherent and systematic fashion.

The dream is a 'nodal point' in a boundless web of associations; and Freud's text, similarly, draws together a complex network of ideas and images originating in different periods, and under different circumstances, throughout the development of western society. In re-establishing many of the interconnections within the labyrinth of western ideas about dreams, Freud circumvented the more restrictive intellectualism and rationalism which characterised the orthodoxies of his own day. Read in the context of *fin-de-siècle* culture, it is tempting to view Freud's work in general as expressive of an uneasy sense of inner disintegration; it seems to be trapped in an ambiguous borderland between classical bourgeois individualism and the postmodern age. But in the larger framework of intertextuality his psychology can be seen, yet more provocatively, as recovering the hidden roots of modernity. Freud's domestication of the baroque not only provides an alternative view of the significance of a neglected past, it furnishes the contemporary world with a meaningful image of itself.

NOTES

1 Meier, in Grunebaum and Caillois (1966), pp. 303–19.
2 Mavromatis (1987).
3 Weber (1952), pp. 61–89.
4 Husser (1994), p. vii.
5 Otto (1954), p. 68.
6 Snell (1953), p. 6; see more generally Onians (1951), Regnéll (1967), Claus (1981), Gernet (1981), Vernant (1980, 1991), and for a psychoanalytic perspective Caldwell (1989).
7 Sullivan (1988), p. 29.
8 Dodds (1951), p. 16.
9 Gernet (1981), p. 74.
10 Synesius (1930), p. 328.
11 Ibid., p. 334.
12 Ibid., p. 341.
13 Dodds (1951), pp. 102–34; Trombley (1993), vol. 1, pp. 165–8.
14 Foucault (1990), pp. 1–36.
15 Artemidorus (1975), p. 13.
16 Aristotle (1935).
17 Artemidorus (1975), p. 14.
18 Ibid., p. 15.
19 Ibid., p. 15.
20 Ibid., p. 15.
21 Ibid, pp. 105–6.
22 Le Goff (1985), p. 198.
23 Macrobius (1952).
24 Kruger (1992), pp. 21–5.
25 Macrobius, (1952), p. 90.
26 Kruger (1992), p. 23.
27 MacMullen (1984) draws attention to the normality of visions in this context.
28 Le Goff (1985), pp. 212–14.

29 Brown (1989), pp. 190, 232.
30 Bauer (1971).
31 Rudolph (1983); Filoramo (1990).
32 Fischer (1978), pp. 26–8.
33 Piehler (1971); Spearing (1976); Fischer (1978); Kruger (1992).
34 Alan of Lille, quoted in Gurevich (1985), p. 61.
35 Mâle (1972), p. 29.
36 Alan of Lile, quoted in Gurevich (1985), p. 59.
37 Grabes (1982) p. 4.
38 Ferguson (1990), pp. 85–92.
39 This vast and intriguing subject can only be hinted at; see Ong (1958); Yates (1966); Carruthers (1990).
40 Bakhtin (1968).
41 Parr (1974).
42 Foucault (1970), pp. 3–16; Riley (1962), p. 48.
43 As an unjust reader might blame Mirbeau for the Rat Man's fantasy.
44 Cervantes (1950), p. 534, 555.
45 Ibid., p. 317.
46 Ibid., p. 616.
47 Forcione (1970), pp. 16–17.
48 Ortega y Gasset, quoted in Gilman (1989), p. xiv.
49 Weiger (1988), p. 139.
50 Alter 'Partial Magic', quoted in Weiger (1988), p. 7, the sentence continues 'and it begins with Cervantes'.
51 Palley (1983).
52 Ibid., p. 213.
53 Hofmannsthal was deeply influenced by Calderón; see Curtius (1973), pp. 135–68.
54 The entire play illustrates the notion that 'Man cannot know himself immediately'; Cascardi (1984), p. 4.
55 Reiss (1982) argues that Kepler's *Somnium* is a genuine point of transiton between a 'patterning' discourse and an 'analytico-dedictive' discourse.
56 Kristeller (1943); Walker (1958); Yates (1964, 1985); Shumaker (1972); Garin (1978); Couliano (1987).
57 Nicolson (1948) particularly mentions John Donne.
58 Ibid., p. 41.
59 Hallyn (1990), p. 174.
60 Ibid., p. 175.
61 Simon (1979), pp. 8–9.
62 The phrase is taken from the title of Hallyn's exciting book (Hallyn 1990).
63 Quoted in Koyré (1973), p. 133. The aesthetic dimension is also emphasised in Simon (1979); see also Caspar (1959).
64 White (1957).
65 Simon (1979), pp. 134–6.
66 Martin (1977), p. 12.
67 Maravall (1986); Buci-Glucksmann (1994); Deleuze (1993).
68 Quoted in Maravall (1986), p. 38.
69 Maravall (1986), p. 90.
70 Ibid., p. 163.
71 See Resnik (1987) for an approach to the dream as a theatrical performance. The theatre was the most popular art form in Freud's Vienna.
72 Greer (1991).
73 Warnke (1972), p. 70; Parker (1988).

74 Cascardi (1984), p. 23.
75 E. W. Hesse quoted in Maravall (1986), p. 210.
76 Camporesi, in a series of remarkable studies (1988, 1989, 1991).
77 Barkan (1975); Koenigsberger (1979).
78 Camporesi (1988), p. 181.
79 Camporesi (1988), p. 184; Corbin (1990) and Süskind (1991) are still able to invoke this almost vanished sensibility. See also Classen (1993).
80 Martin (1977), p. 14.
81 Warnke (1972), p. 73.
82 Martin (1977), p. 14.
83 Deleuze (1993), p. 3.
84 For various suggestions here see Nisbet (1972); Capek (1971, 1976); Freudenthal (1986); Burwick (1986).
85 'The Puritan wanted to work in a calling, we are forced to do so', Weber (1930), p.181.
86 Foucault's (1977) treatment of this transition shows the way in which coercion itself becomes rationalised. His treatment of public torture is an exemplary description of many of the central themes of the baroque.

7

HYPERTEXT

Freud and sociological theories
of modern society

It is tempting to regard Freud's 'theory of society' as an elaboration upon the mechanism of repression. Shame, guilt and moral repugnance are the individuated and inward expression of conventions through which society is established and maintained. Of the three great sources of unhappiness which Freud identifies in the opening pages of *Civilisation and its Discontents* – 'the superior power of nature, the feebleness of our own bodies and the inadequacy of the regulations which adjust the mutual relationship of human beings' – he does not hesitate to identify 'what we call our Civilisation' as the most significant cause of misery.[1] The fact that society is the source of innumerable satisfactions, that it has devolved upon us God-like powers of self-mastery and domination of nature seems, in the end, to count for nothing. Society superimposes upon the primary organic repression, associated with the adoption of an erect posture and a radical reorganisation of the sensorial, further restrictions on the availability of instinctual gratification. But the acquisition of a fully internalised sense of disgust, which is the phylogenetic precondition of the power of society over us, does not in itself account for our wholly conscious unhappiness. Freud argues that it is 'primary mutual hostility' that is the underlying source of human antipathy to, and estrangement from, social life:

> Civilisation has to use its utmost efforts in order to set limits to man's aggressive instincts and to hold the manifestations of them in check by psychical reaction-formations.
>
> (SE 21, p. 112)

The common interest in work is insufficient of itself to control aggression, which Freud gradually acknowledged to be 'an original, self-subsisting instinctual disposition'. The forced renunciation of this instinctual gratification through its subjection to external authority is gradually replaced by the power of an internal and ever-vigilant conscience. Originally guilt corresponded to remorse over the consequences of an aggressive act; but for the internal authority of a super ego the distinction between act and

194

intention is insignificant, so that guilt flows from the impulse itself. Thus, 'the price we pay for our advance in civilisation is a loss of happiness through the heightening of the sense of guilt'.[2]

To the extent that instinctual impulses can be diverted into other channels they provide a store of 'energy' which can be used for the 'higher' purposes of civilisation. A simple 'pleasure principle' is overtaken by a harsh 'reality principle' and 'sublimation' and 'compromise-formations' of all sorts are the tolerable substitutes for the direct means of instinctual gratification.

This is a caricature of Freud's views, though one which his later works to some extent encouraged; and it is the view of Freud's work which has become orthodox in the more general social sciences literature.[3] Yet it is hardly justified, either as a logical elaboration and extension of his psychology, or as an insight into the character of modern society. Freud's real contribution to our understanding of society lies elsewhere; and to make this more obvious it is helpful to bring his work into a closer relation with those major sociological figures for whom modernity was a central intellectual preoccupation.

FREUD AND WEBER: MODERNITY AS EGO

In terms of temperament, moral outlook and general 'orientation to the world' Freud seems closer to Max Weber than to any other major sociological figure, and for that reason if for no other some discussion of the relation between their views of modernity is an obvious starting point.

They were both conservative in their mode of life, immensely hard-working and ambitious. They were both secular intellectuals who sought to understand the meaning and significance of various religious traditions which, they believed, no longer played a fundamental part in shaping people's lives. They were both pessimistic about the possibilities of human self-improvement, and sceptical of movements which proclaimed the real possibility of a radically different future. And for all their differences in approach, in terms of a strong interest in the ancient world and in the history of civilisation, they shared a common background of knowledge which was rooted in a classical German education. Additionally, Max Weber himself suffered a mental breakdown and, we might suppose, this provided him with personal insights which might have attracted him to Freud's work.[4]

Yet they seem to have had no interest in each other's writings, and there has been little enthusiasm for bringing their ideas together. To determine a potentially fruitful point of contact between their respectively vast but seemingly divergent realms of discourse, it is important to bear in mind the most general tendencies of their thought. Weber was concerned, above all, with the historical processes of 'rationalisation', that is with 'ego construction'; while Freud, similarly, was preoccupied primarily with efforts to understand the processes of ego formation as the rationalising power of consciousness. Both were extremely interested in non-rational and even irrational forces or 'values', but conceived them as part of the relational field against which the ego (rational action) could define itself.

Indeed, the general context of Weber's sociological view of the development of western society as a continuous process of 'rationalisation' might be considered as a history of the ego, while his most celebrated work, *The Protestant Ethic and the Spirit of Capitalism*, can be read as a sophisticated analysis of the social mechanism through which the ego became inextricably bound to the development of modernity. Weber argues that, in western society, religion has played a key role in social development. Paradoxically, it has been religious ideas and institutions which have been the 'carrier' of the process of rationalisation. In the most inclusive sense of the term, Weber refers to a general and continuous process of harmonisation, systematisation and growth of internal coherence in all aspects of social life. This process is conditioned by specific extra-rational values in terms of which all social action becomes subjectively meaningful for the social actors themselves. In western society the particular character of religion is not only to ground action in a system of 'ultimate values', but to do so in terms of specific religious assumptions which themselves carry forward the rationalising process. It is, in particular, the primary commitment to belief in a single, transcendental and omnipotent God, upon whom human salvation depends and in relation to whom the human encounter with evil must be worked out, that has engendered a powerful internal dynamic. The 'givenness' of a transcendental God together with a belief in salvation introduced an inevitable tension between the experience of the everyday world and the religious promise of happiness.[5] Rational theology, emerging in the tradition breaking innovations of prophecy, and developing in response to the encounter between the religious traditions of Ancient Judaism and secular Greek culture, was further strengthened by this tension which continually led to demands for religious 'explanations' of the world. And as the western God was wholly transcendent, human reason itself, within the limits set by foundational religious assumptions, became the final arbiter of theological ideas and drove their development towards systematic completion.

According to Weber, this completion took place in the theology of Calvin, in whom:

> That great historic process in the development of religions, the elimination of magic from the world which had begun with the old Hebrew prophets and, in conjunction with Hellenistic scientific thought, had repudiated all magical means to salvation as superstition and sin, came here to its logical conclusion.
>
> (Weber 1930, p. 105)

The Reformation swept aside all residual magical elements from western Christianity, laid bare its underlying principles with unambiguous clarity, and inter-related its elements with uncompromising logic. What emerged was a wholly rational, but humanly unreasonable, set of religious precepts. The absolute character of God's otherness form everything human, and at the same time the helpless dependence upon His grace for salvation, resulted in a state of acute spiritual insecurity. Weber outlines the implications of the doctrine of predestination with a clarity of his own:

> In its extreme inhumanity this doctrine must above all have had one consequence for the life of a generation which surrendered to its magnificent consistency. That was a feeling of unprecedented inner loneliness of the single individual. In what was for the man of the age of the Reformation the most important thing in life, his eternal salvation, he was forced to follow his path alone to meet a destiny which had been decreed for him from eternity. No one could help him.
>
> (Weber 1930, p. 104)

As Weber points out, 'the decisive problem is: How was this doctrine borne?' He argues that, in fact, in its original and wholly consistent form it was not. The tension between the demands of everyday life and religious doctrine was productive of a 'compromise-formation' that proved to be equally damaging to both. It was, above all, in the 'practical pastoral work, which had immediately to deal with all the suffering caused by the doctrine', that a resolution was found.[6] Firstly, the doctrine of predestination was relaxed to the extent that a religious duty of self-confidence was placed upon the believer. If the individual could summon the inner strength required to sustain an unshakeable conviction that they were among the chosen, then this certainty itself was interpreted as a token of faith and, thus, a sign of grace. This notion of faith, of course, transgressed the fundamentals of the dogmatic position, but it nonetheless proved to be irresistible. Secondly, 'in order to attain that self-confidence intense worldly activity is recommended as the most suitable means'.[7] Weber, of course, was concerned particularly with the economic and social consequence of this peculiar form of 'inner-worldly asceticism', but his account is, above all, a compelling piece of historical psychology. It was in the form of Puritanism that the modern ego was born from the womb of spiritual anxiety. Weber's account parallels Freud's analysis of obsessive and compulsive behaviour. Relentless work and self-denial was considered to be 'the most suitable means of counteracting feelings of religious anxiety'. And, for the Puritan it was through ascetic practices that in the formal sense of the term, the personality was created.[8] Self-mastery, rational conduct and the suppression of emotion all became internalised as spiritual duties, and simultaneously laid the psychological groundwork for the emergence of the autonomy of the modern individual. One is reminded of Freud's early remark to Fliess that the ego is just a specific type of 'compulsive idea'.

A significant implication of Weber's analysis is that, within a very short period, Calvin's rational theology gave rise to a religious practice which was, in its own way, as magical as anything that had gone before. The asceticism of the Puritan was conceived, implicitly and sometimes explicitly, as a specific religious *means* of attaining personal salvation, but in making of salvation an end which could be obtained by the rational conduct of life its inner religious character was destroyed. It was for this reason that modern society was able to establish itself on a purely secular basis, and continually transform its institutions in conformity with the best available means to obtain specific and stated ends. That is to say, social action could no longer be judged in terms of its capacity to express an inner value.

The withering away of religious sentiments which had inspired the initial stages of the emergence of modern society did nothing, however, to lessen the compulsive character of its egoism:

> The Puritan wanted to work in a calling; we are forced to do so. For when asceticism was carried out of monastic cells into everyday life, and began to dominate worldly morality, it did its part in building the tremendous cosmos of the modern economic order. This order is now bound to the technical and economic conditions of machine production which to-day determines the lives of all the individuals who are born into this mechanism, not only those concerned with economic acquisition, with irresistible force.
>
> (Weber 1930, p. 181)

The ego, in other words, has become linked to the 'object-world' in a decisive fashion. But that world has itself been completely emptied of ultimate meaning and significance. Within this 'iron cage' of modern rational capitalism the ego is forced to live on in 'mechanised petrifaction'. Like Ivan Ilych, in Tolstoy's story, or a character from Chekhov, the individual discovers the senselessness of modern life but is left with no alternative but to live on in a wholly 'disenchanted' world.

Paradoxically, however, the experience of modernity is not always, or even normally, that of a tensionless void. The nihilism of the iron cage implies the elimination of ultimate values from collective life, but not necessarily from all forms of experience. All non-rational values, including political, aesthetic, erotic and intellectual as well as religious, take on a purely inward significance for the life of the individual and gradually draw apart from one other as specific and antithetical personal values.[9] In this regard Weber makes several pertinent statements about sexuality which brings him into a closer relationship with central Freudian themes. Weber clearly regards religious values, in themselves, to be as elemental as sexuality.

Thus, in a 'primal' state 'the relation of sex and religion was very intimate', indeed the relation among all 'ultimate values' was very close. Sexual intercourse was frequently an aspect of cultic practices, and 'every ecstasy was considered "holy"'.[10] But he is clearly well aware of the significance of the repression of 'natural' sexuality in favour of eroticism, and of its continuous refinement (through rationalisation) into ego-pleasure:

> The tension of religion and sex has been augmented by evolutionary factors on both sides. On the side of sexuality the tension has led through sublimation into 'eroticism', and therewith into a consciously cultivated, and hence, a non-routinized sphere. . . . The extraordinary quality of eroticism has consisted precisely in a gradual turning away from the naive naturalism of sex. The reason and significance of this evolution involve the universal rationalization and intellectualization of culture.
>
> (Weber 1948, p. 344)

Weber makes the loss of 'natural' sexuality much more recent than does Freud: 'The total being of man has now been alienated from the organic cycle of peasant life'. But he sees this process of repression in a similarly ambivalent light. On the one hand it afforded the individual the possibility of pleasure rather than senseless ecstasy: 'Eroticism was raised into the sphere of conscious enjoyment (in the most sublime sense of the term).' On the other hand, in the context of the emergence of modern society:

> This boundless giving of oneself is as radical as possible in its opposition to all functionality, and rationality, and generality. It is displayed here as the unique meaning which one creature in his irrationality has for another, and only for that specific other. . . . It is so overpowering that it is interpreted 'symbolically': as a sacrament.
>
> (Weber 1948, p. 347)

The absolute but irreconcilable differences among values have become internalised within the individual where they play out, as the conflicting and irresolvable demands of the inner personality, the historical struggles driving the development of human cultures. The embattled ego persists, as does modernity, simply by inertia; by the absence of anything in its way.

FREUD AND DURKHEIM: MODERNITY AS HYSTERIA

The works of Freud and Durkheim are frequently viewed as compatible. They seem bound together by a conservative distrust of modernity, and an interest in the pathological consequences of the breakdown of the social regulation of desire.[11] In fact Freud's work can be used to fill what is sometimes perceived to be a gap in Durkheim's sociology, completing at a 'micro' psychological level the analysis of modern life he developed at a 'macro' sociological level. Conversely Durkheim could be viewed as providing, more completely and more suitably than he did for himself, the social perspective in which Freud's writings gain their full meaning. This approach owes most to the authority of Talcott Parsons, and implies the view that Durkheim lacked a fully developed 'social psychology' which given the general framework of his analysis of the character and development of modern society in general, and his attempt to explain suicide in particular, is both surprising and regrettable.[12] Before considering any alternative approaches to linking the work of Freud and Durkhiem, it is worth considering Durkheim's own, somewhat neglected, psychology.

Durkheim, it may be less controversially suggested, provided a general understanding of the social foundation and development of individualism in modern society. In this he self-consciously adopted a position which was opposed to the main traditions of academic psychology then being established in France. His concern was to demonstrate the social character of individual experience, so that, for him, society was composed of 'representations' rather than of people, or of individuals, or of social relations; or, rather, all those elements of social life were themselves representations. Individuals entered into social relations, and social relations defined individual experience, and both were linked together as a society through sets of conventionally defined meanings. The modality of social life is composed entirely of such representations. Furthermore, society, in this sense, is a 'moral community' which exercises a constraining effect on the activity of its members by virtue of its conventional and, therefore, collective nature. Representations confront the individual (which, is itself such a representation) as a 'given', or a series of 'given' realities. Representations, of which language is the most fundamental, are, thus, 'trans-social' realities sustained through the network of everyday social relations.

For Durkheim, the fundamental structuring principle in modern society is the division of social labour. A progressive differentiation and specialisation has affected every aspect of social life and, as a result, binds each part more completely to every other part. It is on the basis of this process of differentiation that a high level of individuation has taken place. Each person's experience of society is somewhat different to, and distinct from that of any other person. Individualism is simply the subjective experience of the division of labour. Unlike conservative social critics who saw in the development of individualism an immanent threat to the stability and dynamism of modern society, Durkhiem argued that individualism was its foundation. The 'cult of the individual' does not, in itself, threaten society with a loss of vital commitment. Apathy, a retreat into private life, and a consequential loss of civic spirit did not seem to Durkheim to raise serious problems for modern society. From this point of view it seems that Durkheim and Freud might be brought together, in relation to the 'normal' development of society, in terms of a social theory of the superego, or, what amounts to the same thing, a psychological theory of collective representations.[13]

Durkheim argued that real difficulties emerged, however, as a consequence of the 'abnormal forms' of the division of labour. Put simply, the process of differentiation and specialisation in the division of labour proceeded automatically and according to its own laws. The subsequent process of adjustment to each 'advance' in the process was contingent, and uncertain in its timing and effectiveness. Two particular problems arose, connected with social isolation and the rapidity and unpredictability of social change, which he subsequently studied in considerable depth. Durkheim argued that it was just these conditions of 'egoism' and 'anomie' which were statistically associated with the development of pathological forms of individual experience, including higher than average suicide rates.

The individualism characteristic of modern society is itself a foundational institution of that society, and is generally associated with a high level of 'dynamic' and 'moral density'. Normal individualism, that is to say, is sustained by a multiplicity of social relationships and a high level of social participation. It is quite the reverse of a 'withdrawal' into private life. In the complex development of modern society, however, conditions arise in which people tend to become isolated, their social relations dwindle in number and intensity and they become poorly integrated with the general processes of social life. This situation of relative social isolation is viewed, from a subjective standpoint, as 'egoistic'. It is sometimes claimed that Durkheim is satisfied merely with attempting to establish statistical regularities, showing, for example, that suicide rates are lower among those who are married compared to the unmarried, and lower still amongst those who are married with children, and this, in some sense, is an indicator of the level of 'integration' into domestic life.[14] But Durkheim is at pains to understand such associations in terms of both its effect on, and meaning for, subjective life.

It is society, and more particularly the social groups into which we are well integrated, that has aroused in us all our humanly more highly developed motives for living:

> The influence of society is what has aroused in us the sentiments of sympathy and solidarity drawing us toward others; it is society which, fashioning us in its image, fills us with religious, political and moral beliefs that control our actions. To play our social role we have striven to extend our intelligence and it is still society that has supplied us with tools for this development by transmitting to us its trust fund of knowledge.
>
> (Durkheim 1952, pp. 211–12)

All these 'higher' forms of human life are 'society itself incarnated and individualised in each one of us'. It follows from this that:

> We can cling to these forms of human activity only to the degree that we cling to society itself. Contrariwise, in the same measure as we feel detached from society we become detached from that life whose source and aim is society.
>
> (Durkheim 1952, p. 212)

We have a double nature, because 'social man necessarily superimposes himself upon physical man'. But if society, which exists only through continuous interaction, dissolves to the extent that 'we no longer feel it in existence', then:

> All that remains is an artificial combination of illusory images, a phantasmagoria vanishing at the least reflection; that is, nothing which can be a goal for our action. . . . Thus we are bereft of reasons for existence; for the only life to which we could cling no longer corresponds to anything actual; the only existence still based upon reality no longer meets our needs. . . . So there is nothing more for our efforts to lay hold of, and we feel them lose themselves in emptiness.
>
> (Durkheim 1952, p. 213)

In such a situation 'the least cause of discouragement may easily give birth to desperate resolutions'. And even where isolation has reduced the individual to a condition of aimless existence, it is a residual sense of social disintegration which provides the very 'cause of discouragement' which may lead to suicide. Isolated and depressed, people become victims of negative currents of social life:

> Since we are its handiwork, society cannot be conscious of its own decadence without the feeling that henceforth this work is of no value. Thence are formed currents of depression and disillusionment emanating from no particular individual but expressing society's state of disintegration. They reflect the relaxation of social bonds, a sort of collective asthenia, or social malaise, just as individual sadness, when chronic, in its way reflects the poor organic state of the individual.
>
> (Durkheim 1952, p. 214)

Even where society remains well integrated, suicide rates are high as a result of periodic crisis. Durkheim points out that the common sense understanding of this connection is faulty. It is not just economic crises causing poverty which are fertile of suicides, 'crises of prosperity have the same result'.[15] This is because sudden changes in the social environment alters the balanced relationship between human 'wants' or 'needs' and the means to satisfy them. In human society, Durkheim points out, needs have very little to do with the satisfaction of organic appetites which are assuaged by more or less fixed quantities of goods. It is otherwise with the needs engendered by social life itself:

> But how to determine the quantity of well-being, comfort or luxury legitimately to be craved by a human being? Nothing appears in man's organic nor in his psychological constitution which sets a limit to such tendencies. . . . Irrespective of any external regulatory force, our capacity for feeling is in itself an insatiable and bottomless abyss.
>
> (Durkheim 1952, p. 247)

Without some form of social regulation the unlimited capacity for feeling 'can only be a source of torment to itself'. This might be seen as Durkheim's version of a 'Constancy Principle'. Of course, in the normal course of social development desires are continually renewed and extended, but only after periodical satisfaction. A state of unsatisfied desire is a continuous torment; and 'to pursue a goal which is by definition unattainable is to condemn oneself to a state of perpetual unhappiness'.[16]

In modern society the condition of anomie has become a normal state, especially in the sphere of trade and industry:

> Reality seems valueless by comparison with the dreams of fevered imaginations; reality is therefore abandoned. . . . A thirst arises for novelties, unfamiliar pleasures, nameless sensations, all of which lose their savour once known. The whole fever subsides and the sterility of all the tumult is apparent, and it is seen that all these new sensations in their infinite quantity cannot form a solid foundation of happiness . . . from now on nothing remains behind or ahead of him to fix his gaze upon . . . in the end he cannot escape the futility of an endless pursuit.
>
> (Durkheim 1952, p. 256)

Not only is Durkheim at pains to make his 'types' psychologically meaningful, he argues cogently, in a little noted discussion, that these types are also distinguished by the manner and affective tone of the final act. In cases of egotistical suicide the individual becomes increasingly melancholic and self-preoccupied. This serves only to heighten the isolation and detachment of the individual:

> the man whose whole activity is diverted to inner meditation becomes insensible to all his surroundings . . . His passions are mere appearances, being sterile. They are dissipated in futile imaginings, producing nothing external to themselves.
>
> (Durkheim 1952, p. 279)

The nothingness of the social world is translated into internal and personal emptiness. And the individual, for whom nothing else exists, 'becomes addicted and abandoned to this with a kind of morbid joy'. This 'pleasure in non-existence' is completed only 'by completely ceasing to exist'. There is nothing 'violent or hasty' in such suicides. Typically such people are possessed, at the end, by 'a calm melancholy'. In a 'dreamy' state the individual ends his or her life by asphyxiation, or the slow decline of starvation.

Anomic suicide, however, is marked by anger, by 'irritation and exasperated weariness'.[17] The confused and heightened emotional state of the anomic makes suicide a somewhat arbitrary, but common, outcome of anger and disappointment. The overthrowing of all settled patterns of expectations in life:

> reduces him to a state of acute over-excitation, which necessarily tends to seek solace in acts of destruction. The object upon which the passions thus aroused are discharged is fundamentally of secondary importance. The accident of circumstances determines their direction.
>
> (Durkheim 1952, p. 285)

Thus, for example, Goethe's Werther, 'enamoured of infinity', kills himself from disappointed love.

Durkheim's psychology, it should be noted, is more developed than is usually acknowledged, and it is tempting to view it as compatible with, if not, indeed, as a component part of, Freud's approach to the understanding of modern life. Durkheim's views on the danger of 'over-stimulation' and the need for an adequate level of social regulation of desire seem to promise that his more general theory might provide a framework conducive to the synthesis of sociological and psychological perspectives. This involves redefining Freud's theory of the instincts as the 'deep' social institutions of modernity. In this sense Freud's work 'fills out' Durkheim's sketchy psychology, rather than 'fills up' a gap in his work which, in fact, does not exist.

More specifically Freud and Durkheim can be linked through the common context of the emergence of a 'consumer society' throughout Europe, and particularly in France, during the latter part of the nineteenth century. The over-stimulation which threatened psychic stability had its specific cause in the development of new and aggressive forms of selling. The 'frenzy' of life in Paris, which so impressed Freud during his stay there in 1885, was focused on the new department stores which had been constructed on such a lavish scale. These immense concentrations of commodities displayed, on an unprecedented scale of luxury, objects of all sorts. The exotic and unusual mingled with the mundane and practical. Above all it seemed to make everything readily available. The distance between individuals and the objects through which their needs could be satisfied was reduced. Every effort was made to break down the physical and psychological barriers between the commodity and its potential consumer.[18]

The new consumerism, however, was not founded upon the regulation (stimulation) of desire, but upon the liberation of wishful fantasies. Desire is essentially a conception of ego-psychology, and belongs to the classical period of bourgeois modernity. It is predicated on an essential 'distance' between the ego and a valued object, the lack of which is felt as the tension of a 'want' or 'need'. It is just this tension which motivates the rational action directed towards the attainment of the object. Desire is directly linked to the notion of consumption as possession and, ultimately, to the social relations of property. But the notion of desire also links consumption to self-expression, and to notions of taste and discrimination. The individual expresses himself or herself through their possessions. But for advanced capitalist society, committed to the continuing expansion of production, this is a very limiting psychological framework which ultimately gives way to a quite different psychic 'economy'. The wish replaces desire as the motivating force of consumption. Durkheim describes this as a dangerous pathology of modernity. But what he regarded as the anomic frenzy of modern life has in reality become its normal condition.

The most effective way to sell is to elevate the casual whim into a legitimate reason for a purchase. In the context of late nineteenth-century ideas, women were seen as pre-adapted for their role as modern consumers. Women were not regarded as 'rational' customers, seeking to satisfy a 'need' or 'desire' through an appropriate commodity. Indeed, given the enormous expansion of the quantity and range of commodities available, it was not possible to behave as a rational consumer. It was impossible to survey the entire stock of the city and relate what was available to what one might need or want. And though collecting together large numbers of individuals, the frenzy of consumption was not genuinely a phenomenon of imitation, or of social facilitation. Durkheim's criticisms of those pre-Freudian psychological theories were well founded. It was, rather, to adopt Freud's language, a process of regression, occurring simultaneously in many people, due to the particular circumstances and surroundings. And as women were already known to be 'emotional' and 'suggestible' it was not difficult to treat them as if they were children.[19]

Interestingly the context in which anomie was most prevalent in French society, as of Viennese society, was among middle-class women. They were the group most exposed to the 'shock of the new'. Unconstrained by the demands of work or a public role, they became the first shoppers of the consumer society. Rather than see hysteria as a consequence of the repression of their domestic life, it is possible to view it in terms of the organised provocation of wishfulness and fantasy.

Thus, each dazzling array of frivolous and inessential goods might tempt from its hiding place the artful lunge of an irresistibly potent 'cathexis' of psychical energy, temporarily endowing some indifferent object with the significance of a mnemic image. These hypnotically induced symptoms soon passed, whatever had been purchased lost its charm, and the whole process could be undergone again and again. This amounted to a regulated de-regulation of desires; to periodic and organised outbursts of hysterical wish-fulfilment, which provided the essential 'psychical-energy' for the perpetual expansion of consumption, and, therefore, of production. Freud and Durkheim come together in describing the pathology of modernity (hysteria) in which the symptoms of the postmodern age were most evident.[20]

FREUD AND MARX: MODERNITY AS PSYCHOSIS

A successful union of Freud's and Marx's critical unveiling of the real nature of life in modern society has seemed, from time to time, to hold the promise both of a revolutionary form of self-understanding and of a liberation from the constraints of modernity. But it has remained unclear how such a potent amalgamation could best be effected and, more frequently, followers of either master have remained indifferent to, or expressed hostility towards, the other. For Marxists, Freud's evident conservatism was all too likely to be viewed with suspicion and made the excuse for a hasty dismissal of his work in its entirety while, for Freudians, Marx's historical objectivity was likely to be viewed as a blatant disregard of psychological issues. It has, thus, tended to the more unorthodox followers of both, as in the case of Wilhelm Reich and Herbert Marcuse, who have been boldest in their attempts to distil the libertarian essence from both Marx and Freud into a radical vision of social transformation.[21]

Reich, himself a trained analyst and a second-generation disciple of Freud, was the first to argue that psychoanalytic insights could be reformulated as a radical social and political programme. Freud's 'therapeutic nihilism' had already been one of the issues which had divided him from Jung, who had argued that the therapist should provide in addition to a comprehensible account of the origin of the patient's symptoms, the hope of a cure. Reich went much further. This hope could only be founded on a decisive rejection of the bourgeois family, whose internal dynamics were the source of the neurotic symptoms psychoanalysis had been called into existence to treat. For him, 'the relation between sexual suppression and human exploitation' began in the treatment of children within the privatised western nuclear family. It was there that 'the economic and sex-economic situation of patriarchal authoritarian society are interwoven'.[22] The patriarchal family is 'the factory in which the state's structure and ideology are molded'; it is an 'authoritarian state in miniature'. Its role is to instil 'morality' in the child; a morality whose 'aim is to produce acquiescent subjects who, despite distress and humiliation, are adjusted to the authoritarian order'.[23] The typical 'character-structure' to which the modern family gives rise (where it does not lead directly to crippling symptoms) is that 'authoritarian personality' upon which fascism depended for its rise.[24]

Reich regarded psychoanalysis as a genuine critique of bourgeois morality; it was the very repressiveness of bourgeois morality which led to an intensification and generalisation of neurotic disorders and produced the raw material upon which Freud built his science. This science, in turn, revealed the real consequences of such a morality, and, Reich claimed, justified its abolition.[25]

Reich was virtually unknown when his libertarian politics were revived in the more influential, and more sophisticated, version of Herbert Marcuse, which focused on the irrational and paradoxical persistence of repression in a society where the problem of need has been more or less effectively solved. Written at a high-point of American affluence and (misdirected) technological mastery over nature, Marcuse argued that the fundamental relation which Freud saw between the development of civilisation and the repression of instinctual gratification no longer held. If it was scarcity which had at one time required that we master ourselves so that we might win in the relentless struggle against nature, modern conditions had liberated us into a new world in which we need no longer cower, anxious and helpless, in the face of an ineluctable force over which we have no control. But so successfully had repression been enjoined on our predecessors, and so completely had they grasped the reality principle to which it had given rise that they had, in effect, solved the problems which first required that we embrace that principle. We can now afford to 'desublimate' repressed forms of gratification and reach a new and less one-sided relationship with reality. In contemporary society, therefore, sexual liberation becomes a key political issue. The persistence of repression serves only the vested interests of a ruling class who profit from the unnecessary work of the mass of people. Marcuse makes it clear that it is the liberation of pre-genital sexuality that is the fundamental issue; the process of normal sexual development stultifies the potential for forms of gratification which are only hinted at in the surviving traces of dispersed 'erotogenic zones'. Repression means:

> a quantitative and qualitative restriction of sexuality: the unification of the partial instincts and their subjugation under the procreative function (which) alter(s) the very nature of sexuality: from the autonomous 'principle' governing the entire organism it is turned into a specialized temporary function, into a means for an end.
>
> (Marcuse 1955, p. 45)

And repression is an essential aspect of the instrumentality of work:

> the partial instincts do not develop freely into a 'higher' stage of gratification which preserves their objectives, but are cut off and

reduced to subservient functions. This process achieves the socially necessary desexualization of the body: the libido becomes concentrated in one particular part of the body, leaving most of the rest free for use as the instrument of labor.

(Marcuse 1955, p. 49)

Rather than see 'pleasure' as the qualitative gain for renouncing instinctual (and indifferent) gratification, Marcuse insists we see it as a mere fragment of the richer store of human happiness from which it was wrenched. Yet, such is the entrenched and institutionalised character of the forces of 'surplus-repression' in modern society that any effort to regain this lost domain is anathematised:

Against a society which employs sexuality as a means for a useful end, the perversions uphold sexuality as an end in itself; they thus place themselves outside the domination of the performance principle and challenge its very foundation. They establish libidinal relationships which society must ostracize because they threaten to reverse the process of civilisation which turned the organism into an instrument of work.

(Marcuse 1955, p. 50)

But Marcuse was not afraid to embrace at least the symbolic value of Freud's phylogenetic speculation.[26] And he saw in the dominance of the distance sense, vision, over the proximate senses of taste, smell and touch, the initial triumph of social domination over instinctual gratification.

Marcuse's libertarian politics thus finds its Archimedean point in a Freudian interpretation of Marx's notion of alienation. For him, the process of repression is guided by social imperatives; by the need to transform 'body and mind into alienated labor'.[27] Clearly Marcuse has in mind a possible future in which there would be not only a 'desublimation' of work into instinctual gratification but, simultaneously, a 'de-alienation' of human labour into free activity. It is through a simultaneously social and psychological process that the worker (and not 'man' in general) creates 'reality' in a distorted and oppressive form. Indeed, Marx himself described the process of alienation as the creation, out of an inner plenitude, of a new and constraining 'reality' principle, so that:

the more the worker exerts himself in his work, the more powerful the alien, objective world becomes which he brings into being over against himself, the poorer he and his inner world become, and the less they belong to him . . . . The worker places his life in the object; but now it no longer belongs to him but to the object . . . . What the product of his labour is, he is not. Therefore the greater this product, the less he is himself. The externalization (*Entäusserung*) of the worker in his product means not only that his labour becomes an object, and *external* existence, but that it exists *outside him*, independently of him and alien to him, and begins to confront him as an autonomous power; that the life which he has bestowed on the object confronts him as hostile and alien.

(Marx 1975, p. 324)

The worker 'loses himself' in the product of his labour, which exists, so to speak, at his (or her) expense. As work satisfies needs only indirectly, through the creation of specific objects, these objects, alienated as private property, confront the worker as an obstacle to, rather than a means of, gratification.

Marcuse's radical vision involves the end of private property as one of the conditions for the fulfilment of instinctual impulses. It also seemed to involve a continuous and orderly flow of goods, produced with effortless technological sophistication and requiring no more than a minimal quantity of instinctual renunciation in work. Marx's view of the real possibility of unalienated labour, with its sharp reversal in the historically significant tendency towards the increasing fragmentation of the division of labour and its assumption of a 'primal' period in which human beings laboured freely and in common is not, then, dissimilar to Freud's view of a 'primal' world in which sexual gratification was also freely available.

Marcuse's refreshing views, coming at a time when orthodox opinion regarded both Freud and Marx (whatever their differences) as rather stern and even puritanical in their devotion to their own versions of truth, stimulated a good deal of fruitful discussion, and is still influential.[28] Interestingly the reaction to libertarian claims in respect of each has been surprisingly similar. 'Respectable' followers of both Marx and Freud claimed the mantle of 'scientific' for their respective masters and dismissed 'humanist' versions of Marx, as well as radical readings of Freud, as without foundation. Critics who were hostile to either primarily in terms of moral and political objections were not slow to take up this new opportunity and claimed to 'disprove' not only the libertarian synthesis, but the original theories upon which they were supposedly based. Debates over the scientific status of Marx's work were just as vigorous (and ultimately just as inconclusive) as discussions over the validity of clinical findings in psychoanalysis.[29]

What Marcuse had proposed was, in effect, a Marxian reading of Freud. A Freudian reading of Marx was equally possible, and equally fruitful. The pioneering work along these lines is Josef Gabel's book *False Consciousness* which, strongly influenced by Bergson and Minkowski, as well as by Freud, takes its point of departure in a 'psychiatric' version of Marx's alienation hypothesis. Here the point of contact between Marx and Freud is in the notion of ideology and in the development of a social theory of *projection*. For Freud projection is the psychical mechanism of narcissism and is particularly evident in the regressive character of psychotic delusions. The basis of schizophrenia, for him, is the withdrawal of affect from the external world, usually as a consequence of 'social humiliations and slights':[30]

> The patient has withdrawn from the people in his environment and from the external world generally the libidinal cathexis which he has hitherto directed on to them. Thus everything has become indifferent and irrelevant to him, and has to be explained by means of a secondary rationalization as being 'miracled up, cursorily improvised'. The end of the world is the projection of this internal catastrophe; his subjective world has come to an end since his withdrawal of his love from it.
>
> (SE 12, p. 70)

The psychotic delusional system, as Freud made clear, is not the primary symptom of schizophrenia but, in effect, an attempt to recover by projecting into the deadened world a remnant of human life and feeling. The world is rebuilt:

> so that he can once more live in it. He builds it up by the work of his delusions. The delusional formation, which we take to be the pathological product, is in reality an attempt at recovery, a process of reconstruction. Such a reconstruction after the catastrophe is successful to a greater or lesser extent, but never wholly so.
>
> (SE 12, p. 71)

For Gabel it is modern reality, and not the psychiatric patient, that is psychotic. The central features of schizophrenia – loss of affect, isolation, sense of oppression, suspicion, withdrawal and projection into the world of a private reality – is nothing other than a fearlessly accurate description of the social relations of capitalism; it is 'a reificational syndrome'.[31] The psychotic is not so much suffering from 'false-consciousness', in the sense of misrepresenting the world, as he or she is accurately reflecting a false and inverted world. Capitalism is created through the production and exchange of commodities and, in terms of its exchange-value, the commodity has a purely objective existence. Although the 'vast accumulation of commodities' is a consequence of specific social relations, it has the appearance of a natural order. The most fundamental process in capitalism thus remains strangely invisible, and social life seems to be dominated by the universal and necessary relations among things themselves. This 'fetishism' of commodities is no simple-minded error, but the indirect expression of the real nature of these hidden social relations.

The core of Marx's argument hinges on the distinction between, and the actual social separation of, the 'use-value' and 'exchange-value' of commodities. Commodities are 'useful things' but, unlike the useful goods produced in other societies, in capitalist society these things are produced in order to be exchanged. Capitalism is simply the universalisation of a particular form of exchange. Where, in his earlier work, he stressed the objective presence of the products of labour as a source of oppression and estrangement, he later came to view the commodity in terms of exchange. The commodity undergoes a curious process of dematerialisation. It loses all its 'qualitative' determinants and retains 'substance' only as the carrier of a purely abstract value. Thus, 'as soon as it emerges as a commodity, it changes into a thing which transcends sensuousness'.[32] As labour power can itself be conceptualised as a commodity, and its actual existence divided into quite distinct components of use and exchange, it enters into the process of exchange as a specific value. The 'use-value' of commodities is suppressed, nothing but 'fair' exchange takes place so that the accumulation of profit seems to be a miraculous side-effect of the entire process which is regulated by the apparently natural relationships among things themselves:

> The mysterious character of the commodity-form consists therefore simply in the fact that the commodity reflects the social character-istics of men's own labour as objective characteristics of the products of labour themselves, as the socio-natural properties of these things. . . . It is nothing but the definite social relations between men themselves which assumes here, for them, the fantastic form of a relation between things.
>
> (Marx 1976, p. 165)

In Gabel's view psychotics accept the fetishism of commodities as a living reality and treats people as things. For them personal identity is assimilated to the rigid objectivity of commodity relations. The coldness of the schizo-phrenic, their typical 'loss of vital contact' and 'morbid rationalism', is simply a reflection of the thing-like imperviousness of the social world. Most significantly of all, because the commodity is viewed as the carrier of an abstract and, therefore, eternal value, the schizophrenic experiences the world wholly in terms of spatial categories. For the schizophrenic time has no more significance than it has for the commodity which has been removed from the real world of labour and preserved in an idealised domain of timeless relations. Indeed it is this transformation which has encouraged a misplaced aesthetic infatuation with the psychotic.[33] The schizophrenic loses all dialectical elasticity in relation to the world, while, inversely, the neurotic insists on treating every transient relation as an authentic human encounter, and thus negates the objective givenness of the social world.

Where, for Marcuse, the fundamental point of agreement between Freud and Marx lies in their stress on repression, on the ultimate triumph of the reality principle (that is of self-repression under a reality principle), for Gabel the crucial point is the way in which they describe the conditions under which reality becomes an illusion, albeit (given those conditions) a necessary illusion. It is not the objectivity and 'weight' of commodities which repress people but, rather, their ethereal abstraction and lightness. Reality is nothing more than an appearance; a 'veil' behind which real presence lies obscured.

Both reality and appearance are generated from the same processes and are, so to speak, cut from the same cloth. Such a view of modernity, which was articulated at a phenomenological and biographical level by Rousseau, in fact receives decisive and characteristically different treatments by Freud and Marx. In other words, they are linked but also distinguished by their separate responses to the Romantic tradition against which they both reacted. Where Romanticism, in its literary and in its philosophical forms, sought the union, or rather the reunion, of subject and object in a new 'higher' reality, Marx and Freud in their different ways conceived of modernity in terms of a series of inescapable and irresolvable conflicts. For them, we are bound to the surface of life and imagine that we might depart from it only to the extent that such hopes, in fact, restrain us all the more securely. The followers of what Marx called the 'German Ideology' found in ideas the liberation they were denied in reality; but, as ideas were powerless in themselves to change the social world, this amounted to nothing more than an imaginative reconciliation to the very conditions (of injustice and constraint) which they had thought to overturn. Romanticism, that is to say, might be viewed in terms of Freudian characterisations as a *symptom* of modernity.

It is as critics of Romanticism, and of the metaphysical longings upon which it was based, that Deleuze and Guattari have linked Freud and Marx in a work with the promising title *Anti-Oedipus: capitalism and schizophrenia*.[34] Given that modern society presents itself to us as a deceptive appearance, it is no simple matter to distinguish between the critical understanding of social life and ideal fabrications. It would be quite impossible (and against the spirit of their enterprise) to attempt, however briefly, an 'exposition' of their fascinating 'anti-book'. It defies summary, but does invite the casual theft of insights relevant to the present discussion.

Modernity involves a complete mechanisation of experience in which the insights of Freud and Marx are relocated, or better, mapped on to a living surface charged both with libidinal flows and with economic exchanges. Marx and Freud, still seeking the completeness and closure of knowledge, abstract from these singular flows separate and distinct domains of representation. But, in reality, there is only the endless coupling of machines, draining of energy, and through this the creation of objects and partial objects. Deleuze and Guattari, reading Freud and Marx in the light of Nietzsche and Bergson, attempt to reinstate the fluidity which they see as the underlying reality of their still too perfect abstractions.

This simple reality – the flow of energy across a surface – they term desire. But this is no bourgeois ego-concept of self-identity and self-realisation. It is a process drained of romanticism: 'Desire constantly couples continuous flows and partial objects that are by nature fragmentary and fragmented.'[35] Desire here is both demonic and playful. Modernity stripped of its seductive veil of reason and ideals is revealed to be a world of perpetual and meaningless production. But, where Gabel had focused on the psychotic's delusional system as a symbolic transformation of the fetishism of commodities, Deleuze and Guattari locate the truth of schizophrenia in production itself. 'The schizophrenic', they declare, 'is the universal producer.'[36] What remained for Marx a fearful abyss between the constrained process of labour and the liberation of the product is dissolved into a continuous flow of ever-renewed acts of producing. Nothing gets 'beyond' this process, in which the whole of existence has become bound up.

The perfect fluidity of desire, the continuous flow of libidinal and economic energies, and endless process of coupling and producing, defines the human body as an aspect of this process; as an organic process. But, as a pure process, it has no structure and organisation of its 'own', no identity as an articulated assembly of parts and no organs. The schizophrenic discovers this hidden truth within capitalism, that pure production (which is the foundation of modern reality) has not only abolished self-identity (which is, in fact, nothing but a romanticised *image* of the body), but has annihilated the body itself. The schizophrenic is a body deprived of organs. Schreber felt himself to be empty.[37] He is 'the body without an image', where the Romantic might be seen as an image without the body. The bourgeois ideal – the embodied image (ego) – was never more than the sporadic hope of capitalism, which instead produced imageless bodies. This in turn produces disembodied images (delusions). The schizoid takes seriously what we all know, that the ego is the 'vanishing point' (Kierkegaard) of modernity.

Deleuze and Guattari, in viewing desire as a continuous process of producing, as a flow of energy, and nothing more, at a stroke abolish the 'ideal' or 'fantasised' world which, for bourgeois psychology, is the corollary of longing. Desire, for bourgeois ego-psychology, is defined as the lack of a real object, literally the *want* of an object, and this want calls into existence an entire world of imaginary beings towards which desire is seen as straining, and in the service of which the entire resources of reason and intention are concentrated within the ego. But it is just this 'lack' which is illusory:

Desire does not lack anything; it does not lack its object. It is rather, the *subject* that is missing in desire, or desire that lacks a fixed subject; there is no fixed subject unless there is repression. Desire and its object are one in the same thing: the machine, as a machine of a machine.

(Deleuze and Guattari 1977, p. 26)

And desire is not a longing which is satisfied or fulfilled in the object, but a process with continuous interruptions, couplings, ruptures and breakdowns which creates a whole series of 'partial-objects' which briefly come into existence and are then reabsorbed into the continuous flux. This can only be misconceived if it is thought of as a unity:

> We live today in an age of partial objects, bricks that have been shattered to bits, and leftovers. We no longer believe in the myth of the existence of fragments that, like pieces of an antique statue, are merely waiting for the last one to be turned up, so that they may all be glued back together to create a unity that is precisely the same as the original unity. We no longer believe in a primordial totality that once existed, or in a final totality that awaits us at some future date.
>
> (Deleuze and Guattari 1977, p. 42)

In this context, of course, the 'triangulation' of the Oedipus myth 'reduces all of desire to a familial determination that no longer has anything to do with the social field actually invested by the libido'.[38]

This is also the domain or 'deterritorialised' flow of Lyotard's *Libidinal Economy*, which begins, like Foucault's *Discipline and Punish*, with a baroque evisceration of the body. Indeed, the recovery of the sensuous has been so marked that, quite suddenly, Marcuse and the 'radical' Freudians seem curiously dated. And the distance from Weber's defensive egoism has become abysmal. The transition from classical bourgeois culture, which is rooted firmly in the psychic economy of the ego, to advanced societies requires the 'transvaluation' of that economy. The work of advanced civilisation no longer requires the surplus-repression of sexuality but, rather, the over-production of commodities. This implies consumerism, which in turn requires a more or less complete abandonment of repression, and the creation of a world which was at one time only conceivable as a psychotic delusion.

FREUD AND SIMMEL: MODERNITY AS DREAM

In marked contrast to the other classical sociologists Simmel did not take an historical and institutional approach to the understanding of modernity, but sought, rather, to delineate the characteristic 'forms of sociation' through which it was experienced. Given this emphasis it is perhaps unsurprising that, more than any other classical sociologist, he also developed a strong interest in psychology and that consequently an affinity between Simmel and Freud, though little discussed, is clearly evident.[39]

For Simmel, individual experience depends not only upon qualitatively distinct life-contents but also upon the social forms typical of modernity. And more generally, it might be argued that the double character of the instincts and the persistent dualism in their conceptualisation (pleasure/

need, ego/libido, individual/species, life/death), which is characteristic of Freud's work, is mirrored both by Simmel's methodological commitment to a Kantian dualism of form and content and by its application in specific cases. Simmel, in fact, views every aspect of experience in a double perspective; as processes of individuation and as forms of sociation. Each person 'exists both for society and for himself', and does so simultaneously. Paradoxically society is composed 'of beings which, on the one hand, feel themselves to be complete social entities and, on the other hand – and without thereby changing their content at all – complete personal entities'.[40] The individual, thus, 'is contained in sociation and, at the same time, finds himself confronted by it'.

A good deal more than the coincidence of their date of publication, then, links *The Interpretation of Dreams* to *The Philosophy of Money*. To grasp the significance of these links it is helpful first to view Freud's developing theory of the 'psychical apparatus' in the light of Simmel's essay on 'The Metropolis and Mental Life'.

Simmel begins by noting that:

> The psychological basis of the metropolitan type of individual consists in the *intensification of nervous stimulation* which results from the swift and uninterrupted change of outer and inner stimuli.
>
> (Simmel 1950 pp. 409–10)

The 'rapid crowding of changing images, the sharp discontinuity in the grasp of a single glance, and the unexpectedness of onrushing impressions' establishes quite new and fateful psychological conditions. The vastly increased diversity of stimuli, the continuous flux of metropolitan experience, engenders both 'a heightened awareness and a predominance of intelligence' in the psychic economy. To cope with the new conditions of experience:

> The reaction to metropolitan phenomena is shifted to that organ which is least sensitive and quite remote from the depth of the personality. Intellectuality is thus seen to preserve subjective life against the overwhelming power of metropolitan life.
>
> (Simmel 1950, pp. 410–11)

The metropolis encourages, and even makes necessary, the development of indifference, a blasé attitude and impersonal and anonymous relationships in which reserve plays a significant element. In all these 'seemingly insignificant traits, which lie upon the surface of life, the same psychic currents unite'. These are traits generated primarily from the incapacity of the human subject to register, or to react to, any but a few selected events in a metropolitan environment which has outgrown the boundaries of personal experience and confronts the individual with 'an overwhelming fullness of crystallised and impersonalised spirit'.

Yet we do react, in subtle and almost unconscious ways, to the myriad of images which pass before us in a dissociated stream:

> Our psychic activity still responds to almost every impression of somebody else with a somewhat distinct feeling. The unconscious, fluid and changing character of this impression seems to result in a state of indifference. Actually this indifference would be just as unnatural as the diffusion of indiscriminate mutual suggestion would be unbearable. From both these typical dangers of the metropolis, indifference and indiscriminate suggestibility, antipathy protects us.
>
> (Simmel 1950, p. 416)

Reserve and, he might have added, joking allow the individual 'a kind and an amount of personal freedom which has no analogy whatever under other conditions'. But, at the same time, metropolitan conditions militate against the expression of this freedom. The 'extravagances of mannerism, caprice, and preciousness' are, therefore, attempts to establish differences where, in fact, indifference is unavoidable.

The metropolis predisposes all relationships towards superficiality. Simmel describes the 'currents' and 'flows', 'sociation' and 'dissociation' of its social life, such that, although the individual is free to define, within a protective shell of anonymity, any unique and fantastic self-identity, this never amounts to the acquisition of a definite character. In the metropolis:

> life is made infinitely easy for the personality in that stimulations, interests, uses of time and consciousness are offered to it from all sides. They carry the person as if in a stream, and one hardly needs to swim for oneself.
>
> (Simmel 1950, p. 422)

In describing the specific effects of money within the metropolitan environment Simmel also uses the image of being swept along in a stream. And in drawing attention to the tendency of the money economy to degrade all qualitative 'coloration' and to define all objects, persons and relations in terms of its own universal quantity, he remarks that 'All things float with equal specific gravity in the constantly moving stream of money'.

No individual can be more than a spectator amidst the flux of impressions which constitute metropolitan experience. The social world appears with all the inconsequential charm and excitement of a dream. The varied and unconnected vistas, the distant, colourless scenes with emotionally indifferent content and stereotypically cold interactions are pictured with dreamlike lucidity. Simmel describes the social world of 'the man without qualities' as he moves blindly through a dreamscape of 'objectified spirit' in which everything is both an absolutely compelling physical reality and a fantastic amalgamation of images.

The indifference of the dream, in Freud's view, conceals a wish which, at the same time, it represents as fulfilled. And for Simmel the dreamy landscape of the metropolis is linked to the invisible but ever-present movements and restless transformations of the social unconscious; money. It is money which carries modern life-contents and distributes them across the psychic space of the metropolis. The process of 'monetisation' is the large-scale 'dream-work' which transforms the social space of the modern city into a fantastic theatre.

This 'social-work' operates by first dissolving all psychic contents into an undifferentiated stream of purely objective value. The process of exchange ideally, and through the general use of money actually, 'removes . . . objects from the sphere of merely subjective significance' and 'confronts the individual as an objective realm'.[41] But as the 'autonomous manifestation of the exchange relation', money transforms every object into an expression of its own colourless and characterless form. Money, in terms of its functionality, is wholly abstract and, so to speak, takes on a substantial form only as a matter of convenience:

> As a visible object, money is the substance that embodies abstract economic value, in a similar fashion to the sound of words which is an acoustic-physiological occurrence but has significance for us only through the representation that it bears or symbolizes.
>
> (Simmel 1978, p. 120)

'The philosophical significance of money' for modern society in which almost every object is the carrier of symbolic values which 'express the relations among various elements of our existence', is as a common medium of such representations and, thus, 'the clearest formula of all being'.[42] Money 'represents pure interaction in its purest form'.

The indifference of money to any particular subjective value, its characterless dimensionality, the purity of its being as a relation and its endless circulation, transforms every interaction into a means and abolishes to an infinitely remote distance the final consummation of subjectively valued ends. But, paradoxically, this does not usher in an age of rational instrumentality in social life. Quite the contrary, money, which expresses and promotes the growth of social complexity, draws the individual into an objective realm within which the ego, and thus all notion of intentionality, purposiveness and rationality is abolished. The individual is literally 'lost' within the infinite complexity of relations made possible through money. The endless chain of 'teleological causes' which is the money relation, as it does not terminate in the satisfaction of a particular value, but persists as an ever-expanding and developing network of relations, withdraws from us the possibility of attaining any ultimate value. Thus 'what we call the ultimate purpose is floating above the teleological sequence' and seems to retreat from us with the same speed that we approach.[43] Money has the effect, in this, of relativising all values:

217

Out of the endless series of possible volitions, self-developing actions and satisfactions, we almost arbitrarily designate one moment as the ultimate end, for which everything preceding it is only a means; whereas an objective observer or later even we ourselves have to posit for the future the genuinely effective and valid purposes without their being secured against a similar fate . . . . As the expression and equivalent of the value of things, and at the same time as a pure means and an indifferent transitional stage, money symbolizes the established fact that the values for which we strive and which we experience are ultimately revealed to be means and temporary entities.

(Simmel 1978, p. 236)

Just as Freud demonstrates how unconscious processes find a mode of representation as wishes by association with indifferent material of the day residues, and thus lure these current memories into a vast network of half-forgotten mnemic images, so Simmel shows the way in which the instrumentality of money lures the ego into a labyrinth within which its underlying irrationality comes to the surface. And, like the Freudian repressed, the continuous pressure which money exerts in its endeavour to form 'mnemic images' as valued objects can be described as *wishfulness.*

Temporarily realising itself in an object, money value is infinitely transposable and interchangeable. As money creates a fundamentally uniform substance from the irreducible qualitative distinctions among things, it allows these quite different objects to be substituted for each other and to be displaced, condensed and related together according to seemingly logical principles.

Not only does money, by infiltrating every relation with an uncanny power of dematerialisation, render modern experience dreamlike; it creates a new order of social perversions. The pure instrumentality of money does not, in fact, transform every relation into the common denominator of a cold and calculating rationality. The relationship with money itself takes on a specific 'colour', and can be exaggerated in a number of directions to a variety of irrational extremes. The 'evaluation of money as an absolute purpose' might be thought of as corresponding to sexual practices which derive gratification from pre-genital forms of libidinal organisation. They wrench money from the context of its larger social purpose and make it an end in itself.

Avarice and greed, thus, are 'pathological deformations of the interest in money', and, in treating money as an end in itself, have the effect of relativising all other ultimate values:

Money is not content with being just another final purpose of life alongside wisdom and art, personal significance and strength, beauty

218

and love; but in so far as money does adopt this position it gains the power to reduce the other purposes to the level of means.

(Simmel 1978, p. 241)

The miser, thus, 'loves money as one loves a highly admired person who makes us happy simply by his existence'. And the avaricious person is fascinated with money as a store of unlimited potentiality, as the certainty of future satisfaction which is stored up by its possession. The love of money itself eliminates the risk of disappointment which otherwise spoils the enjoyment of any other possessions because in the other cases there is always some incommensurability between the anticipation of the wish and the actual enjoyment bestowed by possession of the object. But this is not the case with money, which:

> is not expected to achieve anything for the greedy person over and above its mere ownership. We know more about money than any other object because there is nothing to be known about money and so it cannot hide anything from us. It is a thing absolutely lacking in qualities and therefore cannot, as can even the most pitiful object conceal within itself any surprises or disappointments. Whoever really and definitely only wants money is absolutely safe from such experiences.

(Simmel 1978, p. 244)

The avaricious person, on the contrary, does not love money at all, but invests his or her entire 'cathexis' of energy in relation to objects themselves which, however insignificant in appearance, take on in their eyes an absolute value. And again, in a form of extravagance which seems to be logically related to, and not simply suggestive of, the sexual perversions, the miser hordes money through an exaggerated interest in the foreplay of possession. Here the accumulation of wealth itself becomes pleasurable and in the service of which the miser will make many sacrifices. The spendthrift, on the other hand, derives pleasure from the extravagance of purchase, rather than from the gratification of consumption, and is 'willing to pay for the enjoyment of this moment at the price of squandering all more concrete values'.[44]

Money seems to bring about the 'transvaluation of all psychical values' which Freud observed in the displacement from latent dream thought to manifest dream image. Money is nothing other than the 'common currency' of modern life, in which all other values are dissolved and reformed according to a qualitatively indifferent standard.

The juxtaposition of Simmel and Freud suggests a sociological interpretation of the dream as an image of the experience of modernity, in which money plays the part of the latent dream thought and the metropolis provides the phantasmagoria of its manifest content. When they are brought together in this way additional points of contact quickly suggest themselves. The image of a 'stream of life' in which one is carried along is common to both, and gives rise to a number of related metaphors: variation in volume ('flooding' and 'drying-up') and speed of flow (energetic 'torrents' and lethargic 'pools'), the process of 'branching', 'meandering' and 'joining', momentary disappearance into underground passages, and reappearance, as the vicissitudes of life's fundamental contents. Both give prominence to the role of the inertial forces contained within this flow. Freud, for example, accorded increasing significance to repetition as an elemental property of life, an insight expressed by Simmel not only in the notion of the inertia of sentiments as a constitutive part of social life but as the persistence of social forms as such. In a characteristic essay 'Faithfulness and Gratitude' he argues that:

> Sociological connectedness, no matter what its origin, develops a self-preservation and autonomous existence of its form that are independent of its initially connecting motives. Without this inertia of existing sociations, society as a whole would constantly collapse, or change in an unimaginable fashion.
>
> (Simmel 1950, pp. 380–1)

He also discusses the importance of play in social life. Sociability itself is a 'play-form' of, and not an 'instinct' for, society.

The development of modernity brings into prominence all the features of superficiality, playfulness and autonomy of social forms as such; it is 'the fulfilment of a relation that wants to be nothing but relation'.[45]

PLEASURE AND ECSTASY

These informal dialogues suggest a number of possible developments for any contemporary sociology concerned with the nature of experience. More significantly, perhaps, from the present perspective, they act as something of a corrective to 'vulgar Freudianism' (extrapolated uncritically from *Civilisation and its Discontents*).

Firstly, 'pleasure' is possible only in relation to the ego and depends upon the process of repression. The 'primary process' is originally undifferentiated with respect to 'quality', that is to say the satisfaction of *any* need gives rise to gratification which can be conceptualised only as the removal of a generalised state of tension. It is difficult to imagine what such gratification 'feels like'; indeed, the whole basis of 'feeling' depends upon inhibiting the primary process and developing from it a series of distinguishable states. The temptation, however, has been to identify 'pleasure' with the primary process itself, and the ego as an agency of some sort through which we experience its primordial gratification. But this view ignores the fact that the ego is itself constructed through a process of repression, so that, just as we cannot push the ego into the unconscious to examine its contents but become aware of these only through a variety of surface 'deformations', we cannot place ourselves in the midst of the primary process to investigate its feeling tone. If the 'quality' of pleasure is ignored, repression appears in a negative light as the continuous shrinking and dilution of an original state of abundance.

Secondly, the process of sublimation and compromise formation places at our disposal a continuously expanding field of new sources of pleasure. Not only are sublimated pleasures still pleasures, they represent a continuous modification and 'refinement' of the primary process through which pleasure is itself created. Thus, for example, in relation to sexuality Freud discusses the mechanism of 'fore-pleasure' through which 'a slight feeling of pleasure' is amplified into a greater resultant or 'end-pleasure'.[46] This is a mechanism unknown in childhood. Indeed, it is difficult to understand how a child could be forced to abandon primary narcissism if repression were not itself the condition of pleasure. From an economic viewpoint the gain of pleasure (and not improved survival prospects) is the immediate benefit which accrues to the expenditure of energy required by the process of repression.

It is not 'pleasure' but a kind of organic ecstasy which is repressed.[47] 'Feeling' emerges only as the satisfaction of needs is associated with mnemic images through which they can be connected to the experience of the world. But once feeling is harnessed to the representation of the everyday world, new possibilities of pleasure emerge. Freud, it must be remembered, devoted his greatest efforts to elucidating the experience of unpleasure. His patients, turning away from what for a variety of reasons had become the intolerable reality of everyday life, sought pleasure through ineffectual methods of regression. Normal and effective mechanisms created pleasure from processes which had become, to a large extent, independent of the instinctual gratification from which they derived their 'psychical energy'.

Pleasure is a mnemic symbol for the ego and not for the primary process which is more nearly represented by religious sensibilities. Freud himself claimed to be incapable of the feeling described to him by Romain Rolland as a 'sensation of eternity, a feeling as of something limitless, unbounded – as it were oceanic'; a feeling which he acknowledges to be the foundation of religious sentiments.[48] This sense of merging with the world, however, is only one side of religious feeling which, in its other aspect, is a shattering confrontation with the numinous as the awfulness and dreadfulness of an absolutely given reality.[49] The *mysterium tremendum*, though still experienced as a primordial and contentless anxiety, is capable of its own development; from demonic possession to highly intellectualised and conventionalised expressions of abjection.[50] It is drawn out through the 'vicissitudes' –

displacement, transformation and rationalisation – of ordered religious practices in which the ego once again comes to play a central role. Sufficient of its ecstatic elements remain, however, for it to be clear that, in spiritual terms, the 'primary process' should not be confused with the personal comfort and security which accrues, in fact, as a consequence of *its* inhibition.

Pleasure is inhibited, and thus differentiated and qualified Eros, just as spiritual happiness is inhibited and transformed ecstasy.[51] The primary process is bereft of 'quality', which emerges only through the process of repression. Freud's psychological theory is about the creation of pleasure *through* repression; and not about the repression of pleasure.

THE BODY AS SELF-IMAGE OF THE PRESENT

Freud's psychoanalytic writing provides a sensitive description of the central features of the experience of life in advanced modern societies. Though his own understanding of 'civilisation', his career and his private life were modelled on the unquestioned assumptions of classical bourgeois liberalism, especially as expressed through the pre-sociological writings of German aesthetic philosophies, Freud brought to life, in illness and in dreams, all those deformations of the ego which were symptomatic of 'styles of life' which had left those certainties behind. In his work, and in spite of the strenuous rearguard action he mounted in its defence, the ego dissolves into a series of loosely related processes from which it cannot be recovered other than by an arbitrary act of 'secondary revision' on the part of the analyst.

However, even if Freud is treated (or mistreated) as the Hegel of postmodernity and turned back on his feet, so that everything 'pathological', 'perverted' and 'abnormal' becomes exemplary of a new age, there is no straightforward way in which his insights can be assimilated to sociological understandings of the characteristic tendencies within *fin-de-siècle* life and culture. The instability of any reading of Freud, and of his relationship with sociological thought, is itself indicative of the wide range of these tendencies and of intellectual responses to them. The more extensively Freud's influence can be felt the less likely does it seem that a coherent interpretation of his work might be proposed. Increasingly parts of his work are broken off and used for specific purposes. There is an 'analytic' Freud, a 'metapsychological' Freud, a cultural historian, an interpreter of dreams and so on. Reading Freud in the context of his own biography, or of social and cultural life of late imperial Vienna, seems hardly more likely to produce a unified view. Thus we seem driven to accept fragmentations and dispersal as the very essence of his work, and welcome him into the pantheon of postmodern gurus, however much he might have rejected that honour himself.

This is not, however, the necessary conclusion to the kind of contextual reading favoured here. Freud mapped the experience of modernity as a domain of representations. In his view both nature and the soul, withdrawn to an infinitely remote point as the ultimate (and therefore uninteresting) causes of experience, were unknowable forms of 'otherness'. What could be known were representations which, once formed, could interact on the same 'level', or on the same surface, as interchangeable quantities of excitation. Freud's psychology is the 'working through' of the implications of Copernicanism, and the emergence of an apparently autonomous realm of representation, for all its loss of substance, promises both intellectual control and practical mastery of the world which it is instrumental in creating. Does not psychoanalysis, then, as all other discourses, depend upon and end in, a theory of language? This possibility has been pursued both within and beyond psychoanalysis.[52]

It should, however, be treated with caution. Freud himself 'placed' language firmly in the pre-conscious, and the idea that 'the unconscious is structured like a language' (Lacan), seems either contradictory or obscure. Furthermore, Freud's fundamental problem – the elucidation of the meaning, significance and origin of mnemic symbols – led him to postulate the existence of pre-linguistic body images as the primordial *schemata* of consciousness. Indeed, he had to invent a language in which to describe these.

The focus on language is nonetheless useful in overcoming the antithesis between nature and freedom which has tended to polarise much writing on Freud. The range of contemporary readings of Freud, from within and outside sociology, run from the 'materialism' and 'determinism' of post-Darwinian biology to the 'idealism' and 'freedom' of post-Kantian hermeneutics, which are themselves extensions and variants of the important traditions of scientific medicine and of Romantic literature which influenced Freud himself. Both suggestions are initially attractive in re-establishing the centrality of the 'unconscious' in Freud's texts and, thus, offer an antidote to the development of 'ego-psychology' which was the dominant theme in, especially American, psychoanalytic literature after his death. It ought to be remembered, in fact, that, in the latter part of his life, Freud's strong interest in the psychology of the ego was primarily an attempt to understand its emergence on the basis of unconscious processes, and not as an immanent movement within the psychical apparatus towards 'self-actualisation'.

The antitheses of nature and freedom provide alternative images through which the ego is negated; two distinctive ways in which the self is 'carried away' or 'lost' to forces in the face of which it is helpless. Freud talked a good deal of the tyranny of nature and of the human response to its own helplessness, but what should be kept in mind is the extent to which both his analytic practice and his general psychology is a rejection of all views of human reality, either potentially or actually, as a domain of freedom. Anxiety is a reaction to, or better an immediate intuition of, the dizzying freedom of the human. The analysis of dreams, as of neurotic symptoms, does not terminate in meaning, but continually opens itself, spreading outwards a network of life contents. The dreamy texture of modern life is suffused by hyper-sensitivity to this freedom, as to a blinding light, which is sensed as a fundamental arbitrariness in the entire process of representation through which the world is both grasped and constructed.

We are continually in danger of recognising that it is 'just' a dream. The interminable process of analysis, the never-ending interpretation of life's text, is itself an illness from which we recover by chaining ourselves to the specificity of definite symptoms. Illness, whatever its 'secondary gains', provides the never-failing consolation of a voluntary loss of freedom.

Freud's rejection of the absolute antitheses of biological determinism and Romantic expressionism took the form of a baroque merging of subject and object in which all sensuous categories were spiritualised and spiritual categories were sensualised. His understanding of the psychical mechanism allowed him to see the formation of consciousness not only functionally, in terms of the discharge of excitation and the emergence of a reality-testing mechanism, but schematically, in terms of the organising principles given in a limited range of non-contingent body images. One way, then, in which his understanding of modern life might be reconciled with a variety of sociological views is through a social and cultural history (rather than a biological fantasy) of the body-image. Of course these types co-exist in every society, and constitute, in different combinations, the normal forms of human experience. But, throughout the development of western society, first one, then another, has taken its turn in being elevated into a position of privilege and cultural pre-eminence; representing for its period a dominant mode of valuation.[53]

Thus, in the ancient world, a disunited assembly of organs, which bears some resemblance to the earliest erotogenic zones, is evident. Neither the Homeric body, nor the body in the Ancient Judaic tradition acts and thinks as a unity; its various organs are subject to specific passions of which it is the passive victim.[54] Both Christianity and neoplatonism imposed upon this 'primary process' a spatial differentiation of 'inside' and 'outside' with a consequential unification in terms of spiritual values over organic processes. The 'orality' of the ancient world was gradually 'oedipalised'; that is, its openness to the abundance of spiritual value which flowed ceaselessly from its gods became closed-off and made conditional on acts of obedience and, ultimately, upon the spontaneous conformity of an inner will. Subsequently, in the context of the development particularly of feudal society, this unification was reconceptualised as a microcosmic order, which operated both as a mirror and as a replica of the macrocosmic structure of the world. These developing body-images, related to the Freudian discussion of anal eroticism, might be elaborated in terms both of the symbolic order of everyday life and of the organisation of nature. Renaissance body-images established the separateness of the human realm and understood the cosmological structure in terms of its mirroring in the mind, rather than in terms of direct participation in the substantial unity of creation. Withdrawn, and therefore privileged, the human body took on the character of a world apart. The reflective body-image, redefined within the bourgeois epoch as the infinite inwardness of the human subject, became self-sufficient and cut-off from the cosmos of which it could only dream. Then as advanced societies broke down the absolute distinctions introduced into the post-feudal epoch as characterising human dignity, the body once again opened itself towards, and fused with, the world; giving rise to a surface across which energetic and playful forces shocked first one, then another, element of consciousness into life.

Freud rediscovered these historic body-images as contemporary residues and as alternative dreamworlds. They co-exist on the surface of modern life; indeed, they are its texture. The experience of modernity is nothing other than this texture, which should not be understood as a series of metamorphoses in some undefined, protean substratum but, rather, as the juxtaposition of alternative and exclusive modes of being. There is nothing 'in-between' to which these worlds adhere, and through which we might hope to regain a sense of continuity, coherence and depth. And there is something deceptive, therefore, in proposing a sociological 'history' of body-images which transforms the inherently incomprehensible lunges from one to another into a meaningful succession of valued forms.

The contemporary 'postmodern' body-image, thus, is not one but many. It is simply the availability of all these 'previous' images in a new way as so many equivalent consumables. This has the rather odd effect of 'doubling' the repertoire of possibilities; each of which is now presented to us in an 'authentic' (historical) mode and as its copy in contemporary hyperreality.

The entire domain of experience is viewed by Freud as *neither* nature *nor* freedom. Equally, it is viewed as *both* nature *and* freedom. The way in which these non-human extremities come together is central to his notion of play, which is fundamental to his later metapsychology. Here the simplest of rules, repetition, liberates spirit from nature and begins the process of world-creation while, at the same time it binds this newly-born world to the universality and necessity of a natural process.[55] Repetition is the inexplicable 'leap' by which we are removed from one world and thrust into another. It is from the inertial force of repetition that we learn the art of forgetting, and of repression, and thus build for ourselves the possibility of pleasure.

Not only for Freud, but for the development of twentieth-century 'human sciences' generally, the body has become a central preoccupation. Its dispersal, openness and fragmentation has become a kind of negative point of reference for contemporary social and philosophical reflection; and, thus, the point of intersection for innumerable contradictory and incompatible ideas. It is now the body which thinks, as well as feels; its order and structure has become the defining moment of contemporary life; the body resensualised, the senses reorganised, the order of life corporealised. In a curious way ancient body images are rediscovered in the wishfulness and dreamlike indifference of contemporary consumerism. Liberated wishes effortlessly carry the body, as if on a turbulent stream, in no particular direction.

NOTES

1 SE 21, p. 86.
2 SE 21, p. 134.
3 As for example in Bocock (1976, 1983).
4 Mitzman (1985), pp. 148–63.
5 Ferguson (1992) for a general discussion.
6 Weber (1930), p. 111.
7 Ibid., p. 112.
8 Ibid., p. 119.
9 Weber (1948), pp. 323–62.
10 Ibid., p. 343.
11 For a vigorous rejection of this judgement see Pearce (1989).
12 Parsons (1937), pp. 301–450.
13 This is the approach adopted by Parsons.
14 E.g. Douglas (1967); Taylor (1982).
15 Durkheim (1952), p. 246.
16 Ibid., p. 248.
17 Ibid., p. 284.
18 Miller (1981); Williams (1982).
19 Dijskra (1986) Russett (1989).
20 Mestrovic (1991) for a sympathetic re-reading of Durkheim in this context.
21 There have, of course, ben many unorthodox Marxists who, influenced in a more general way by Freud, have sought to assimilate (rather than amalgamate with) his work. Walter Benjamin and Ernst Bloch are, perhaps, the most significant examples.
22 Reich (1970), p. 29.
23 Ibid., p. 30.
24 The notion of the auhoritarian pesonality was exhaustively studied during the Second World War by emigré sociologists and psychologists from the Frankfurt School for Social Research, a group influenced by both Freud and Marx.
25 Robinson (1972), p. 31; see also Rieff (1965), Giddens (1992).
26 Marcuse (1955), p. 57.
27 Ibid., p. 48.
28 E.g. Kovel (1988).
29 The latter debate has proved longer lasting. A new round in the dispute was inaugurated by Grünbaum (1984), and continued in Clark and Wright (1988).
30 SE 12, p. 60.
31 Gabel (1975), p. 78.
32 Marx (1976), p. 163.

33 Jaspers (1963) is an inexhaustible source and expression of this infatuation. For a comprehensive study see Sass (1992).
34 Elliott (1994), pp. 194–5 somewhat unfairly criticises them on the grounds of their 'Romanticism'; where, in fact, he objects to their extreme anti-Romantic realism.
35 Deleuze and Guattari (1977), p. 5.
36 Ibid., p. 7.
37 Schilder (1935) describes the normal body-image as a sensitive surface; about the insides of our bodies, he says, 'we know nothing'.
38 Ibid., p. 62.
39 An affinity which, obviously enough, has conditioned the preceding discussion. On Simmel's interest in academic psychology see Frisby (1992), pp. 20–43.
40 Simmel (1950), p. 350–1.
41 Simmel (1978), p. 79.
42 Ibid., pp. 128–9.
43 Ibid., p. 235.
44 Ibid., p. 248.
45 Wolff (1950), p. 53.
46 SE 7, p. 210–11.
47 Several recent French writers have referred to this as *jouissance.*
48 SE 21, p. 64.
49 Feelings prominent in Otto (1959).
50 Kristeva (1982) on non-religious versions in modern society.
51 George Bataille's writings attempt to preserve the original unity of the primary process, and he thus interprets the sexual and the religious in terms of each other. Whatever the shortcomings of his exposition (which altogether ignores, so far as is possible, the development of the ego) it has the merit of restating in uncompromising terms the qualitative difference between pleasure and ecstasy.
52 Lacan's work is, of course, highly suggestive: Lacan (1979); Forrester (1980).
53 Feher (1989).
54 On the disunited body-image in Ancient Judaism see Pedersen (1926); Johnson (1964); Adkins (1970); Wolff (1974); Gundry (1976).
55 Ricoeur (1966) analyses the body-image in terms of the merging of freedom and nature which makes voluntary movement possible.

BIBLIOGRAPHY

Adkins, A. W. H. (1970) *From the Many to the One*, London, Constable.
Adorno, Theodor W. (1989) *Kierkegaard: The Construction of the Aesthetic*, trans. and ed. Robert Hullot-Kentor, Minneapolis, University of Minnesota Press.
Anzieu, Didier (1986) *Freud's Self-Analysis*, trans. Peter Graham, London, Hogarth Press and Institute of Psycho-Analysis.
Appignanesi, Lisa and Forrester, John (1993) *Freud's Women*, London, Virago.
Arendt, Hannah (1978) *The Jew as Pariah*, New York, Grove Press.
Aristides, P. Aelius (1981) *The Complete Works*, vol. II, trans. Charles A. Behr, Leiden, E. J. Brill.
Aristotle (1912) *The Works of Aristotle*, vol. V, ed. J.A. Smith and W. D. Ross, Oxford, Oxford University Press.
—— (1935) *Parva Naturalia*, trans. W. S. Hett, London, Loeb Classical Library.
Arnold, Denis (1990) *Monteverdi*, London, Dent.
Artemidorus (1975) *The Interpretation of Dreams*, trans. and commentary Robert J. White, Park Ridge, N.J., Noyes Press.
Aschheim, Steven E. (1982) *Brothers and Strangers*, Madison, Wisconsin, University of Wisconsin Press.
Babinski, J. and Froment, J. (1918) *Hysteria or Pithiatism*, trans. J. D. Rolleston, London, University of London Press.
Bachelard, Gaston (1968) *The Psychoanalysis of Fire*, trans. Alan C. M. Ross, Boston, Beacon Press.
—— (1969) *The Poetics of Reverie*, trans. Daniel Russell, Boston, Beacon Press.
Bachofen, J. J. (1967) *Myth, Religion and Mother Right*, trans. Ralph Mannheim, Princeton, N.J., Princeton University Press.
Bacon, Edward (1976) *The Great Archaeologists*, London, Secker & Warburg.
Bahr, Hermann (1925) *Expressionism*, trans. R. T. Gribble, London, Henderson.
Bain, Alexander (1868) *Mental and Moral Science*, London, Longman, Green and Co.
Bakhtin, Mikhail (1968) *Rabelais and his World*, trans. H. Iswolsky, Cambridge, Mass., MIT Press.
Bakan, David (1958) *Sigmund Freud and the Jewish Mystical Tradition*, Boston, Mass., Beacon Press.
Balmary, Marie (1982) *Psychoanalyzing Psychoanalysis*, trans. and intr. Ned Lukacher, Baltimore and London, Johns Hopkins University Press.
Bauer, Walter (1971) *Orthodoxy and Heresy in Earliest Christianity*, Philadelphia, Fortress Press.
Beard, George M. (1881) *American Nervousness: its causes and consequences*, New York, G. P. Putnam.

Becker, Raymond de (1968) *The Understanding of Dreams*, trans. Michael Heron, London, Allen & Unwin.

Beckford, William (1971) *Dreams, Waking Thoughts and Incidents*, ed. and intr. Robert J. Gennett, Cranbury, N.J., Associated Universities Press.

Béguin, Albert (1946) *L'Âme Romantique et Le Rêve*, Paris, Linraire José Corti.

Behler, Ernst (1993) *German Romantic Literary Theory*, Cambridge, Cambridge University Press.

Bell, Charles (1830) *The Nervous System of the Human Body*, London, Longman.

Beller, Steven (1989) *Vienna and the Jews 1867–1938*, Cambridge, Cambridge University Press.

Bennett, Benjamin (1988) *Hugo von Hofmannsthal: the theatre of consciousness*, Cambridge, Cambridge University Press.

Bergson, Henri (1915) *Dreams*, trans. and intr. Edwin E. Slosson, London, Swan Sonnenschein.

Berkley, George E. (1988) *Vienna and its Jews: the tragedy of success*, Cambridge, Mass., Madison Books.

Bernheim, H. (1980) *Bernheim's New Studies in Hypnotism*, trans. Richard S. Sander, New York, International Universities Press.

Bernheimer, Charles and Kahane, Charles (1985) *In Dora's Case: Freud-Hysteria–Feminism*, London, Virago.

Binet, Alfred (1977) *Alterations of Personality / On Double Consciousness*, ed. and preface Daniel N. Robinson, New York, University Publications of America.

Bleuler, Eugene (n.d. 1916) *Textbook of Psychiatry*, trans. A. A. Brill, London, Allen & Unwin.

—— (1950) *Dementia Praecox, or the Group of Schizophrenias*, trans. Joseph Zirkin, New York, Allen & Unwin.

Bliss, Eugene L. (1986) *Multiple Personality, Allied Disorders and Hypnosis*, Oxford, Oxford University Press.

Bloch, Ernst (1986) *The Principle of Hope*, trans. Neville Plaice, Stephen Plaice and Paul Knight, Oxford, Blackwell.

Blumenberg, Hans (1987) *The Genesis of the Copernican World*, trans. and intr. Robert M. Wallace, Cambridge, Mass., MIT Press.

Bocock, Robert (1976) *Freud and Modern Society*, London, Nelson.

—— (1983) *Sigmund Freud*, London and New York, Tavistock.

Bousquet, Jacques (1964) *Les Thèmes du Rêve dans la Littérature Romantique*, Paris, Didier.

Bowie, Malcolm (1987) *Freud, Proust and Lacan* Cambridge, Cambridge University Press.

Boyer, John (1981) *Political Radicalism in Late Imperial Vienna*, Chicago and London, Chicago University Press.

Braid, James (1899) *Braid on Hypnotism: Neurypnology*, ed. Arthur Edward Waite, London, George Redway.

Braudel, Fernand (1975) *The Mediterranean and the Mediterranean World in the Age of Philip II*, 2 vols., trans. Siân Reynolds, London, Fontana.

Brazier, Mary A. B. (1984) *A History of Neurophysiology in the 17th and 18th Centuries*, New York, Raven Press.

—— (1987) *A History of Neurophysiology in the 19th Century*, New York, Raven Press.

Brentano, Franz (1973) *Psychology from an Empirical Standpoint*, ed. Oskar Krauss and Leslie L. McAlister, London, Routledge.

Broch, Hermann (1984) *Hugo von Hofmannsthal and his Time: the European Imagination 1860–1920*, trans. and ed. Michael P. Steinberg, Chicago and London, Chicago University Press.

—— (1986) *The Sleepwalkers*, trans. Willa and Edwin Muir, London, Quartet.

Brown, Peter (1989) *The Body and Society: men, women and sexual renunciation in early Christianity*, London, Faber & Faber.

Büchner, Ludwig (1884) *Force and Matter: or Principles of the Natural Order of the Universe*, London, Ascher.

Buci-Glucksmann, Christine (1994) *Baroque Reason: the aesthetics of modernity*, trans. Patrick Cammiller, intr. Bryan S. Turner, London, Sage.

Burkert, Walter (1972) *Homo Necans: the anthropology of Ancient Greek sacrificial ritual and myth*, trans. Peter Bing, Berkeley, Los Angeles and London, University of California Press.

Burrow, J. W. (1966) *Evolution and Society*, Cambridge, Cambridge University Press.

Burwick, Frederick (1986) *The Damnation of Newton: Goethe's color theory and romantic perception*, Berlin and New York, Walter de Gruyter.

Bynum, W. F., Roy Porter and Michael Shepherd (eds) (1988) *The Anatomy of Madness, vol. III: the asylum and its psychiatry*, London, Routledge.

Calder III, William M. and David A. Traill (eds) (1986) *Myth, Scandal and History: the Heinrich Schliemann controversy*, Detroit, Wayne State University Press.

Calderón de la Barca, Pedro (1991) *Plays: One*, trans. and intr. Gwynne Edwards, London, Methuen.

Caldwell, Richard (1989) *The Origin of the Gods*, Oxford, Oxford University Press.

Calvi, Giulia (1989) *Histories of a Plague Year: the social and the imaginary in Baroque Florence*, trans. David Biocca and Bryant T. Ragan Jr, Berkley, Los Angeles and Oxford, University of California Press.

Camporesi, Piero (1988) *The Incorruptible Flesh: bodily mutation and mortification in religion and folklore*, trans. Tania Croft-Murray and Helen Elson, Cambridge, Cambridge University Press.

—— (1989) *Bread of Dreams: food and fantasy in early modern Europe*, trans. David Gentileone, Oxford and Cambridge, Polity Press.

—— (1990) *The Fear of Hell: images of damnation and salvation in early modern Europe*, trans. Lucinda Byatt, Cambridge, Polity.

Capek, Milic (1971) *Bergson and Modern Physics*, Dordrecht and Boston, Reidl.

—— (ed.) (1976) *The Concepts of Space and Time*, Dordrecht and Boston, Reidl.

Carruthers, Mary (1990) *The Book of Memory: a study of memory in medieval culture*, Cambridge, Cambridge University Press.

Cascardi, Anthony J. (1984) *The Limits of Illusion: a critical study of Calderón*, Cambridge, Cambridge University Press.

—— (1992) *The Subject of Modernity*, Cambridge, Cambridge University Press.

Caspar, Max (1959) *Kepler*, London and New York, Abelard-Schuman.

Certeau, Michel de (1986) *Heterologies: discourses on the other*, trans. Brian Massumi, Manchester, Manchester University Press.

Cervantes, Miguel de (1950) *Don Quixote*, trans. J. M. Cohen, Harmondsworth, Penguin.

—— (1972) *Exemplary Stories*, trans. C. A. Jones, Harmondsworth, Penguin.

Chapple, Gerald and Hans H. Schulte (1981) *The Turn of the Century: German literature and art 1890–1915*, Bonn, Bouvier Verlag.

Charcot, Jean-Martin (1889) *Clinical Lectures on Diseases of the Nervous System*, 3 vols, trans. Thomas Savill, London, The New Sydenham Society.

—— (1987) *Charcot the Clinician: the Tuesday lessons (1887/88)*, trans. and commentary Christopher G. Gretz, New York, Raven Press.

Chartier, Roger (1994) *The Order of Books*, trans. Lydia G. Cochrane, Cambridge and Oxford, Polity Press.

Clare, George (1984) *Last Waltz in Vienna: the destruction of a family 1842–1942*, London.

Clark, Peter and Crispin Wright (1988) *Mind, Psychoanalysis and Science*, Oxford, Blackwell.

Clark, Ronald W. (1982) *Freud: the man and the cause*, London, Granada.

Clarke, Edwin and L. S. Jacyna (1987) *Nineteenth-Century Origins of Neuroscientific Concepts*, Berkeley, Los Angeles and London, University of California Press.

Classen, Constance (1993) *Worlds of Sense*, London, Routledge.

Claus, Carl (1889) *Elementary Textbook of Zoology*, 2 vols, trans. Adam Sedgwick, London.

Claus, David B. (1981) *Toward the Soul*, New Haven and London, Yale University Press.

Clifford, William Kingdom (1879) *Lectures and Essays*, 2 vols, London, Macmillan.

—— (1885) *The Common Sense of the Exact Sciences*, London, Kegan, Paul & Trench.

Cohen, I. Bernard (1980) *The Newtonian Revolution*, Cambridge, Cambridge University Press.

Cole, J. Preston (1971) *The Problematic Self in Kierkegaard and Freud*, Princeton, N.J., Princeton University Press.

Collier, Peter and Judy Davies (eds) (1990) *Modernism and the European Unconscious*, Cambridge and Oxford, Polity Press.

Colquhoun, J. C. (1851) *An History of Magic, Witchcraft, and Animal Magnetism*, 2 vols, London, Longman, Brown, Green and Lougmans.

Corbin, A. (1994) *The Foul and the Fragrant*, London, Picador.

Cottingham, John (1986) *Descartes*, Oxford, Blackwell.

Couliano, Ioan P. (1987) *Eros and Magic in the Renaissance*, trans. Margaret Cook, Chicago and London, Chicago University Press.

Crankshaw, Edward (1938) *Vienna: the image of a culture in decline*, London, Macmillan.

—— (1963) *The Fall of the House of Habsburg*, London, Longmans.

Cuddihy, John Murray (1987) *The Ordeal of Civility*, Boston, Beacon Press.

Curtius, E. R. (1973) *Essays on European Literature*, trans. Michael Kowal, Princeton, N.J., Princeton University Press.

Daniel, Glyn (1981) *A Short History of Archaeology*, London, Thames & Hudson.

David-Ménard, David (1988) *Hysteria from Freud to Lacan*, trans. Catherine Porter, Ithaca, N.J., and London, Cornell University Press.

deBois, Page (1988) *Sowing the Body: psychoanalysis and ancient representations of women*, Chicago and London, University of Chicago Press.

Decker, Hannah S. (1977) *Freud in Germany: revolution and reaction in science, 1893–1907*, New York, International Universities Press.

—— (1991) *Freud, Dora, and Vienna 1900*, New York and Toronto, The Free Press.

Dedijer, Vladimir (1967) *The Road to Sarajevo*, London, Macgibbon and Kee.

Deleuze, Gilles (1993) *The Fold: Leibniz and the Baroque*, trans. Tom Conley, London, Athlone.

—— (1994) *Difference and Repetition*, trans. Paul Patton, London, Athlone.

Deleuze, Gilles and Felix Guattari (1977) *Anti-Oedipus: capitalism and schizophrenia*, trans. Robert Hurley, New York, Viking Press.

Dember, William N. (1964) *Visual Perception: the nineteenth century*, New York and London, Wiley.

Descartes, René (1984) *The Philosophical Writings of Descartes, volume I*, eds John Cottingham, Robert Strothoff and Dugald Murdoch, Cambridge, Cambridge University Press.

Descartes, René (1985) *The Philosophical Writings of Descartes, volume II*, eds John Cottingham, Robert Srothoff and Dugald Murdoch, Cambridge, Cambridge University Press.

Detienne, Marcel (1979) *Dionysos Slain*, trans. Mireille Muellneu and Leonora Muellneu, Baltimore and London, The Johns Hopkins University Press.

Dijkstra, Bram (1986) *Idols of Perversity: fantasies of feminine evil in fin-de-siècle culture*, Oxford, Oxford University Press.

Dilman, Ilham (1984) *Freud and the Mind*, Oxford, Blackwell.

Dodds, E. R. (1951) *The Greeks and the Irrational*, Berkeley and Los Angeles, University of California Press.

Douglas, J. (1967) *The Social Meanings of Suicide*, Princeton, N.J., Princeton University Press.

Drinka, George (1984) *The Birth of Neurosis: myth, malady and the Victorians*, New York, Simon & Schuster

Duerr, Hans Peter (1985) *Dreamtime*, trans. Felicitas Goodman, Oxford, Blackwell.

Durkheim, Emile (1933) *The Division of Labour in Society*, trans. George Simpson, New York, Free Pres

—— (1952) *Suicide: a study in sociology*, trans. John A. Spaulding and George Simpson, London, Routledge & Kegan Paul.

Edmunds, Lowell and Alan Dundes (eds) (1984) *Oedipus: a folklore casebook*, New York and London, Garland.

Ellenberger, Henri F. (1970) *The Discovery of the Unconscious: the history and evolution of dynamic psychiatry*, London, Allen Lane.

Elliott, Anthony (1994) *Psychoanalytic Theory: an introduction*, Oxford, Blackwell.

Emmerton, Norma E. (1984) *The Scientific Reinterpretation of Form*, Ithaca and London, Cornell University Press.

Erichsen, John Eric (1866) *On Railway and Other Injuries of the Nervous System*, London, Walton and Maberly.

Ferguson, Harvie (1990) *The Science of Pleasure: cosmos and psyche in the bourgeois world view*, London, Routledge.

—— (1992) *Religious Transformation in Western Society: the end of happiness*, London, Routledge.

—— (1995) *Melancholy and the Critique of Modernity: Søren Kierkegaard's religious psychology*, London, Routledge.

Feher, M., Nadaff, R. and N. Tazi (eds) (1989) *Fragments for a History of the Human Body*, 3 vols., New York, Urzone Inc.

Field, Frank (1967) *The Last Days of Mankind: Karl Krauss and his Vienna*, London and New York, Macmillan.

Filoramo, Giovanni (1990) *A History of Gnosticism*, Oxford, Blackwell.

Fingarette, Herbert (1969) *Self-Deception*, London, Routledge & Kegan Paul.

Firth, Raymond (1973) *Symbols: public and private*, London, George Allen & Unwin.

Fischer, Steven R. (1978) *The Dream in the Middle High German Epic*, Bern, Frankfurt and Los Angeles, Peter Leng.

Fisher, Seymour (1970) *Body Experience in Fantasy and Behaviour*, New York, Appleton-Century-Crofts.

Forcione, Alban K. (1970) *Cervantes, Aristotle, and the Persiles*, Princeton, N.J., Princeton University Press.

Forrester, John (1980) *Language and the Origins of Psychoanalysis*, London, Macmillan.

Fosgate, Blanchard (1850) *Sleep: psychologically considered with reference to sensation and memory*, New York, Putnam.

Foucault, Michel (1970) *The Order of Things: an archaeology of the hunman sciences*, London, Tavistock.

—— (1977) *Discipline and Punish: the birth of the prison*, trans. Alan Sheridan, London, Allen Lane.

—— (1979) *The History of Sexuality, vol. I*, trans. Robert Hurley, London, Viking.

—— (1990) *The Care of the Self*, trans. Robert Hurley, Harmondsworth, Penguin.

Foucault, Michel and Ludwig Binswanger (1993) *Dream and Existence*, ed. Keith

Hoeller, trans. Forrest Williams and Jacob Needleman, Atlantic Highlands, N.J., Humanities Press.

Foulkes, David (1978) *A Grammar of Dreams*, Hassocks, Harvester.

Freud, Sigmund (1953–74) *The Standard Edition of the Complete Psychological Works of Sigmund Freud*, 24 vols, ed. and trans. James Strachey with Anna freud, Alix Strachey and Alan Tyson, London, The Hogarth Press and the Institute of Psycho-Analysis.

—— (1953) *On Aphasia: a critical study*, New York, International Universities Press.

—— (1961) *Letters of Sigmund Freud 1873–1939*, ed. Ernst L. Freud, trans. Tania and James Stern, London, The Hogarth Press.

—— (1974) *Cocaine Papers by Sigmund Freud*, ed. Robert Byck, Stonehill, New York.

—— (1985) *The Complete Letters of Sigmund Freud to Wilhelm Fliess*, trans. and ed. Jeffrey Moussaieff Masson, Cambridge, Mass. and London, Harvard University Press.

—— (1987) *A Phylogenetic Fantasy: overview of the transference neuroses*, ed. and with essays Ilse Grubrich-Simitis, trans. Axel Hoffer and Peter T. Hoffer, Cambridge, Mass. and London, Harvard University Press.

—— (1990) *The Letters of Sigmund Freud to Eduard Silberstein 1871–1881*, ed. Walter Boehlich, trans. Arnold J. Pomerans, Cambridge, Mass. and London, Harvard University Press.

Freud, Sigmund and Karl Abraham (1965) *A Psycho-Analytic Dialogue: the letters of Sigmund Freud and Karl Abraham, 1907–1926*, ed. Hilda C. Abraham and Ernst L. Freud, trans. Bernard Marsh and Hilda C. Abraham, London, The Hogarth Press and the Institute of Psycho-Analysis.

Freud, Sigmund and Carl Jung (1974) *The Freud-Jung Letters: the correspondence between Sigmund Freud and C.G. Jung*, ed. William McGuire, trans. Ralph Manheim and R. F. C. Hull, The Hogarth Press and Routledge & Kegan Paul.

Freudenthal, Gideon (1986) *Atom and Individual in the Age of Newton: on the genesis of the mechanist world view*, Dordrecht and Lancaster, Rediel.

Frisby, David (1981) *Sociological Impressionism: a reassessment of Georg Simmel's social theory*, London, Heinemann.

—— (1984) *Georg Simmel*, London and New York, Tavistock.

—— (1992) *Simmel and Since: essays on Simmel's social theory*, London, Routledge.

Frosh, Stephen (1991) *Identity Crisis: modernity, psychoanalysis and the self*, London, Macmillan.

Gabel, Joseph (1975) *False Consciousness: an essay on reification*, Oxford, Basil Blackwell.

Gardiner, Muriel (ed.) (1971) *The Wolf-man by the Wolf-man*, New York, Basic Books.

Gardner, Sebastian (1993) *Irrationality and the Philosophy of Psychoanalysis*, Cambridge, Cambridge University Press.

Garin, Eugenio (1978) *Science and Civil Life in the Italian Renaissance*, trans. Peter Munz, Gloucester Mass., P. Smith.

Gay, Peter (1978) *Freud, Jews and other Germans*, New York and Oxford, Oxford University Press.

—— (1987) *A Godless Jew: Freud, atheism and the making of psychoanalysis*, New Haven and London, Yale University Press.

—— (1988) *Freud: a life for our time*, London and Melbourne, Dent.

Gedo, John E. and George H. Pollock (eds) (1976) *Freud: the fusion of science and humanism*, New York, International Universities Press.

Gelfand, Toby and John Kerr (eds) (1992) *Freud and the History of Psychoanlysis*, Hillsdale, N.J., The Analytic Press.

Gernet, Louis (1981) *The Anthropology of Ancient Greece*, trans. John Hamilton S.J. and Blaise Nagy, Baltimore and London, The Johns Hopkins University Press.

Giddens, Anthony (1991) *Modernity and Self Identity: self and society in the late modern age*, Cambridge and Oxford, Polity.

—— (1992) *The Transformation of Intimacy*, Cambridge and Oxford, Polity.

Gill, Merton and Karl Pribram (1976) *Freud's 'Project' Re-assessed*, London, Hutchinson.

Gilman, Sander L. (1986) *Jewish Self-Hatred: anti-Semitism and the hidden language of the Jews*, Baltimore and London, The Johns Hopkins University Press.

—— (1993) *The Case of Sigmund Freud: medicine and identity at the fin-de-siècle*, Baltimore and London, The Johns Hopkins University Press.

Gilman, Stephen (1989) *The Novel According to Cervantes*, Berkley, Los Angeles and London, University of California Press.

Glover, Jane (1978) *Cavalli*, London, Batsford.

Goethe, Johann Wolfgang von (1949, 1959) *Faust*, 2 vols, trans. Philip Wayne, Harmondsworth, Penguin.

—— (1952) *Goethe's Botanical Writings*, trans. Bertha Mueller, Woodbridge, Conn., Ox Bow.

—— (1970) *Italian Journey*, trans. W. H. Auden and Elizabeth Mayer, Harmondsworth, Penguin.

—— (1971) *Elective Affinities*, trans. R. J. Hollingdale, Harmondsworth, Penguin.

—— (1989) *The Sorrows of Young Werther*, trans. Michael Hulse, Harmondsworth, Penguin.

Goff, Jacques Le (1988) *Medievel Civilization*, trans. Julia Barrow, Oxford, Basil Blackwell.

—— (1988) *The Medieval Imagination*, trans. Arthur Goldhammer, Chicago and London, Chicago University Press.

Goldscheider, Calvin and Alan S. Zuckerman (1984) *The Transformation of the Jews*, Chicago and London, University of Chicago Press.

Goldstein, Jan (1987) *Console and Classify: the French psychiatric profession in the nineteenth century*, Cambridge, Cambridge University Press.

Goody, Jack (1993) *The Culture of Flowers*, Cambridge, Cambridge University Press.

Gordon, R. L. (ed.) (1981) *Myth, Religion and Society*, Cambridge and Paris, Cambridge University Press.

Goux, Jean-Joseph (1993) *Oedipus, Philosopher*, trans. Catherine Porter, Stanford, Stanford University Press.

Gould, Stephen Jay (1977) *Ontogeny and Phylogeny*, London and Cambridge, Mass., Harvard University Press.

Grabbes, Herbert (1982) *The Mutable Glass*, trans. Gordon Collier, Cambridge, Cambridge University Press.

Greer, Margaret Rich (1991) *The Play of Power: mythological court dramas of Calderón de la Barca*, Princeton, N.J., Princeton University Press.

Gregory, Tullio (ed.) (1985) *I Sogni nel Medioevo*, Rome, Edizioni dell'Ateneo.

Grinstein, Alexander (1980) *Sigmund Freud's Dreams*, New York, International Universities Press.

—— (1990) *Freud at the Crossroads*, Maddison, Conn., International Universities Press.

Groddeck, Georg (1949) *The Book of the It*, trans. V. M. E. Collins, London, Vision Press.

Grünbaum, Adolf (1984) *The Foundation of Psychoanalysis: a philosophical critique*, Berkeley, University of California Press.

—— (1993) *Validation in the Clinical Theory of Psychoanalysis*, Madison, Conn., International Universities Press.

Grunebaum, G. E. von and Roger Caillois (1966) *The Dream and Human Societies*, Berkeley and Los Angeles, University of California Press.

Grunwald, Max (1936) *History of the Jews in Vienna*, Philadelphia, The Jewish Publication Society of America.

Gulick, Charles A. (1948) *Austria: from Habsburg to Hitler, vol. I, Labour's Workshop of Democracy*, Berkeley and Los Angeles, University of California Press.

Gundry, Robert H. (1976) *Soma in Biblical Theology*, Cambridge, Cambridge University Press.

Gurevich, A. J. (1985) Categories of Medieval Culture, trans. G. L. Campbell, London, Routledge & Kegan Paul.

Guthrie, W. K. G. (1950) *The Greeks and their Gods*, London, Methuen.

Hacking, Ian (1995) *Rewriting the Soul: Multiple Personality and the Science of Memory*, Princeton, N.J., University of Princeton Press.

Haley, Bruce (1978) *The Healthy Body and Victorian Culture*, Cambridge, Mass. Harvard University Press.

Hallyn, Fernand (1990) *The Poetic Structure of the World: Copernicus and Kepler*, trans. Donald M. Leslie, New York, Zone.

Harrington, Anne (1987) *Medicine, Mind, and the Double Brain*, Princeton, N.J., University of Princeton Press.

Haywood, Bruce (1959) *Novalis: the veil of imagery*, 'S-Gravenhage, Mouton.

Heine, Heinrich (1891) *Pictures of Travel*, 2 vols, trans. Charles Godfrey Leland, London, Sampson, Low, Marston.

Helmholtz, H. (1884) *Popular Lectures on Scientific Subjects*, trans. E. Atkinson, London.

Hirschmüller, Albrecht (1989) *The Life and Work of Josef Breuer: physiology and psychoanalysis*, New York and London, New York University Press.

Hobbes, Thomas (1962) *Leviathan*, ed. John Plamenatz, London, Fontana.

Hoffmeister, Gerhart (1983) *German Baroque Literature*, New York, Frerick Unger.

Holt, Robert R. (1989) *Freud Reappraised: a fresh look at psychoanalytic theory*, New York and London, The Guilford Press.

Hughes, Judith M. (1994) *From Freud's Consulting Room*, Cambridge, Mass., Harvard University Press.

Husser, Jean-Marie (1994) *Le Songe et la parole: etude sur le rêve et sa fonction dans l'ancien Israel*, Berlin and New York, Walter de Gruyter.

Iggers, Wilma Abeles (1967) *Karl Krauss: a Viennese critic of the twentieth century*, The Hague, Martinus Nijhoff.

Isbister, J. N. (1985) *Freud: an introduction to his life and work*, Cambridge and Oxford, Polity Press.

Jackson, John Hughlings (1931) *Selected Writings of John Hughlings Jackson*, 2 vols., ed. James Taylor, London, Hodder & Stoughton.

Jacques, Francis (1991) *Difference and Subjectivity: dialogue and personal identity*, trans. Andrew Rothwell, New Haven and London, Yale University Press.

Janet, Pierre (1898) *Névroses et idées fixes*, 2 vols, Paris, Alcan.

—— (1925) *Psychological Healing: a historical and clinical study*, trans. Eden and Cedar Paul, London, George Allen & Unwin.

—— (1965) *The Major Symptoms of Hysteria*, New York, Hafner.

—— (1977) *The Mental State of Hystericals*, ed. and intr. Daniel N. Robinson, trans. Caroline Rollin Carson, Washington D.C., University Publications of America.

Jaspers, Karl (1963) *General Psychopathology*, trans. J. Hoenig and Marian W. Hamilton, Manchester, Manchester University Press.

Jászi, Oscar (1961) *The Dissolution of the Habsburg Monarchy*, Chicago and London, Chicago University Press.

Johnson, Aubrey R. (1964) *The Vitality of the Individual in the Thought of Ancient Israel*, Cardiff, University of Wales Press.

Johnston, William M. (1972) *The Austrian Mind: an intellectual and social history 1848–1938*, Berkeley, Los Angeles and London, University of California Press.

Jones, Ernest (1953–57) *The Life and Work of Sigmund Freud*, 3 vols, New York, Basic Books.

Kamen, Henry (1985) *Inquisition and Society in Spain: in the sixteenth and seventeenth centuries*, London, Weidenfeld & Nicolson.

Kanzer, Mark and Jules Glenn (eds) (1980) *Freud and His Patients*, New York, Jason Aronson.

Katz, Jacob (1987) *Toward Modernity: the European Jewish Model*, New Brunswick and Oxford, Transaction Books.

Kerr, John (1994) *A Most Dangerous Method*, London, Sinclair-Stevenson.

Kierkegaard, Søren (1987) *Either/Or*, 2 vols, ed. and trans. Howard V. Hong and Edna H. Hong, Princeton, N.J., Princeton University Press.

Kitcher, Patricia (1992) *Freud's Dream: a complete interdisciplinary science of mind*, Cambridge, Mass., MIT Press.

Klages, Ludwig (1929) *The Science of Character*, trans. W. H. Johnston, London, George Allen & Unwin.

Klein, Dennis B. (1981) *Jewish Origins of the Psychoanalytic Movement*, New York, Praeger.

Kline, Paul (1972) *Fact and Fantasy in Freudian Theory*, London, Methuen.

Koenigsberger, Dorothy (1979) *Renaissance Man and Creative Thinking: a history of the concept of harmony, 1400–1700,*, Hassocks, Harvester.

Kohut, Heinz (1971) *The Analysis of the Self*, New York, International Universities Press.

—— (1977) *The Restoration of the Self*, New York, International Universities Press.

Kokoschka, Oskar (1974) *My Life*, trans. David Britt, London, Thames and Hudson.

Kovel, Joel (1988) *The Radical Spirit: essays on psychoanalysis and society*, London, Free Association Books.

Koyré, Alexandre (1957) *From the Closed World to the Infinite Universe*, Baltimore and London, The Johns Hopkins University Press.

—— (1973) *The Astronomical Revolution*, London, Methuen.

Kristeller, Paul Oskar (1943) *The Philosophy of Marsilio Ficino*, New York, Columbia University Press.

Kristeva, Julia (1982) *Powers of Horror: an essay on abjection*, trans. Leon S. Roudiez, New York, Columbia University Press.

Kruger, Steven F. (1992) *Dreaming in the Middle Ages*, Cambridge, Cambridge University Press.

Krüll, Marianne (1986) *Freud and His Father*, trans. Arnold J. Pomerans, New York and London, W. W. Norton.

Kuzniar, Alice (1987) *Delayed Endings: nonclosure in Novalis and Holderlin*, Athens and London, University of Georgia Press.

Lacan, Jacques (1967) *The Language of the Self: the function of language in psycho-anlysis*, trans. Anthony Wilden, Baltimore and London, The Johns Hopkins University Press.

—— (1977) *Écrits: a selection*, trans. Alan Sheridan, London, Tavistock.

—— (1979) *The Four Fundamental Concepts of Psycho-Analysis*, trans. Alan Sheridan, Harmondsworth, Penguin.

Lang, Bernhard (ed.) (1985) *Anthropological Approaches to the Old Testament*, Philadelphia, Portress Press and London, SPCK.

Lansky, Melvin R. (ed.) (1992) *Essential Papers on Dreams*, New York, New York University Press.

Laplanche, J. and J.-B. Pontalis (1988) *The Language of Psycho-Analysis*, London, Karnac Books and Institute of Psycho-Analysis.

Laycock, Thomas (1840) *A Treatise on the Nervous Diseases of Women*, London.

Lear, John (1965) *Kepler's Dream*, Berkeley and Los Angeles, University of California Press.

Lehmann, Jennifer M. (1993) *Deconstructing Durkheim*, London, Routledge.

Lesky, Erna (1976) *The Vienna Medical School of the 19th Century*, trans. L. Williams and I. S. Levy, Baltimore and London, The Johns Hopkins University Press.

Levin, David Michael (1985) *The Body's Recollection of Being*, London, Routledge.

Lockwood, Michael (1989) *Mind, Brain and Quantum: the compound 'I'*, Oxford, Blackwell.

López Piñero, José M. (1983) *Historical Origins of the Concept of Neurosis*, trans. D. Berrios, Cambridge, Cambridge University Press.

Lovejoy, Arthur O. (1960) *The Great Chain of Being*, New York, Harper.

Loewenstien, R. M., Newman, L. M., Schur, M. and Solnit, A. J. (eds) (1966) *Psychoanalysis – A General Psychology*, New York, International Universities Press.

Lukes, Steven (1973) *Emile Durkheim, his life and work*, London, Allen Lane.

Lyotard, Jean-François (1993) *Libidinal Economy*, trans. Hamilton Grant London, Athlone Press.

Macartney, C. A. (1971) *The Habsburg Empire 1790–1918*, London, Weidenfeld & Nicolson.

McGrath, William J. (1974) *Dionysian Art and Populist Politics in Austria*, New Haven and London, Yale University Press.

—— (1986) *Freud's Discovery of Psychoanalysis: the politics of hysteria*, Ithaca and London, Cornell University Press.

Mach, Ernst (1989) *Contributions to the Analysis of the Sensations*, Peru, Ill. Open Court.

Macmillan, Malcolm (1990) *Freud Evaluated: The Closing Arc* Amsterdam, North Holland.

MacMullen, Ramsay (1994) *Christianizing the Roman Empire: AD 100–400*, New Haven and London, Yale University Press.

McNish, Robert (1830) *The Philosophy of Sleep*, Glasgow, W. R. M'Phun.

—— (1834) *Aphorisms by a Modern Pythagorean*, Glasgow.

Macrobius (1952) *Commentary on the Dream of Scipio*, trans. and intr. William Harris Stahl, New York, Columbia University Press.

Mahony, Patrick J. (1984) *Cries of the Wolf Man*, New York, International Universities Press.

—— (1986) *Freud and the Rat Man*, New Haven, Yale University Press.

—— (1987) *Freud as a Writer*, New Haven and London, Yale University Press.

—— (1989) *On Defining Freud's Discourse*, New Haven and London, Yale University Press.

Mâle, Emile (1972) *The Gothic Image: Religious Art in France of the Thirteenth Century*, trans. Dora Mussey, New York and London, Harper & Row.

Maravall, José Antonio (1986) *Culture of the Baroque*, trans. Terry Cochran, Manchester, Manchester University Press.

Marcuse, Herbert (1955) *Eros and Civilisation*, New York, The Beacon Press.

Maritain, Jacques (1946) *The Dream of Descartes*, trans. Mabelle L. Andison, London, Editions Poetry.

Martin, John Rupert (1977) *Baroque*, London, Allen Lane.

Marx, Karl (1975) *Early Writings*, trans. Rodney Livingstone and Gregor Benton, intr. Lucio Colletti, Harmondsworth, Penguin.

—— (1976) *Capital Vol. I*, trans. Ben Fowkes, Harmondsworth, Penguin.

Masson, Jeffrey (1985) *The Assault on Truth*, London, Fontana.

Maury, Alfred (1862) *Le Sommeil et les rêves*, Paris, Librairie Académique.

Mavromatis, Andreas (1987) *Hypnagogia: the unique state of consciousness between wakefulness and sleep*, London, Routledge.

May, Arthur J. (1951) *The Habsburg Monarchy 1867–1914*, Cambridge, Mass. and London, Harvard University Press.

Meige, Henry and E. Feindel (1907) *Tics and their Treatment*, trans. S. A. K. Wilson, London, Appleton.

Meissner, W. W. (1984) *Psychoanalysis and Religious Experience*, New Haven and London, Yale University Press.

Meltzer, Françoise (ed.) (1988) *The Trial(s) of Psychoanalysis*, Chicago and London, University of Chicago Press.

Merleau-Ponty, Maurice (1974) *The Conflict of Interpretations*, Evanston Ill., Northwestern University Press.

Mestrovic, Stjepan G. (1991) *The Coming Fin-de-Siècle*, London, Routledge.

Meyerson, Emile (1930) *Identity and Reality*, trans. Kate Lowenberg, London, Allen & Unwin.

Meynert, Theodor (1885) *Psychiatry: a clinical treatise on diseases of the fore-brain*, trans. B. Sachs, New York and London, Putnam.

Miles, David H. (1972) *Hofmannsthal's Novel Andreas: memory and self*, Princeton, N.J., Princeton University Press.

Miller, Michael B. (1981) *The Bon Marché: bourgeois culture and the department store, 1869–1920*, Princeton, N.J., Princeton University Press.

Mirbeau, Octave (1986) *Le Jardin des supplices*, Paris, Union Générale D'Éditions.

—— (1990) *Les vignts et un jours d'un neurasthénique*, Paris, Editions de Septembre.

Mitchell, S. Weir (1885a) *Fat and Blood: an essay on the treatment of certain forms of neuresthenia and hysteria*, Philadelphia.

—— (1885b) *Lectures on Diseases of the Nervous System: especially in women*, London.

Mitzman, Arthur (1985) *The Iron Cage*, New Brunswick and Oxford, Transaction Books.

Morse, George L. (1985) *Nationalism and Sexuality: respectability and abnormal sexuality in modern Europe*, New York, Howard Fertig.

Morton, Frederic (1979) *A Nervous Splendor: Vienna 1888/1889*, London, Weidenfeld & Nicolson.

Muensterberger, Warner (ed.) (1969) *Man and His Culture: psychoanalyic anthropology after 'Totem and Taboo'*, London, Rapp & Whiting.

Murillo, L. A. (1988) *A Critical Introduction to* Don Quixote, New York, Peter Lang.

Musil, Robert (1968) *The Man Without Qualities*, 3 vols, trans. Eithne Wilkins and Ernst Kaiser, London, Panther.

—— (1982) *On Mach's Theories*, trans. Kevin Mulligan, Washington, D.C., Catholic University of America Press.

Nicolson, Marjorie Hope (1948) *Voyages to the Moon*, New York, Macmillan.

Nietzsche, Friedrich (1973) *Beyond Good and Evil*, trans. R.J. Hollingdale, Harmondsworth, Penguin.

Nisbet, H. B. (1972) *Goethe and the Scientific Tradition*, London, University of London Press.

Nolan, Edward Peter, (1990) *Now Through a Glass Darkly: specular images of being and knowing from Virgil to Chaucer*, Ann Arbor, University of Michigan Press.

Nordentoft, Kresten (1972) *Kierkegaard's Psychology*, trans. Bruce Kirmmse, Pittsburgh, Duquesne University Press.

Novalis (Friedrich von Hardenberg) (1989) *Pollen and Fragments*, trans. and intr. Arthur Versluis, Grand Rapids, Michigan, Phanes Press.

—— (1992) *Hymns to the Night and Spiritual Songs*, trans. George MacDonald, London, Temple Lodge.

Ong, Walter J. (1977) *Interfaces of the Word: studies in the evolution of consciousness and culture*, Ithaca and London, Cornell University Press.

Onians, Richard Broxton (1951) *The Origins of European Thought about the Body, the Mind, the Soul, the World, Time and Fate*, Cambridge, Cambridge University Press.

Oppenheim, A. Leo (1956) *The Interpretation of Dreams in the Ancient Near East*, Transactions of the American Philosophical Society, N.S. 46, 1956.

Oppenheim, Janet (1991) *'Shattered Nerves': doctors, patients and depression in Victorian England*, Oxford, Oxford University Press.

Oring, Elliott (1984) *The Jokes of Sigmund Freud*, Philadelphia, University of Pennsylvania Press.

Orrù, Marco (1987) *Anomie: history and meaning*, Boston, Allen & Unwin.

Otto, Rudolph (1959) *The Idea of the Holy*, trans. John W. Harvey, Harmondsworth, Penguin.

Otto, Walter F. (1954) *The Homeric Gods*, trans. Moses Hadas, Cambridge, Cambridge University Press.

Owen, Alex (1989) *The Darkened Room: women, power and spiritualism in late nineteenth century England*, London, Virago.

Palley, Julian (1983) *The Ambiguous Mirror: dreams in Spanish literature*, Velencia, Chapel Hill, University of North Carolina Press.

Parker, Alexander A. (1988) *The Mind and Art of Calderón*, Cambridge, Cambridge University Press.

Parr, James A. (1974) *Don Quixote: anatomy of subversive discourse*, Newark, Delaware, Juan de la Cuesta.

Parsons, Talcott (1937) *The Structure of Social Action*, New York, The Free Press.

Pearce, Frank (1989) *The Radical Durkheim*, London, Unwin Hyman.

Pederson, Johannes (1926) *Israel: its life and culture I-II*, London and Copenhagen, Oxford University Press.

Pfefferkorn, Kristin (1988) *Novalis: a romantic's theory of language and poetry*, New Haven and London, Yale University Press.

Piehler, Paul (1971) *The Visionary Landscape: a study in medieval allegory*, London, Edward Arnold.

Piñero, José M. López (1988) *Historical Origins of the Concept of Neurosis*, trans. D. D. Berrois, Cambridge, Cambridge Univeristy Press.

Pirrotta, Nino and Elena Poveledo (1982) *Music and Theatre from Poliziano to Monteverdi*, trans. Karen Eales, Cambridge, Cambridge University Press.

Plato (1955) *The Republic*, trans. Desmond Lee, Harmondsworth, Penguin.

Poulet, Georges (1956) *Studies in Human Time*, trans. Elliott Coleman, Baltimore and London, The Johns Hopkins University Press.

Preus, J. Samuel (1986) *Explaining Religion: criticism and theory from Bodin to Freud*, New Haven, Conn. and London, Yale University Press.

Prince, Morton (1906) *The Dissociation of a Personality*, New York and London, Longmans, Green.

—— (ed.) (1910) *Psychotherapeutics: a symposium*, London, Longmans, Green.

Pulzer, Peter (1988) *The Rise of Political Anti-Semitism in Germany*, London, Peter Halban.

Quevedo, Franciso de (1989) *Dreams and Discourses*, trans. and intr. R. K. Britton, Warminster, Aris and Phillips.

Regnéll, Hans (1967) *Ancient Views on the Nature of Life*, Lund, CWK Gleerup.

Reich, Wilhelm (1970) *The Mass Psychology of Fascism*, London, Souvenir.

—— (1972) *Reich Speaks of Freud*, London, Souvenir.

Reik, Theodor (1949) *The Inner Experiences of a Psychoanalyst*, London, Allen & Unwin.

Reiss, Timothy J. (1982) *The Discourse of Modernity*, Ithaca and London, Cornell University Press.

Resnik, Salomon (1987) *The Theatre of the Dream*, trans. Alan Sheridan, London and New York, Tavistock.

Ribot, Theodore (1882) *Diseases of Memory*, London.

Rice, Emanuel (1990) *Freud and Moses*, Albany, State University of New York Press.

Richards, Barry (1989) *Images of Freud: cultural responses to psychoanalysis*, London, Dent.

Ricoeur, Paul (1966) *Freedom and Nature: the voluntary and the involuntary*, trans. Erazim Kohák, Evanston, Northwestern University Press.
—— (1970) *Freud and Philosophy: an essay on interpretation*, trans. Denis Savage, New Haven, Conn. and London, Yale University Press.
Rider, Jacques le (1993) *Modernity and Crisis of Identity: culture and society in fin-de-siècle Vienna*, trans. Rosemary Morris, New York, Continuum.
Rieff, Philip (1965) *Freud: the mind of the moralist*, London, Methuen.
Riley, E. C. (1962) *Cervantes' Theory of the Novel*, Oxford, Clarendon Press.
Ritvo, Lucille B. (1990) *Darwin's Influence on Freud*, New Haven, Conn. and London, Yale University Press.
Roazen, Paul (1976) *Freud and His Followers*, London, Allen Lane.
Robert, Marthe (1966) *The Psychoanalytic Revolution*, trans. Kenneth Morgan, London, Allen & Unwin
—— (1976) *From Oedipus to Moses: Freud's Jewish identity*, trans. Ralph Manheim, New York, Anchor/Doubleday.
Robertson, Ritchie and Edward Timms (eds) (1991) *The Austrian Enlightenment and its Aftermath*, Edinburgh, Edinburgh University Press.
Robinson, Paul A. (1972) *The Sexual Radicals*, London, Paladin.
Rohde, Erwin (1925) *Psyche: the cult of souls and belief in immortality among the Greeks*, trans. W. B. Hillis, London, Kegan, Paul, Trench and Trubner.
Róheim, Géza (1950) *Psychoanlysis and Anthropology*, New York, International Universities Press.
Roith, Estelle (1987) *The Riddle of Freud: Jewish influence on his theory of female sexuality*, London, Tavistock.
Rorty, Richard (1980) *Philosophy and the Mirror of Nature*, Oxford, Oxford University Press.
Roth, Joseph (1974) *The Radetzky March*, trans. Eva Tucker, London, Allen Lane
Roth, Michael S. (ed.) (1994) *Rediscovering History: culture, politics and the psyche*, Stanford, Calif., Stanford University Press.
Rousseau, G. S. (ed.) (1990) *The Language of the Psyche: mind and body in Enlightenment thought*, Berkeley, Los Angeles and London, University of California Press.
Rousselle, Aline (1988) *Porneia: on desire and the body in antiquity*, trans. Felicia Pheasant, Oxford, Blackwell.
Roy, Alec (ed.) (1982) *Hysteria*, New York, Wiley.
Rozenblit, Marsha L. (1983) *The Jews of Vienna 1867–1914: assimilation and identity*, Albany, State University of New York Press.
Rudnytsky, Peter L.(1987) *Freud and Oedipus*, New York, Columbia University Press.
Rudolph, Kurt (1983) *Gnosis: the Nature and Histiory of an Ancient Religion*, Edinburgh, T. & T. Clark.
Russett, Cynthia Eagle (1989) *Sexual Science: the Victorian construction of womanhood*, Cambridge, Mass. and London, Harvard University Press.
Said, Edward (1978) *Orientalism*, Harmondsworth, Penguin.
Saint-Denys, Hervey de (1982) *Dreams and How to Guide Them*, trans. Nicholas Fry, London, Duckworth.
Sass, Louis A. (1992) *Madness and Modernism: insanity in the light of modern art, literature and thought*, Cambridge, Mass. and London, Harvard University Press.
Schilder, Paul (1935) *The Image and Appearance of the Human Body*, London, Routledge & Kegan Paul.
Schivelbusch, Wolfgang (1986) *The Railway Journey: the industrialization of time and space in the 19th century*, Hamburg and New York, Berg.
Schlechter, Solomon (1945) *Studies in Judaism: first series*, Philadelphia, The Jewish Publication Society of America.

Schliemann, Heinrich (1978) *Memoirs of Heinrich Schliemann*, ed. Leo Devel, London, Hutchinson.
Schnitzler, Arthur (1971) *My Youth in Vienna*, trans. Catherine Hunter, London, Weidenfeld & Nicolson.
Schorske, Carl E. (1980) *Fin-de-Siècle Vienna: politics and culture*, London, Weidenfeld & Nicolson
Schur, Max (1972) *Freud: Living and Dying*, London, The Hogarth Press and The Institute of Psycho-Analysis.
Showalter, Elaine (1987) *The Female Malady: women, madness and English culture 1830–1980*, London, Virago.
—— (1992) *Sexual Anarchy: gender and culture at the fin-de-siècle*, London, Virago.
Shumaker, Wayne (1972) *The Occult Sciences in the Renaissance*, Berkeley and Los Angeles, University of California Press.
Sidis, Boris and Simon P. Goodhart (1905) *Multiple Personality*, London.
Simmel, Georg (1950) *The Sociology of Georg Simmel*, trans. and intr. Kurt H. Wolff, Glencoe, Ill., The Free Press.
—— (1955) *Conflict and Web of Group Affiliations*, trans. Kurt H. Wolff and R. Bendix, Glencoe, Ill., The Free Press.
—— (1978) *The Philosophy of Money*, trans. T. Bottomore and D. Frisby, London, Routledge.
Simon, Gérard (1979) *Kepler: astronome astrologue*, Paris, Éditions Gallimard.
Skram, Amalie (1992) *Under Observation*, trans. Katherine Hanson and Judith Messick, Seattle, Women in Translation.
Skrine, Peter N. (1978) *The Baroque: literature and culture in seventeenth-century Europe*, London, Methuen.
Smith, Joseph, H. (ed.) (1980) *The Literary Freud*, New Haven, Conn. and London, Yale University Press.
Smith, W. Robertson (1889) *Lectures on the Religion of the Semites*, London, A. & C. Black.
Snell, Bruno (1953) *The Discovery of the Mind*, Cambridge, Mass., Harvard University Press.
Spearing, A. C. (1976) *Medieval Dream-Poetry*, Cambridge, Cambridge University Press.
Spector, Jack J. (1972) *The Aesthetic of Freud*, London, Allen Lane.
Spillane, John D. (1981) *The Doctrine of the Nerves*, Oxford, Oxford University Press.
Spurling, Laurence (ed.) (1989) *Sigmund Freud: critical assessments vol. 1*, London, Routledge.
Steed, Henry Wickham (1969) *The Hapsburg Monarchy*, New York, Fertig.
Steedman, Carolyn (1995) *Strange Dislocations: childhood and the idea of human interiority 1780–1930*, London, Virago.
Stepansky, Paul E. (1986, 1988) *Freud: appraisals and reappraisals*, 2 vols, New York, The Analytic Press.
Stewart, Susan (1984) *On Longing: narratives of the miniature, the gigantic, the souvenir, the collection*, Baltimore and London, The Johns Hopkins University Press.
Sullivan, Shirley Darcus (1988) *Psychological Activity in Homer*, Ottawa, Carleton University Press.
Sulloway, Frank J. (1980) *Freud: Biologist of the Mind*, London, Fontana.
Sully, James (1881) *Illusions: a psychological study*, London, Kegan & Paul.
Synesius of Cyrene (1930) *The Essays and Hymns of Synesius of Cyrene*, 2 vols, trans. and intr. Augustine Fitzgerald, Oxford, Oxford University Press.
Tal, Uriel (1975) *Christians and Jews in Germany*, trans. Noah Jonathan Jacobs, Ithaca and London, Cornell University Press.
Taylor, S. (1982) *Durkheim and the Study of Suicide*, London, Hutchinson.
Thompson, Bruce (1990) *Schnitzler's Vienna: image of a society*, London, Routledge.

BIBLIOGRAPHY

Timms, Edward (1986) *Karl Krauss: apocalyptic satirist*, New Haven, Conn. and London, Yale University Press.

Timpanaro, Sebastiano (1976) *The Freudian Slip*, trans. Kate Soper, London, New Left Books.

Todorov, Tzvetan (1977) *Theories of the Symbol*, trans. Catherine Porter, Oxford, Blackwell.

Townshend, Rev. Chauncy Hare (1844) *Facts in Mesmerism*, London, Bailliere.

Trombley, Frank R. (1993) *Hellenic Religion and Christianization C. 370–529*, 2 vols, London, New York and Köln, E. J. Brill.

Turner, Bryan S. (1984) *The Body and Society*, Oxford, Blackwell.

Turner, Frank Miller (1974) *Between Science and Religion*, Yale University Press, New Haven, Conn. and London.

Tylor E. B. (1871) *Primitive Culture*, 2 vols, London, J. Murray.

Veith, Ilza (1965) *Hysteria: a history of a disease*, Chicago and London, University of Chicago Press.

Vernant, Jean-Pierre (1962) *The Origins of Greek Thought*, London, Methuen.

—— (1980) *Myth and Society in Ancient Greece*, trans. Janet Lloyd, Brighton, Harvester.

—— ((1991) *Mortals and Immortals: collected essays*, ed. Froma Zeitlin, Princeton, N.J., Princeton University Press.

Vernant, Jean-Pierre and Pierre Vidal-Naquet (1988) *Myth and Tragedy: in ancient Greece*, trans. Janet Lloyd, New York, Zone.

Vitz, Paul C. (1988) *Sigmund Freud's Christian Unconscious*, New York and London, The Guilford Press.

Walker, D. P. (1958) *Spiritual and Demonic Magic from Ficino to Campanella*, London, University of London Press.

Wallace, Edwin R. (1983) *Freud and Anthropology: a history and reappraisal*, New York, International Universities Press.

Warnke, Frank J. (1972) *Versions of Baroque, European Literature in the seventeenth century*, New Haven, Conn. and London, Yale University Press.

Warren, Richard M. and Rosyln P. Warren (1968) *Helmholtz on Perception*, New York and London, Wiley.

Weber, Max (1930) *The Protestant Ethic and the Spirit of Capitalism*, trans. Talcott Parsons, London, Allen & Unwin.

—— (1948) *From Max Weber*, ed. and trans. Hans Gerth and C. Wright Mills, London, Routledge.

—— (1952) *Ancient Judaism*, New York, The Free Press.

Weiger, John G. (1988) *In the Margins of Cervantes*, Hanover and London, University Press of New England.

Weininger, Otto (1906) *Sex and Character*, London.

Weinstein, Arnold (1981) *Fictions of the Self: 1500–1800*, Princeton, N.J., Princeton University Press.

Wertheimer, Jack (1987) *Unwelcome Strangers: East European Jews in Imperial Germany*, Oxford, Oxford University Press.

White, John (1957) *The Birth and Rebirth of Pictorial Space*, London, Faber & Faber.

Williams, Rosalind H. (1982) *Dream Worlds: mass consumption in late nineteenth-century France*, Berkeley, Los Angeles and London, University of California Press.

Wistrich, Robert S. (1990) *The Jews of Vienna in the Age of Franz Joseph*, Cambridge, Cambridge University Press.

Wolff, Hans Walter (1974) *Anthropology of the Old Testament*, trans. Margaret Kohl, London, SCM Press.

Wollheim, Richard (1971) *Freud*, London, Fontana.

Wortis, Joseph (1975) *Fragments of an Analysis with Freud*, New York, McGraw-Hill.

Yack, Bernard (1986) *The Longing for Total Revolution*, Princeton, Princeton University Press.

Yates, Frances (1964) *Giordano Bruno and the Hermetic Tradition*, London, Routledge.

—— (1966) *The Art of Memory*, London, Peregrine.

Yates, Frances A. (1985) *Llull and Bruno: Collected Essays, vol. 1*, London, Routldege & Kegan Paul.

Yerushalmi, Yosef Hayim (1991) *Freud's Moses: Judaism Terminable and Interminable*, New Haven, Conn. and London, Yale University Press.

Young, Robert M. (1970) *Mind, Brain and Adaptation in the Nineteenth Century*, Oxford, Clarendon Press.

Zanuso, Billa (1986) *The Young Freud: the origins of psychoanalysis in late nineteenth-century Viennese culture*, Oxford, Blackwell.

Zborowski, Mark and Elizabeth Herzog (1952) *Life is with People: the Jewish Little Town of Esatern Europe*, New York, International Universities Press.

Ziolkowski, Theodore (1990) *German Romanticism and its Institutions*, Princeton, N.J., Princeton University Press.

Zweig, Stefan (1943) *The World of Yesterday: an autobiography*, London, Cassell.

NAME INDEX

Emmy von N. 45–8

Faria, Abbé 39
Faust 112
Fechner, Gustav Theodor 123
Felida X 40, 42
Ferenczi, Sándor 143
Feuchtersleben, Baron Ernst von 14
Ficino, Marsilio 9, 182
Field, Frank 22
Fioxhilde 181
Fleischl von Marxow, Ernst 94–7, 110
Fliess, Wilhelm 62–3, 65, 93–4, 97,
    99–105, 109, 122, 128, 138, 143, 198
Fluss, Gisela 98
Foucault, Michel 214
Frank, Johann Peter 13
Frazer, Sir James 116
Freud, Alexander (brother) 94;
    Amalia (mother) 102; Emanuel
    (half-brother) 100, 102, 104; Jacob
    (father) 100, 102, 104, 110; John
    (nephew) 97, 98, 104; Julius
    (brother) 97, 102; Martin (son)
    128; Oliver (son) 128; Pauline
    (niece) 98–9; Philippe
    (half-brother) 100–2, 104
Freud, Rebecca 100
Freud, Sigmund (biographical) 6–7,
    9–105, 115, 128

Gabel, Josef 209–11, 213
Galen 35
Galilei, Galileo 181–82
Gall, Franz Josef 13
Goethe, Johann Wolfgang von 14–15,
    22, 66, 103, 204–5
Gorgon, the 111
Goux, Jean-Joseph 110–11
Groos, Karl 152
Grunebaum, C. E. von 2, 3
Guattari, Felix 212–14

Hallyn, Fernand 184
Hamilcar 75
Hannibal 74
Hartley, David 39
Heine, Heinrich 50
Heliodorus 177
Helmholtz, Hermann 14
Hirsch-Hyacinth 50
Hobbes, Thomas 5
Hoffmann, E. T. A. 148

Hoffmeister, Gerhart 187
Hofmannsthal, Hugo von 22, 179
Homer 167, 178
Hume, David 6

Irma 62, 65
Ilych, Ivan 198

Jacyna, L. S. 13
Janet, Pierre, 42–4, 47
Jason 111
Jean Paul (A. Richter) 50
Jocasta 109, 111
Joseph (biblical) 76, 96
Joseph II 24, 96
Julius Caesar 96
Jung, Carl Gustav 134–5, 206

K., Frau 81–5
K., Herr 81–5
Kant, Immanuel 6, 13, 130
Kepler, Johannes 9, 167, 181–85, 187–8
Kierkegaard, Søren 31, 58, 71, 213
Kokoschka, Oskar 19
Koller, Carl 64
Königstein, Dr Leopold 64–6
Koyré, Alexandre 184
Kraepelin, Emil 136
Kruger, Steven 167
Kuzniar, Alice 11

Lacan, Jacques 223
Laïus 109, 111
Lear, John 181
Le Goff, Jacques 162, 168
Leibniz, Gottfried Wilhelm 188–9
Leroy, Maxine 6
Lesky, Erna 15
Lessing, Gotthold Ephraim 57
Lichtenberg, Georg Christoph 52
Liébeault, Ambroise 38–9
Little Hans 108, 147–8, 151
Locke, John 39
Lueger, Karl 26
Lyotard, Jean-François 214

Mach, Ernst 17, 22
McNish, Robert 40
Macrobius 167
Marcuse, Herbert 206–9, 211, 214
Maria Theresa 24
Martin, John Rupert 187
Marx, Karl 206, 208–13

SUBJECT INDEX